THE
USAGI
YOJIMBO
SAGA

D1501292

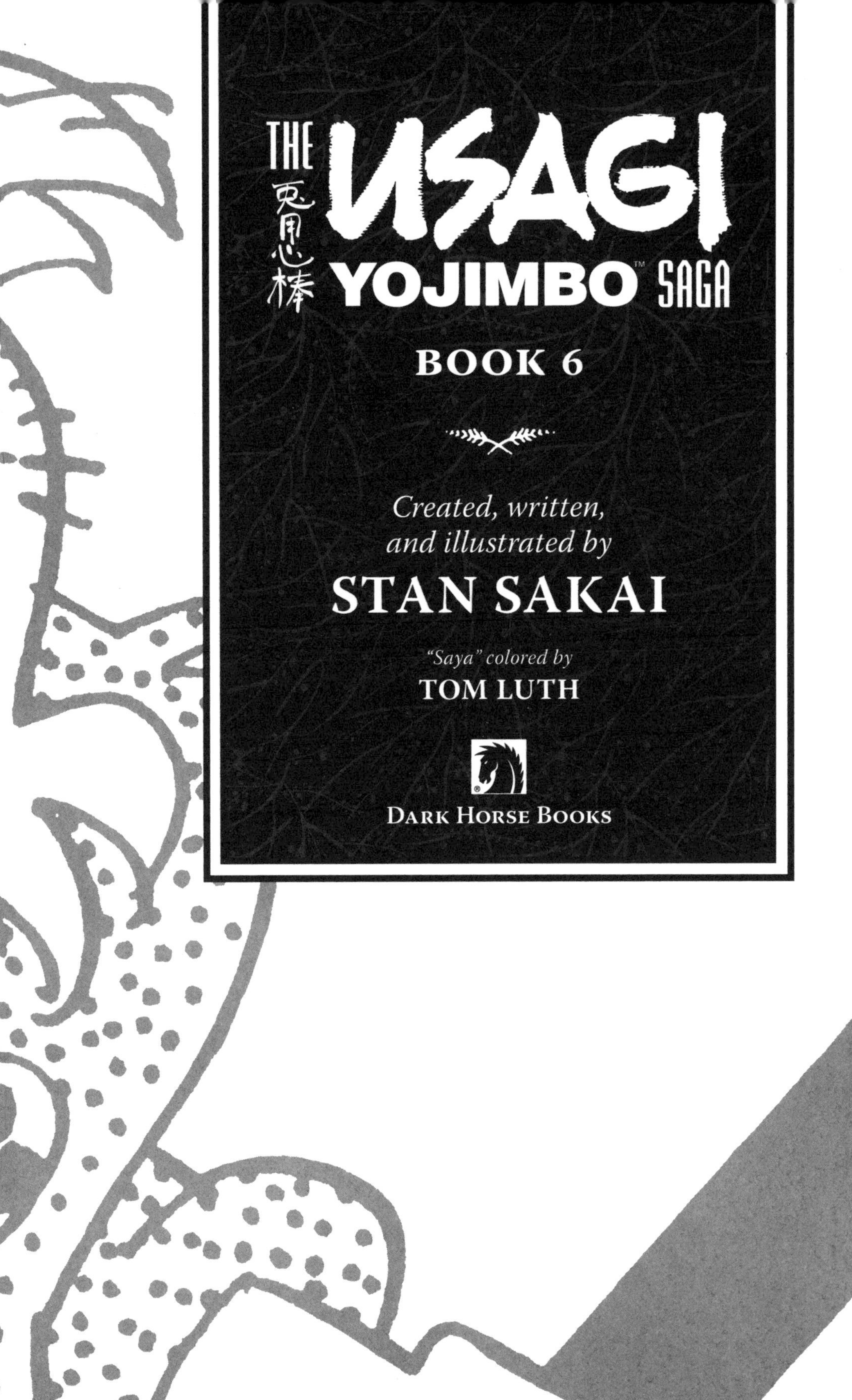

THE USAGI YOJIMBO™ SAGA

兎用心棒

BOOK 6

Created, written, and illustrated by

STAN SAKAI

"Saya" colored by

TOM LUTH

DARK HORSE BOOKS

Publisher
MIKE RICHARDSON

Series Editor
DIANA SCHUTZ

Series Assistant Editors
KATIE MOODY, DAVE MARSHALL, *and* **BRENDAN WRIGHT**

Collection Editors
BRENDAN WRIGHT *and* **AARON WALKER**

Assistant Editors
JEMIAH JEFFERSON *and* **RACHEL ROBERTS**

Designer and Digital Art Technician
CARY GRAZZINI

THE USAGI YOJIMBO™ SAGA Book 6

This volume collects issues #95–#116 of the Dark Horse comic book series *Usagi Yojimbo Volume Three* and "Saya" from *MySpace Dark Horse Presents* #18.

StanSakai.com
UsagiYojimbo.com

Published by Dark Horse Books
A division of Dark Horse Comics, Inc.
10956 SE Main Street
Milwaukie, OR 97222
DarkHorse.com

To find a comics shop in your area, call the Comic Shop Locator Service toll-free at (888) 266-4226.
International Licensing: (503) 905-2377

Library of Congress Cataloging-in-Publication Data

Names: Sakai, Stan, author, illustrator. | Luth, Tom, illustrator.
Title: The Usagi Yojimbo saga. Book 6 / created, written, and illustrated by Stan Sakai ; "Saya" colored by Tom Luth.
Description: First edition. | Milwaukie, OR : Dark Horse Books, 2016. | Summary: "The continuing adventures of Stan Sakai's long-eared samurai is one of the most critically acclaimed and beloved adventure series of all! This sixth volume of the definitive Usagi Yojimbo compilations includes the storylines "Bridge of Tears," in which a new love tempts the rabbit ronin to abandon his wandering lifestyle, "The Darkness and the Soul," revealing at last the origin of the demon Jei, and "Sparrows," featuring Jei's terrifying return, as well as Usagi's travels with bounty hunter Gen and the landmark Usagi Yojimbo #100, a celebratory "roast" issue by several of the best writers and artists in comics, including Frank Miller, Matt Wagner, Jeff Smith, Sergio Aragones, and more! Collects Usagi Yojimbo Volume Three #94-#116"-- Provided by publisher.
Identifiers: LCCN 2015048521| ISBN 9781616556143 (paperback) | ISBN 9781616559151 (hardcover)
Subjects: LCSH: Graphic novels. | CYAC: Graphic novels. | Samurai--Fiction. | BISAC: COMICS & GRAPHIC NOVELS / Fantasy.
Classification: LCC PZ7.7.S138 Us 2016 | DDC 741.5/973--dc23
LC record available at http://lccn.loc.gov/2015048521

First edition: April 2016
ISBN 978-1-61655-614-3

Limited edition: April 2016
ISBN 978-1-61655-915-1

10 9 8 7 6 5 4 3 2 1

PRINTED IN CHINA

This one is for
Masayo Nishikawa—Auntie Mas.

BRIDGE OF TEARS

RETURN OF THE BLACK SOUL

FOX HUNT

After the death of Lord Mifune in the battle of Adachi Plain, retainer **MIYAMOTO USAGI** chose the warrior's pilgrimage, becoming a wandering *ronin* in search of peace. Practicing the warrior code of *bushido*, Usagi avoids conflict whenever possible, but when called upon, his bravery and fighting prowess are unsurpassed.

MAYUMI works as a waitress in a small, gang-ridden town when she first meets Usagi. With no family or friends to tie her down, she longs for a better life somewhere—anywhere—else, and is determined to leave the town behind as soon as she can.

A descendant of samurai nobility, **MURAKAMI "GEN" GENNOSUKE** fell into poverty while his family pursued a vendetta and, vowing never to be poor again, turned to bounty hunting. Gen never fails to stick Usagi with the check for a meal or an inn and swears to be concerned only for himself, but his soft side sometimes briefly emerges.

A bounty hunter with a gruff and ruthless demeanor, **INUKAI (STRAY DOG)** secretly donates most of his earnings to a struggling orphanage. In many instances Stray Dog and Gen find themselves working together, but just as often the two are fiercely at odds with each other.

After a tragedy left his only son dead, the samurai **SANSHOBO** quit to become a monk. He retains his fighting skills, however, and as a warrior priest Sanshobo has many times proven to be an invaluable friend and ally to Usagi.

Inhabiting the body of the swordswoman **INAZUMA** since his apparent death, the demon **JEI** again haunts the countryside with his black blade. Despite claiming to be an emissary of the gods sent to wipe out evil on earth, Jei appears indiscriminate in his killing and has specifically targeted Usagi for death.

BRIDGE OF TEARS

INTRODUCTION

STAN SAKAI IS A *RONIN.*

I've never met the man, and I know it's a mistake to confuse artists with their work, but in the world of comics, a cartoonist who creates, owns, and controls his or her own characters is the closest thing we have to a masterless samurai.

(Which is not to diminish the steady hand of Dark Horse editor extraordinaire Diana Schutz, but I think she'd be the first to admit she's anything but Stan's "master.")

Unlike those of us who've toiled away in the world of corporate-owned superheroes, Stan Sakai is beholden to no one except his own muse, freely roaming the creative landscape and taking his long-eared protagonist anywhere Stan's imagination desires.

In reading some of the other introductions to past collections, I realized that just as Miyamoto Usagi has selflessly bettered the lives of countless characters over the years, so too has Stan enriched an untold number of writers, artists, filmmakers, and other devoted fans.

Stan shouldn't be blamed for my inferior work, but *Usagi* was profoundly influential on my writing, particularly with the Vertigo series I cocreated with artist Pia Guerra, *Y: The Last Man.* I was impressed and inspired by Stan's thorough and thoughtful research, the elegant way he introduced a massive supporting cast throughout a breathless cross-country journey, and the confidence with which he allowed his pictures to speak volumes, always saying so much with seemingly so little.

That said, I only wrote my humble little book for a mere sixty issues, a feat that nearly killed me. Stan has written *and* drawn *and* lettered (oh, the beauty of his calligraphy!) every single panel of his masterpiece for more than *one hundred and sixty issues* (with the hundredth Dark Horse installment included in this very collection).

Forget the oft-repeated and relatively meaningless fact that he's somehow found the discipline to put out these issues on time every time—how about the fact that the book has been consistently outstanding since its very first page? In an era when even the best television shows often become stale after just a few seasons, Stan has found a way to keep his serialized epic fresh for decades, always being brave enough to try new things while never being fickle enough to forget what made his story connect with so many readers across the world in the first place.

If you've never read *Usagi Yojimbo* before, any collection is a fine place to start (especially this one), thanks to Stan's gift of writing instantly relatable characters into surprisingly accessible adventures. And just because *Usagi* features a talking bunny, don't be fooled into thinking this is only a book for kids (though it's one of the few comics out there that I'll happily share with my young nephew). The stories are sophisticated, thrilling, hilarious, and heartbreaking, not in spite of the furry creatures, but because of them.

From *Uncle Scrooge* to *Maus,* comics have had a rich tradition of using anthropomorphic animals to escort us into unfamiliar worlds, and *Usagi Yojimbo* has taken this gaijin to places in feudal Japan that more traditional guides never could. Rabbits and bats and rhinos transcend race and creed and nationality, and allow us to experience stories, perhaps counterintuitively, on a purely human level.

Usagi Yojimbo is as sharp, skilled, and goodhearted as its hero, and as honorable as its creator.

May they never find masters.

BRIAN K. VAUGHAN
LOS ANGELES, CA
FEBRUARY 2009

USAGI YOJIMBO in NINJA HUNT

SHIZUKIRI

PLEASE--WILL YOU SPARE A FEW COPPERS FOR A POOR CRIPPLE AND HIS SON?

GYAHH! GET AWAY FROM ME, YOU FILTHY SCUM!
B-BUT, WE MEAN YOU NO HARM--!

ARE YOU TRYING TO RUIN MY BUSINESS? GET AWAY FROM HERE!

OOO! I LIKE A FEISTY WOMAN.
A RICH MERCHANT LIKE YOU CAN EASILY AFFORD MY COMPANY FOR TONIGHT.
COME ALONG, FATHER.

YOU SHOULD REST FOR A WHILE.

LET'S SIT HERE. MAYBE GOOD FORTUNE WILL COME TO US FOR ONCE.

REST HERE, FATHER. I'LL FIND US SOMETHING TO EAT.
YOU'RE A GOOD SON.
YOU CAN'T BE SERIOUS! HE ASSURED ME IT IS A FINE BLADE, WITH A DISTINGUISHED HISTORY.
2.

I THINK HE TOOK ADVANTAGE OF YOU. THAT SWORD IS NOT WORTH WHAT YOU PAID.

I TESTED IT MYSELF.
TAMESHIGIRI, EH? WHAT DID YOU TEST IT ON?

ON STRAW POSTS.
STRAW? ANY SWORD CAN CUT STRAW!

HERE COME SOME *SAMURAI*. MAYBE THEY WILL BE GENEROUS.
YOU KNOW THERE IS ONLY ONE TRUE TEST FOR A BLADE.

COPPERS FOR A SON AND HIS FATHER CRIPPLED IN THE WARS?
YOU'RE RIGHT. THERE IS ONLY ONE TEST.

WH-- WHAT ARE YOU DOING?

RUN! GET AWAY FROM THEM!

NO! NO!

NO!
EYAHH!
HA!

NO! NO! NO! NO! NO!

4.

;SOB! SOB! SOB!;
SEE? IT IS A FINE BLADE, AFTER ALL.
FWTT!
YOU'RE RIGHT. I GUESS IT IS WORTH WHAT YOU PAID FOR IT.

IT WILL MAKE A FINE GIFT FOR AKIMITSU.

YOU DOTE ON YOUR SON MUCH TOO MUCH.

WHY SHOULDN'T I? HE WILL BE THE HEIR TO OUR FAMILY NAME.

COME OVER TO MY HOME, AND WE'LL HAVE SOME HOT SAKE.
;SOB! SOB! SOB!;
THANKS. IT'S A COLD NIGHT.

...AND THEY WALKED AWAY WITHOUT EVEN A BACKWARD GLANCE.

BUT WE FOUND OUT WHO IS THE FATHER OF AKIMITSU.
HE IS A HIGH-RANKING *SAMURAI*, WITH HIS OWN STAFF OF RETAINERS.

BECAUSE OF THE LAWS OF THE LAND, THE *SAMURAI* ARE FREE TO KILL ANY OF US, BUT WE ARE NOT ENTITLED TO RETRIBUTION.

THAT IS WHY WE, OF THE UNION OF BEGGARS, WOULD LIKE TO HIRE YOU, SHIZUKIRI-*SAN*.
6.

IF THE LAW WILL NOT PROTECT US, WE MUST PROTECT OURSELVES.

HERE ARE ONE HUNDRED RYO. THERE WILL BE FOUR HUNDRED MORE ONCE THE JOB IS COMPLETED.

IT IS OUR TREASURY FOR A YEAR, BUT IT WILL BE WORTH IT IF WORD GETS AROUND THAT WE ARE NOT TO BE TRIFLED WITH.

YOUR REASONS ARE UNIMPORTANT TO ME. I WILL TAKE YOUR MONEY, AND YOU WILL HAVE YOUR JUSTICE.

SO, YOU UNDERSTAND WHAT WE WANT?

OF COURSE.
7.

I KNEW IT. ANOTHER KILLING. YOU ALWAYS GET DRUNK BEFORE YOU KILL. AT LEAST I HOPE IT'S A LOCAL JOB, THIS TIME.

ONCE, YOU WERE GONE FOR A WEEK, AND WHEN YOU GOT THERE THE GUY WHO HIRED YOU WAS DEAD.

YEAH. KILLED BY TWO RONIN. STILL, THEY GAVE ME WHAT I WAS OWED, DIDN'T THEY?

BUT THAT DIDN'T LAST LONG, DID IT?

I'M TIRED OF ALL THIS DEATH. THIS WILL BE MY LAST JOB! NO MORE KILLING FOR ME.

HAH! YOU ALWAYS SAY THAT, BUT MONEY RUNS THROUGH OUR FINGERS LIKE WATER.
GLUG! GLUG!

BEING AN ASSASSIN IS IN YOUR BLOOD. IT IS YOUR KARMA...

...JUST AS BEING A NIGHTHAWK* IS MINE.
9.

*PROSTITUTE

I MEAN IT THIS TIME. WE'LL LEAVE AFTER THIS JOB AND START A NEW LIFE ELSEWHERE.
IT'S NO USE.

YOU CAN'T ESCAPE KARMA.

MY FATE WAS SET WHEN DROUGHT HIT THE LAND, AND MY FATHER SOLD ME TO THE BROTHEL TO FEED THE OTHERS.

I WAS BORN TO BE A PROSTITUTE, AND THAT IS HOW I WILL DIE.

A PERSON MAKES HIS OWN FATE. THAT IS THE ONLY WAY PEOPLE LIKE US CAN FIND HAPPINESS.

SOME PEOPLE WERE JUST BORN TO SUFFER.
10.

I'LL SEE YOU LATER.
HARUYE.
EH?

DON'T GO OUT TONIGHT.

I MUST. THAT IS WHAT I DO...

...JUST AS YOU WILL GO OUT AND SOMEONE WILL BE KILLED THIS NIGHT.

SO DON'T WORRY ABOUT ME.

I'LL SEE YOU LATER.
11.

BAM! BAM! BAM!

BAM! BAM! BAM!
HOLD ON! HOLD ON! I'M COMING!

WHAT DO YOU WANT? DON'T YOU KNOW WHAT TIME IT IS?
THIS IS URGENT.

OPEN UP, AND LET ME IN. I HAVE GOT SOMETHING FOR YOUR MASTER.

GIVE IT TO ME, AND I'LL MAKE SURE THE MASTER GETS IT.

VERY WELL.
12

YAHH!
HIYAH!

OOG!

YAHH!
WE'RE UNDER ATTACK! WE'RE UNDER ATTACK!

KIYAHH!
GAHH!

WHERE IS YOUR MASTER?
13

WHERE IS YOUR MASTER?
SLAY THE INTRUDER!

YARG!
GYAHH!

ARGH!
CRASH!
14.

WHERE IS YOUR MASTER?
KILL HIM!

URK!
GYAH!

UH--! UH--! UH--!
WHERE IS HE?

AH. THERE YOU ARE.
S-STAY BACK!
15.

WHO ARE YOU?

ASSASSIN FOR HIRE.

ASSASSIN? B-BUT WHO HIRED YOU?!

THE GUILD OF BEGGARS.

BEGGARS?! WHAT DID I EVER DO TO THEM?!
WHY DO THEY WANT TO KILL ME?

I'M NOT HERE FOR YOU.

WHAT?! NO... NO!

A SON FOR A SON.
16.

DA--!

AKIMITSU!

AKIMITSU!

MY AKIMITSU...

CONTRACT COMPLETED.

SOB! SOB!
17.

MY JOB IS DONE. LET ME LEAVE IN PEACE.
KILL HIM!
URK!
YARK!
18.

AKIMITSU--MY ONLY SON--YOU WERE MY HEIR... THE FUTURE OF OUR CLAN.
SOB!

B-BUT I CAN'T LET YOU DIE UNAVENGED... WE'VE GOT TO GET THAT ASSASSIN!

AFTER HE'S DEAD, I'LL GET MY REVENGE ON THOSE BEGGARS. I'LL SLAY THEM ALL!

AFTER HIM! HE KILLED AKIMITSU! DON'T LET HIM ESCAPE!
80
80

WE'VE GOT HIM NOW! KILL HIM!
AVENGE MY SON!
YOU FOOL! I GAVE YOU A CHANCE TO LIVE!
19.

HIYAHHHHHHH

GYAHH!

GURK!

FLOO!

Y-YOU KILLED THEM ALL!
ALL? NOT QUITE. THERE IS ONE STILL ALIVE.

YAHHH!
20.

I WAS JUST HIRED TO KILL YOUR SON.
YOU WOULD HAVE LIVED TO MOURN HIS DEATH...
...BUT NOT ANY-MORE.

I'VE GOT YOU TRAPPED NOW!

HIYAHH!
THERE YOU ARE--SKULKING IN THE SHADOWS!

YOU KILLER!

YOU MONSTER!
TANG!

GYAHH!
21

I MUST BE GETTING OLD FOR HIM TO SNEAK UP ON ME LIKE THAT.

IF HE WAS BEHIND ME, THEN WHO...?

NO--!
HARUYE!

WE WERE TO LEAVE OUR LIVES, HARUYE...

...BUT YOU WERE RIGHT.

WE CANNOT ESCAPE OUR KARMA.
22.

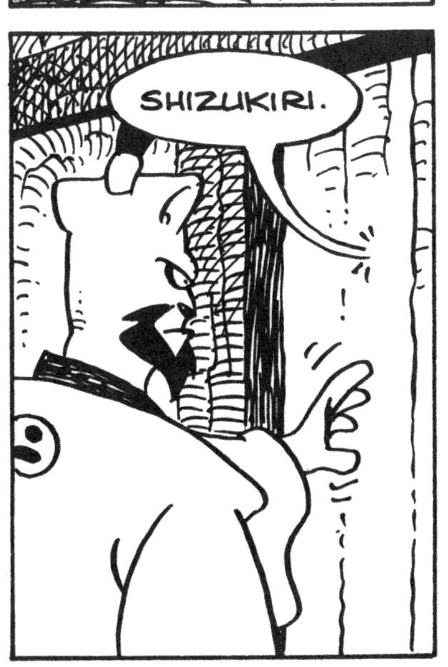
SHIZUKIRI.
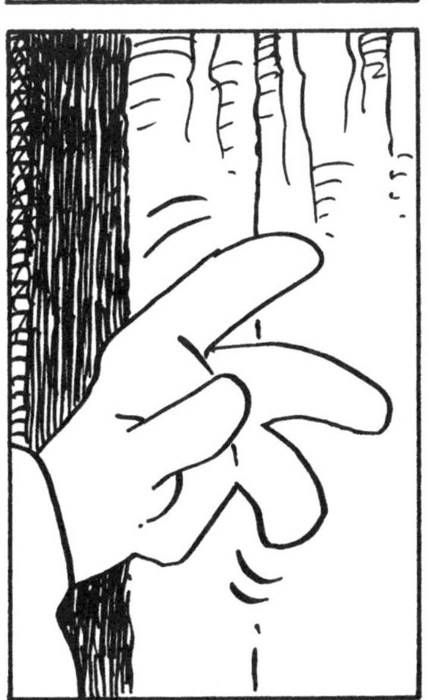

SIGH...

SO... YOU DECIDED TO COME IN, AFTER ALL.
IT IS MY HOME.
23

I CAN IMAGINE WHY YOU HAVE COME TO ME--

--MOTOJIME*.
*HANDLER

I HAVE A NEW ASSIGNMENT. ARE YOU STILL IN THE GAME?

YEAH. I'M IN... UNTIL DEATH. THAT IS MY KARMA.

GOOD. THIS ONE HAS BEEN A THREAT TO OUR LEAGUE OF ASSASSINS FOR A WHILE.

DEAL WITH HIM.

YES.
I KNOW THIS ONE.
宮本兎

THE END

BOSS HAMAKA'S FORTUNE PART ONE

SHAAA--!

I HATE THE RAIN!

1.

YOU KNOW WHERE IT IS! ADMIT IT, *BAKA**!

*IMBECILE

I DON'T KNOW WHAT YOU'RE TALKING ABOUT!
TELL US, OR WE'LL BEAT IT OUT OF YOU!

COMMON SENSE SAYS I SHOULDN'T GET INVOLVED.

BUT I'M SUCH AN IDIOT.
HEY-- WHAT ARE YOU DOING TO HIM?
WHAT?!
WHO ARE YOU?
MIYAMOTO USAGI--A *RONIN**!
*MASTERLESS SAMURAI WARRIOR

THIS IS NONE OF YOUR BUSINESS! GET OUT OF HERE!
TURN AROUND, LEAVE NOW, AND YOU WON'T GET HURT.

IF HE IS A CRIMINAL, TURN HIM OVER TO THE AUTHORITIES. I WON'T STAND BY AND LET YOU BEAT UP ON HIM.

IT'S THREE AGAINST ONE. BEAT IT, *RONIN*!
WELL? WHY ARE YOU STILL STANDING THERE?
HE'S GOT TO BE CRAZIER THAN *BAKA* HERE!
3

YOU ASKED FOR IT!
KILL HIM!
HIYAHHH!
WHAP!
UH!
OW--!
THOK!
YARG!
BONK!
4.

YAHHH!
HA HA
HA HA
HA!

THAT'S RIGHT, COWARDS! RUN, ALL OF YOU!
.....

BLA LA LA LA LA LA!
?

NYAHH!
!

HA! COWARDS!
?
SCUFF! SCUFF!

OH, ARE YOU STILL HERE?
HUH?

WHAT IS IT? LOOKING FOR A REWARD? A HANDOUT? WELL, TOO BAD. YOU'RE NOT GETTING ONE!

I DIDN'T ASK YOU TO BUTT IN! I DIDN'T NEED YOUR HELP!

SO I'M NOT GIVING YOU ANYTHING! UNDERSTAND?!
UH... YEAH.

GOOD. WELL, I'LL SEE YOU LATER, PAL!
UH... SURE.

WHAT A STRANGE PERSON.
6.

WELL, HE'S NOT MY CONCERN.

THIS WON'T KEEP MY HEAD DRY NOW.

!

WHO'S OUT THERE? COME OUT, AND SHOW YOURSELF!
I KNOW SOMEONE IS THERE.

I KNOW THERE IS SOME DANGER OUT THERE--BUT I CAN'T STAY OUT IN THE RAIN ALL DAY.

I'D BETTER HURRY ON TO THE NEXT TOWN.
HE KNEW I WAS WATCHING HIM. HE'S BETTER THAN I THOUGHT.
7.

WHAT A MESS. THIS TOWN LOOKS IN BAD REPAIR.
THIS INN LOOKS OPEN.
AH... IT WILL BE NICE TO BE DRY AGAIN.
8.

YAHH!
IT'S HIM!
THAT RONIN!

YOU CAN'T INTIMIDATE US HERE, RONIN!
THIS IS OUR TOWN!
9.

I WANT TO ENJOY MY MEAL IN *PEACE*.

DO YOU UNDERSTAND ME?
¡GULP!¡
♪
OH! ANOTHER CUSTOMER!

COME ON. LET'S GET OUT OF HERE!

SAKÉ, RONIN?
NO, THANKS. I DON'T CARE FOR IT. TEA WILL BE FINE.

HOW ABOUT A BOWL OF HOT NOODLES, AS WELL?
SURE. THAT SOUNDS DELICIOUS.
10.

I'LL BE RIGHT BACK WITH YOUR TEA AND MEAL.

SAKÉ!
EH--?

AND MAKE SURE IT'S HOT!

HE LOOKS PRETTY FORMIDABLE...
...BUT I'M NOT LOOKING FOR TROUBLE.

HURRY WITH MY SAKÉ!
I WONDER IF HE'S PART OF THAT GANG.
NOT THAT IT'S ANY OF MY BUSINESS.
11.

I'LL CLEAN THIS MESS WHILE YOUR SAKE' IS WARMING, KIN-SAN.
¡HARUMPH!¡

MAYUMI-- THE NOODLES ARE READY!
OH, THANKS!

THERE IS A TENSION IN THE AIR. WHAT IS GOING ON IN THIS TOWN?
WHY DO YOU WANT TO KNOW?

I'M JUST CURIOUS.
LOOKING TO MAKE SOME MONEY, I BET.

WELL, YOU COULD HEAR ABOUT IT EASILY ENOUGH. IF NOT FROM ME, THEN FROM SOMEONE ELSE.

"BOSS HAMANAKA USED TO CONTROL OUR TOWN WITH AN IRON FIST. WE ALL GAVE TRIBUTE TO HIM, IF NOT VOLUNTARILY THEN BY FORCE. BUT IT GOT WORSE AFTER HE DIED--A PEACEFUL DEATH IN HIS SLEEP, MAY HE ROT IN ENMA'S HELL!
12.

"IT WAS HIS SON, JODO, WHO FOUND THE BODY.

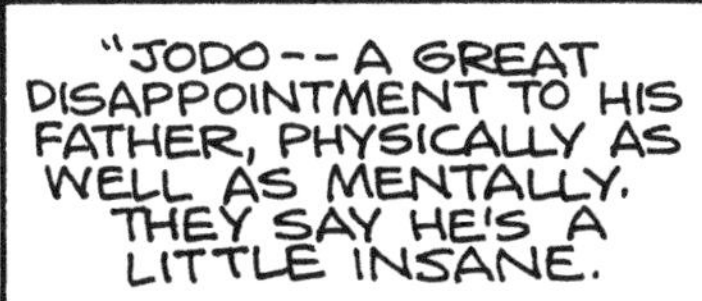

"JODO--A GREAT DISAPPOINTMENT TO HIS FATHER, PHYSICALLY AS WELL AS MENTALLY. THEY SAY HE'S A LITTLE INSANE.

"HAMANAKA DESPISED HIS SON, OFTEN RIDICULING HIM--CALLING HIM '*BAKA.*' JODO WOULD NEVER BE BOSS HAMANAKA'S HEIR.

"THERE WERE TWO LIEUTENANTS, BUT I GUESS BOSS HAMANAKA NEVER FULLY TRUSTED EITHER OF THEM, BECAUSE HE DID NOT APPOINT EITHER ONE TO BE HIS SUCCESSOR."

WHEN HAMANAKA'S MONEY CHEST WAS OPENED, THEY FOUND IT EMPTY. AND NOW THE RACE IS ON TO FIND BOSS HAMANAKA'S FORTUNE. WITH THAT MONEY, ONE OF THEM CAN HIRE SOME THUGS AND CONTROL THE AREA. THEY'VE BEEN TEARING UP THE TOWN LOOKING FOR IT.

;SLURP!; I SEE. AND WHO IS THAT?
KIN? HE'S A *RONIN*, LIKE YOURSELF. HE ARRIVED A FEW DAYS AGO. HE KEEPS TO HIMSELF. I DON'T KNOW WHAT HIS FULL STORY IS.
HEY-- WHERE'S MY DRINK?
I'LL GET IT RIGHT NOW, SIR!

I WONDER IF HE IS THE ONE I SENSED IN THE WOODS. EVEN IF HE'S NOT, I'D BETTER KEEP MY EYE ON HIM!
;SLURP!;
13

HO! SAMURAI!
EH--?

I'M BOSS ITO.
I HEARD YOU ROUGHED UP A FEW OF MY MEN.
ARE YOU LOOKING TO GET EVEN?
NO, JUST THE OPPOSITE.

I COULD USE A GUY LIKE YOU. WHY NOT WORK FOR ME?

THERE'S A LOT OF MONEY IN IT FOR YOU-- ONCE WE FIND THE FORTUNE, THAT IS.

NO, THANKS. MY SWORDS ARE NOT FOR SALE TO YOU.
YOU CAN'T TALK TO BOSS ITO LIKE THAT!

SHEATHE YOUR SWORD. I WON'T BE SO NICE NEXT TIME.
HAVE IT YOUR WAY, *RONIN*, BUT BE CAREFUL AROUND HERE.
GULP!
COME ON-- LET'S GO.
14.

SLURRP!

SAMURAI--I SAW ITO LEAVE. YOU DIDN'T AGREE TO WORK FOR HIM, DID YOU?
I'LL PAY YOU *TWICE* WHAT HE OFFERED.

AND I'LL GET PAID *AFTER* YOU FIND BOSS HAMANAKA'S MONEY? SIP!

OF COURSE! BUT WE'RE GETTING CLOSE TO FINDING IT. AREN'T WE, BOYS?
YEAH, THAT'S RIGHT, BOSS FUGU.
YOU'D BE SMART TO JOIN UP WITH US.

THERE WILL BE A BIG BRAWL WITH BOSS ITO'S GANG WHEN THE MONEY IS FOUND, RIGHT? I DON'T LOOK FOR TROUBLE, SO LEAVE ME ALONE.

HUH! HE SOUNDS LIKE A COWARD. LET'S GET OUT OF HERE.
YEAH. WE WOULDN'T WANT HIM IN OUR GANG.
SIP!
15

YOU TURNED BOTH OF THEM DOWN. I DIDN'T THINK YOU WOULD.
SO YOU KNEW THEY WOULD OFFER ME JOBS, AND CAME IN TO SEE WHAT I WOULD DO.

WHICH ONE OF THEM ARE *YOU* WORKING FOR?

NEITHER. LIKE YOU, I HAVE MY STANDARDS.

HOW DID YOU KNOW I WAS IN HERE, KIN? DID YOU SEE ME COME INTO TOWN? DID ITO'S MEN TELL YOU? SOMEONE ELSE?

STAY OUT OF MY WAY, *RONIN*.
SIP!
16.

*SMALL COPPER COIN

IT WILL ONLY BE A MATTER OF TIME BEFORE THEY FIND THE MONEY. WHEN THAT HAPPENS, THERE WILL BE A BLOODBATH. I DON'T WANT TO BE HERE WHEN THAT HAPPENS.
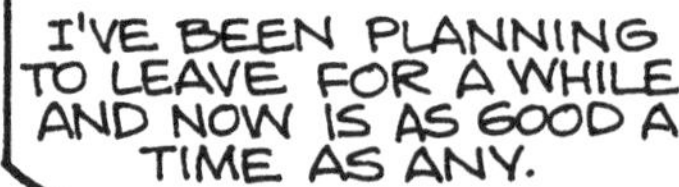
I'VE BEEN PLANNING TO LEAVE FOR A WHILE, AND NOW IS AS GOOD A TIME AS ANY.

IF THE GANGS WERE GONE, THERE WOULD BE NO REASON TO LEAVE.
EVEN IF THERE WERE NO GANGS, THERE WOULD BE NO REASON TO **STAY**!

DON'T YOU HAVE ANY FAMILY? FRIENDS?
NO ONE. THIS IS A DYING TOWN. TAKE MY ADVICE, AND FORGET THE MONEY. LEAVE THIS TOWN TONIGHT.

I WAS NEVER GOOD AT TAKING ADVICE.
I DID NOT THINK YOU WERE.

SEE YOU LATER... AND THANKS FOR THE MEAL.
18

LATER...
I LOVE IT AFTER IT'S RAINED. THE AIR IS SO FRESH AND CLEAN.

HERE'S A TEMPLE. IT'S SOMEPLACE I CAN STAY FOR FREE.

IT'S MUSTY, WITH COBWEBS--BUT AT LEAST IT'S DRY.

OH. I GUESS YOU DID NOT WANT TO SPEND MONEY ON AN INN FOR THE NIGHT EITHER, HUH?
I JUST LIKE MY SOLITUDE.

I KNOW WHAT YOU MEAN. I LIKE TO BE ALONE TOO, SOMETIMES. BUT A FREE, DRY SHELTER IS HARD TO COME BY.

I'LL TRY NOT TO DISTURB YOU.
YOU'RE ALREADY DISTURBING ME.
19

IF YOU'RE NOT WORKING FOR THE BOSSES, WHY ARE YOU STILL IN TOWN?
IT'S NONE OF YOUR BUSINESS.

YOU'RE AFTER THE MONEY, AREN'T YOU?
IN THIS WORLD, WE'RE ALL AFTER MONEY. THAT'S WHY YOU'RE STILL HERE.
ISN'T THAT RIGHT?

FEH! I THOUGHT SO.

GOOD NIGHT, RONIN.

20.

KRT!
KRT!
KRT!

CHOMP!

MUNCH!
MUNCH!

EEP!

ZZZ...

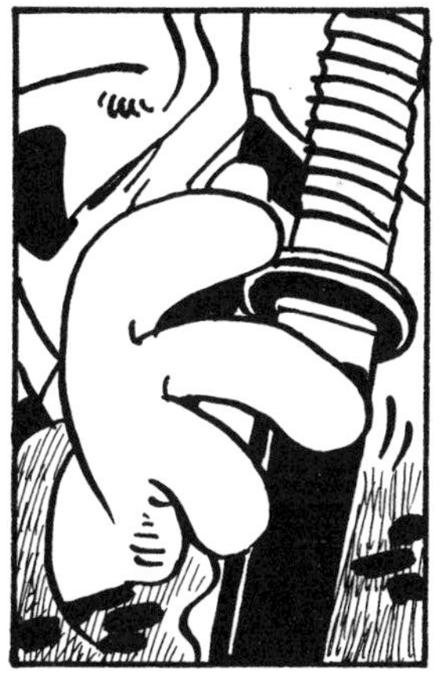

!

EEP!

ZZZ...

ZZZ...

21.

mmm...?

YAWN!

HMM... SOMEONE IS AN EARLY RISER.

THOSE CLOUDS LOOK OMINOUS. IT WILL PROBABLY RAIN LATER.

I HOPE IT'S NOT AN OMEN OF HOW MY DAY WILL END UP.
22.

I WONDER WHAT MAYUMI HAS FOR BREAKFAST.
EH--?

WHAT'S GOING ON?

BOSS ITO'S HOME IS ON FIRE! IT COULD ENGULF THE ENTIRE TOWN!

HELP US, SAMURAI!
23.

HELP! HELP!

THERE ARE STILL PEOPLE IN THERE!

THEY'LL BURN TO DEATH!

BOSS HAMANAKA'S FORTUNE PART TWO

YOU SET FIRE TO BOSS ITO'S HOME!
WE DID NOT! WE SHOULD KILL YOU FOR SLANDERING US!
1

DRAW YOUR SWORD, AND NONE OF YOU WILL WALK AWAY ALIVE!
HA! THAT DOESN'T MAKE SENSE!
IDIOTS!

STOP IT! THE ENTIRE TOWN COULD BURN DOWN WHILE YOU ARGUE!
HEY!

YESTERDAY'S RAINS WILL SLOW THE FIRE DOWN, BUT WE'RE STILL IN DANGER!
HE'S RIGHT! THERE WILL BE NOTHING FOR ANY OF US IF THE TOWN IS DESTROYED!

SET UP A FIRE BRIGADE!

WE NEED MORE BUCKETS--AND WATER!
YOU HEARD HIM--COME ON!

SOME OF YOU--WET YOURSELVES DOWN, AND ATTACK THE FIRE FROM THE INSIDE!
GLUB!

THE REST OF YOU--GRAB MORE BUCKETS! WE NEED WATER!
LOTS OF WATER!

THERE'S KIN, WATCHING FROM THE SIDE. DID HE HAVE SOMETHING TO DO WITH THE FIRE?

I'VE NO TIME TO BOTHER ABOUT HIM NOW, THOUGH.

SOON...
HOORAY! THE FIRE IS OUT!
AND NOT A MOMENT TOO SOON. WE'RE ALMOST OUT OF WATER.
3.

THAT WAS HARD WORK, BUT AT LEAST THE TOWN IS SAFE.
PLIK!
EH--?!

OH, GREAT! WHERE WERE YOU HALF AN HOUR AGO, WHEN WE NEEDED YOU?

ADMIT IT, YOU SCOUNDRELS! YOU SET THE FIRE!

IDIOTS.
BUT I'D BE MORE CONCERNED IF THEY WEREN'T SO INEPT.
WE SHOULD KILL YOU FOR THAT ACCUSATION!
OH, YEAH? GO AHEAD!

HEY! WATCH OUT! BE CAREFUL WITH THAT THING!
YEAH? WHAT ARE YOU GOING TO DO ABOUT IT?

THIS!
HEY, I WAS JUST KIDDING! DON'T WAVE THAT AROUND!
4.

IDIOTS.
WATCH OUT!
YAHHH! BE CAREFUL!
THEY WOULD RATHER ARGUE THAN GET IN OUT OF THE RAIN.

THINGS WILL COME TO A BOIL SOON, AND MANY WILL GET HURT.
BUT NOT TODAY, MAYUMI. MOST OF THOSE THUGS ARE PEASANTS WHO THOUGHT THEY COULD HAVE AN EASIER LIFE AS CRIMINALS.

THEY'RE TOO COWARDLY TO REALLY HURT EACH OTHER.
BUT THEY'LL TAKE THEIR ANGER OUT ON THE TOWNSPEOPLE.

YOU SHOULD HAVE LET THE TOWN BURN DOWN. NO ONE WOULD FIGHT OVER ASHES.
I'LL GET YOU SOME TEA.

THANK YOU, MAYUMI.
ER... USAGI-SAN...
5

YOU SEEM LIKE A DECENT ENOUGH PERSON.
?

WERE YOU SPEAKING THE TRUTH WHEN YOU SAID YOU WERE NOT AFTER THE GOLD?
YEAH.

TAKE ME WITH YOU WHEN YOU LEAVE.
HUH?!

B-BUT I DON'T EVEN KNOW WHERE MY ROAD WILL TAKE ME!
ANYWHERE IS BETTER THAN HERE. I CAN'T STAY IN THIS TOWN ANOTHER DAY!

I CAN'T.
I-I UNDER-STAND.

THEN I'LL HAVE TO TRAVEL ON MY OWN.
THAT CAN BE DANGEROUS.
IT'S NOT YOUR CONCERN.
6.

AS SHE SAID, IT IS NOT MY CONCERN. I CAN'T BE RESPONSIBLE FOR EVERY UNHAPPY PERSON IN THE WORLD.
I HAVE MY OWN LIFE. I CAN'T LOOK AFTER SOMEONE ELSE.

IT LOOKS LIKE THE BOSSES HAVE JOINED THEM.
AT LEAST THEY'VE GOT ENOUGH BRAINS TO GET UNDER COVER.
I'D BETTER FIND SHELTER FOR MYSELF, AS WELL.

I FOUND IT! I FOUND IT!
WHAT?

THAT'S BAKA!

HE'S DISCOVERED THE TREASURE!
7.

I FOUND IT! I FOUND IT!

MOVE ASIDE!
THE GOLD? YOU FOUND THE GOLD?
WHERE?! SHOW IT TO ME!
LOOK! SHINY!

GASP!
IT'S BEAUTIFUL!
LOOK AT THAT!

THERE'S JODO. WHERE IS HE SLINKING OFF TO?

I'LL FOLLOW HIM TO SEE WHAT KIND OF MISCHIEF HE'S UP TO.

THERE'S THE TEMPLE!
HE SAID HE WAS DIGGING IN THE BACK!
OUT OF MY WAY!
I SEE WHERE BAKA WAS DIGGING.

I'LL CHECK IN THE HOLE.

LOOK, BOSS! I'VE FOUND THE GOLD!
9.

IS THAT ALL? IT'S NOT MUCH! THE REST OF MY GOLD MUST BE BURIED DEEPER!
WHAT?!
WHAT DO YOU MEAN YOUR GOLD?! THIS IS ALL MY GOLD!
GET YOUR HANDS OFF ME!
THEY'RE TRYING TO STEAL OUR MONEY! KILL THEM! KILL THEM ALL!
IF THEY GET THE MONEY, YOU DON'T GET PAID!
HYAHH!
GAHH!
ARGH!
AHH!
SO, THEY'VE RAISED THE FIRE UNDER THE COOKING POT...
EYAH!
...AND NOW IT'S GOING TO BOIL OVER!
CLIK!
10.

HA! IT'S ALL STILL HERE--EXCEPT FOR THE FEW COINS I TOSSED IN THE HOLE.
EH--?

YAHH!
SO YOU'RE NOT THE FOOL WE ALL THOUGHT YOU WERE.
11.

HA! IT'S ONLY YOU, RONIN. FOR A SECOND I THOUGHT I WAS IN TROUBLE!
I EXPECTED A DIFFERENT REACTION. MAYBE HE IS CRAZY.

YOU HAD THE GOLD ALL THE TIME.
HA! OF COURSE!

EVERYONE THOUGHT I WAS FEEBLE-MINDED, PHYSICALLY WEAK, AND INSIGNIFICANT.

EVEN MY FATHER HAD NO FAITH IN ME... BUT I SHOWED HIM! I SHOWED THEM ALL!

COULD AN IDIOT HAVE POISONED HIM?

OR HID HIS GOLD BEFORE ALERTING EVERYONE OF HIS DEATH?

BUT I KNEW I COULD NOT TOUCH THE GOLD, NOT WHILE THEY WERE ALL STILL ALIVE, SO I HAD TO BIDE MY TIME.

BUT I COULD NOT WAIT FOREVER. SOONER OR LATER THEY WOULD HAVE STUMBLED ACROSS MY HIDING PLACE UNDER THIS WOOD PILE.
12.

I HAD HOPED THE FIRE I SET AT BOSS ITO'S HOME THIS MORNING WOULD HAVE HAD THEM AT EACH OTHERS' THROATS, BUT YOU MANAGED TO RALLY THEM TOGETHER.

BUT NOW, THEY'RE ALL TAKEN CARE OF!
OH?

WHAT ABOUT ME? WHAT MAKES YOU THINK I WON'T KILL YOU AND TAKE THE MONEY FOR MYSELF?

YOU'RE NOT THAT KIND OF GUY, RONIN. I KNEW THAT WHEN YOU RESCUED ME YESTERDAY. MONEY IS THE LEAST OF YOUR INTERESTS. BESIDES, ALL I HAD TO DO WAS KEEP YOU OCCUPIED FOR A WHILE!

KEEP ME OCCUPIED? WHY? FOR HOW LONG?

JUST UNTIL I GOT HERE, RONIN.

SO THIS IS WHERE YOU HID THE GOLD, EH, BAKA?
I TOLD YOU NOT TO CALL ME THAT!
YEAH. YOU'RE NO FOOL. I'LL GIVE YOU THAT MUCH.
13

WHAT ABOUT THE TWO BOSSES AND THEIR MEN? DID THEY FIND A WAY TO SPLIT THEIR MONEY?

HA HA HA! THEY MAY HAVE BEEN INEPT COWARDS, BUT I'VE NEVER MET A GREEDIER BUNCH. EVEN THE SIGHT OF A *LITTLE GOLD* DROVE THEM INTO A KILLING FRENZY. THOSE THEY DID NOT KILL, I TOOK CARE OF MYSELF.

IT TURNED OUT JUST LIKE YOU PLANNED WHEN YOU HIRED ME.

SO YOU WERE WORKING FOR SOMEONE AFTER ALL--A *THIRD BOSS*.

A THIRD BOSS? YEAH, THAT'S ME--*BOSS JODO!*

NOW SLAY THIS LONG-EARED FOOL, THEN WE CAN GET OUT OF THE RAIN.
SO ORDERS BOSS JODO.

YEAH. WELL, ABOUT THAT...
14.

YOU PROMISED ME TEN PERCENT OF THE GOLD. I DESERVE MORE.

WH- WHAT?!

AFTER ALL, I'M DOING ALL THE WORK.
H-HOW MUCH DO YOU WANT?

NINETY PERCENT.

GASP! N-N- NINETY--?!

AND ANOTHER THING-- I HAVE LOOKED INTO THIS RONIN'S EYES. HE'S GOOD... ALMOST AS GOOD AS I AM...

...AND YOU'RE SO MUCH EASIER TO KILL.
Y-YOU CAN'T MEAN--?

HIYAHH!
STOP!
NOO--!
15

NO!
YAAHHH!!
GYAH!!

HEH. I GUESS HE WAS AN IDIOT AFTER ALL.
FTT!
YOU'RE HEARTLESS! IT WAS NOT NECESSARY TO KILL HIM!
AND NOW WILL YOU TRY TO KILL ME?

NOT AT ALL. AS I SAID, I'M CONTENT WITH NINETY PERCENT OF THE GOLD. YOU CAN HAVE THE REMAINING TEN. PRETTY GOOD WAGES FOR DOING NOTHING.

SO YOU THINK IT CAN END JUST LIKE THAT?
WE GET THE GOLD. IT'S A HAPPY ENDING. WHAT MORE COULD YOU WANT?

THE MONEY DOESN'T BELONG TO US.
WE STOLE IT FROM CRIMINALS. WHO HAS A BETTER RIGHT TO IT THAN US?
16.

THE MONEY BELONGS TO THE TOWNSPEOPLE. WE NEED TO RETURN IT.
GIVE THEM YOUR SHARE. I'M KEEPING MINE.

THAT'S DESPICABLE --AND DISHONORABLE.
WILL HONOR FEED YOU, OR KEEP YOU WARM AND DRY AT NIGHT?

YOU USED TO BE A *SAMURAI.*
BUT NOW I'M JUST A *RONIN.*

SHAAAAA

PIK!
PLIK!
PLIK!
PIK!
PLIK!
PIK!

HYAAHHH!!

TANG!
TANG!
TANG!
TANG!
17.

TANG!

SLIT!

HAH! IT LOOKS LIKE I OVERESTIMATED YOUR ABILITIES, RONIN.
UH--!

SPLOOSH!

OW!
KICK!
18.

SPLAT!

UH--!
CHAK

I'LL KILL YOU FOR THAT, *RONIN!*
YOU MEAN YOU WEREN'T TRYING TO KILL ME EARLIER?

GRR--!

HIYAHHHHH

KYAHHHH!!
19.

AAAAAAAAAHHHHH

20.

SPLOT!
FWTT
SPLAT!
SPLAT!
SPLAT
SPLAT!
21.

TEA.
!

YOU'RE A MESS.

WHAT HAPPENED OUT THERE?
THERE ARE RUMORS OF BODIES FOUND AT THE TEMPLE!

IT'S OVER.
OVER?

THE GANGSTERS ARE ALL DEAD, AND THE MONEY HAS BEEN RECOVERED.
22

IT'S OVER? JUST LIKE THAT? IN ONE DAY?
YEAH.

THE GANGS ARE GONE. THE TOWN CAN CLAIM THE MONEY. NOW YOU DON'T HAVE TO LEAVE.
WHAT?!

YOU *SAMURAI*--YOU DON'T EVEN TRY TO UNDERSTAND, DO YOU? YOU KILL SOME THUGS WITH YOUR SWORD, AND YOU THINK YOU'VE SOLVED ALL OF LIFE'S PROBLEMS!

WELL, YOU'RE WRONG.
I'M STILL GOING.
GULP!

I'LL FETCH YOUR TEA.
.....
23.

WOW.
I WOULD MUCH RATHER FIGHT KIN ONCE MORE IN A THUNDER-STORM THAN HAVE TO FACE HER ANGER AGAIN.
BUT SHE CERTAINLY DOES HAVE SPIRIT.
I KNOW I'M GOING TO REGRET THIS...

I'M LEAVING TOWN AS SOON AS I FINISH MY TEA. IF YOU'RE NOT READY BY THEN, IT'S TOO BAD.
I'M NOT WAITING FOR YOU.
.....

I'LL BE READY.

I'M SUCH AN IDIOT.

THE END

RAIN and THUNDER

Are you talking to me?
YOU KNOW WE ARE, INAZUMA!

You have mistaken me for someone else.

LIAR! WE HAVE YOUR DESCRIPTION! WE'RE AFTER THE REWARD ON YOUR HEAD PUT OUT BY BOSS BAKUCHI!

Heh, heh, heh!

UH... ARE YOU SURE ABOUT THIS, GUYS? I MEAN--HER EYES, HER VOICE...
OF COURSE IT'S HER! STAY OUT OF THIS IF YOU DON'T WANT A SHARE OF THE BOUNTY.
2

SIX AGAINST ONE--
NO MATTER HOW SKILLED
SHE IS, SHE CAN'T WIN
AGAINST ALL OF US!
SPREAD OUT--CIRCLE
AROUND HER! DON'T LET
HER ESCAPE!

Heh, heh, heh.
Don't worry. I have
no intention of
escaping.

KILL HER!
HIIIIYAAAAHHH!!

EYAAHH!
SNORG!
UHHH--!
ARGH!
HACK!
EEGH!
SLASH!
SLICE!
GOUGE
CUT!
SKEWER!
GASP!
KONG!
SHOONK!
3.

Y-YOU KILLED THEM ALL--
--HORRIBLY!
Heh, heh, heh.

P-P-PLEASE... LET ME GO. PLEASE.

I'LL NEVER TOUCH A SWORD AGAIN! I SWEAR IT! PLEASE, INAZUMA!

I told you before...
...I am not Inazuma.

Call me--
--Jei.

YAAHHHHHHHH

SLIT!
SLICE!
CUT!
GOUGE!
HACK!
CHOP!
4.

IT LOOKS LIKE A STORM IS FAST APPROACHING, AUNTY.

Come, dear Keiko. Let us seek suitable shelter.

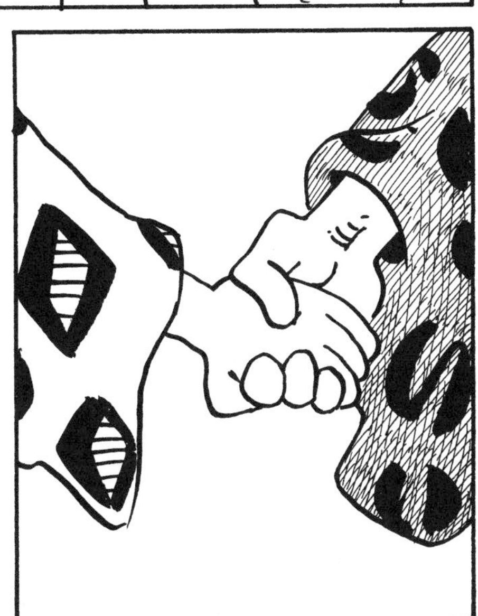

I THINK IT'S GOING TO RAIN SOON.
5.

THERE'S A TEMPLE, AUNTY! WE CAN SPEND THE NIGHT THERE.

You go ahead, Keiko. I cannot set foot in a temple... not again.

THEN LET US FIND A PEASANT WHO WILL SHARE HIS HUT FOR THE NIGHT, AUNTY.

6.

WHAT A HARD DAY! WE ARE NOT AS YOUNG AS WE USED TO BE, WIFE.

SUCH IS THE WAY OF ALL LIVING THINGS, MY HUSBAND.

I WILL BE GLAD FOR SOME OF YOUR DELICIOUS HOT SOUP, WIFE.
OH, YOU MAKE ME BLUSH!

LOOK--SMOKE COMING OUT OF OUR HUT. I KNOW I PUT DOWN THE FIRE THIS MORNING. EMBERS WOULD NOT MAKE SUCH SMOKE. COULD THERE BE SOMEONE INSIDE?

IF THERE IS, I HOPE HE MADE SOME HOT SOUP.

DO YOU THINK IT COULD BE THIEVES?
BUT WE HAVE NOTHING WORTH STEALING.

YOU ARE RIGHT. HOW FORTUNATE WE ARE TO BE SO IMPOVERISHED.
7.

HELLO? IS ANYONE HERE? THIS IS OUR HOME. HELLO?

THERE'S NO ONE HERE. THEY MUST HAVE LEFT.
SOMETHING IS ON THE FIRE. I HOPE IT'S SOUP.

PEE-YUU! WHATEVER THIS IS, IT SMELLS NASTY.

THAT IS OUR MEAL.
GASP!
OH--!

WE APOLOGIZE. WE, ER, DID NOT SEE YOU IN THE SHADOWS.

The Blade of the Gods goes where she is directed.
8.

OF COURSE... ER...BLADE... UH...
I SEE YOU MADE SOME SOUP. ER...WHAT KIND IS IT?

WORMS AND GRUBS. I FOUND THEM MYSELF.
HELP YOURSELVES. SLURP!

UH...WELL... MAYBE NOT TODAY. MY WIFE IS AN EXCELLENT COOK, AND CAN FIX UP A TASTY REPAST...
THERE ARE BUGS IN HERE, TOO!

ER...NOT TO SAY THAT YOUR SOUP DOES NOT LOOK... UH...APPETIZING.
WHAT IS THAT?

YOU ARE, OF COURSE, WELCOME TO SPEND THE NIGHT HERE.

The Blade of the Gods does not need your permission. I stay where my mission takes me.
9

UH... YOUR MISSION? WHAT IS THAT?

To rid the world of evil.

WELL, WE ARE POOR WOODCUTTERS. THERE IS NO EVIL IN US.

Evil exists in many forms...

...even that of poor woodcutters.

UH... BUT, MA'AM...

MA'AM...?

WHIMPER!
10.

CRASH!

HOLD IT, INAZUMA!

HA! I TOLD YOU I COULD TRACK HER DOWN! WE AGREED TO SPLIT THE BOUNTY EVENLY, RIGHT, STRAY DOG?
OF COURSE, GEN!
FOOL!

HEH, HEH! HE'S CRAZY IF HE THINKS I'LL SHARE ANYTHING WITH HIM!

WE'RE HERE FOR YOUR HEAD!
TURN AND FACE US, INAZUMA!
11.

Inazuma? Who is this Inazuma that everyone speaks of?

I am Jei... the Blade of the Gods.

¡GASP!¡

WHAT'S GOING ON, GEN?
IT CAN'T BE YOU! YOU'RE DEAD! I WAS THERE!
Ah, yes. I do recognize you. I speared you in your shoulder. Remember, bounty hunter?

UH--!

GET UP, GEN!
HAUK! COUGH! GAG!
12.

W-WE CAN'T BEAT HER! WE'VE GOT TO GET OUT OF HERE, STRAY DOG!
ARE YOU TURNING COWARD ON ME, GEN?

OR IS THIS SOME TRICK TO MAKE ME DO ALL THE WORK? EITHER WAY, I'M KEEPING ALL THE REWARD MONEY!

GRRR... I'M NOT LETTING YOU STEAL MY MONEY!
THEN STAND UP, YOU FOOL!

I-I'M OKAY NOW. WE CAN TAKE HER!

WHERE IS SHE?
SHE AND THE GIRL ARE GONE!
THEY LOST INTEREST IN ALL OF US WHEN YOUR FRIEND FELL OVER.

YOU'RE SUCH A FOOL, GEN! COME ON!
13

I'M GOING TO BLAME YOU IF SHE GETS AWAY, GEN!
JUST SHUT UP AND FIND HER!
I DON'T KNOW WHAT HAPPENED TO ME IN THERE, BUT I'M OKAY NOW. IT'S IMPOSSIBLE, BUT IF THAT REALLY IS JEI, WE'RE HEADING FOR BIG TROUBLE!

DRAT! IT'S STARTING TO RAIN! I HATE THE RAIN!
THERE'S THE KID... BUT WHERE'S INAZUMA?

WHERE IS THAT SHE-DEVIL YOU WERE WITH?

IT'S RAINING PRETTY HARD. I CAN HARDLY SEE A FEW FEET IN FRONT OF ME!
STOP COMPLAINING ABOUT A LITTLE RAIN! WE WOULD HAVE HAD HER, IF IT WEREN'T FOR YOU!

SHE CAN'T BE FAR AHEAD!
14.

KRAAK!

WHERE IS SHE?!

TANG!
UH--!

GEN-- HELP ME!
SHE FIGHTS LIKE A DEMON!

HYAHHHH!!!

KANG!

CIRCLE AROUND HER! KEEP HER BETWEEN US! DON'T LET HER ESCAPE!
SHE'S JUST STANDING THERE--GRINNING LIKE AN IDIOT!

WE'LL ATTACK HER AT THE SAME TIME!
HYAHHH!

KYAHH

Heh, heh, heh!
16.

TANG!
TANG!
TANG!
TANG!

THAT'S IT-- KEEP HER OFF BALANCE!

SHE ISN'T SO TOUGH, AFTER ALL!
NOT AGAINST BOTH OF US!
17

GET HER--SHE ONLY HAS HER SHORT SWORD!

UHN--!

18.

DON'T LET HER GET AWAY!
I WON'T! I NEED THAT MONEY HER HEAD WILL BRING!

DRAT THE MUD-- AND THESE HILLS!
HOW CAN SHE KEEP HER FOOTING?
DON'T LOSE SIGHT OF HER!
YAHH!

GET UP.
WHERE IS SHE?
HOW COULD SHE HAVE DISAPPEARED SO FAST?

HYAAAAAAHH
19.

EVEN WITH JUST A SHORT SWORD SHE IS A FORMIDABLE OPPONENT!

BUT WE'LL GET HER SOON ENOUGH!

Do you really think so?
ARGH!

NOT AGAIN--!
Now it is just you and me.
AUGHH!

GEN-- GET UP, GEN!
GEN!
20.

TANG! TANG! TANG! TANG!
TANG! TANG! TANG!
TANG! TANG! TANG! TANG!
TANG! TANG! TANG!
TANG! TANG! TANG! TANG!
TANG! TANG!
TANG!
GGHH!
TANG! TANG!
TANG! TANG!
TANG!
Ha! Ha! Ha!

GEN!

UH-- HOLD ON, STRAY DOG, I'M COMING!
UH...

HYAHH

YAHH--!!
Ha! Ha! Ha!
21.

Hahh!!
SPLAT!

.....

Ha! Ha! Ha! Ha!
TANG! TANG! TANG! TANG!
AHHH!

TANG!
UH--!

NOT AGAIN!
OOF!

OOOOOH...

PLOP!
22

.....
UH...

HOW LONG WAS I UNCONSCIOUS?

I'M LUCKY TO STILL BE ALIVE. SHE'S PROBABLY KILLED GEN.
HE WAS A STUPID FOOL... BUT I'LL MISS HIM.

SO, SHE LEFT YOU ALIVE, HUH?
PITY.
UHH...
SHE'S GONE?
IT LOOKS LIKE IT.

SHE KNEW WE WERE AFTER HER, BUT WE WERE AT HER MERCY. WHY DIDN'T SHE KILL US?
WHO KNOWS WHAT GOES THROUGH THE MIND OF THAT DEMON?

YOU ALL RIGHT?
YEAH. MY SHOULDER PAIN IS GONE.
23

YOU'RE AN IDIOT, YOU KNOW THAT? INAZUMA GOT AWAY BECAUSE OF YOU.
THAT WAS NOT INAZUMA.
YOU KNOW A LOT MORE ABOUT THIS THAN YOU'VE TOLD ME.
IF THAT WASN'T INAZUMA, THEN WHO WAS SHE?
A DEVIL I THOUGHT WAS DEAD...
"...AND IF WE REALLY WANT HER BOUNTY, WE'RE GOING TO NEED HELP."
Come, my innocent. We have far to go.
YES, AUNTY.

THE END

BRIDGE OF TEARS

GET OUT OF MY WAY! MOVE ASIDE, YOU CLODS!

I'VE GOT TO GET OUT OF TOWN--
--FAST!

!
TRAITOR!

WE KNEW IF WE SPLIT UP, ONE OF US WOULD FIND YOU!
WE STOLE THAT JADE PIECE TOGETHER, BUT YOU WANTED IT FOR YOURSELF, DIDN'T YOU?

YOU DIRTY, FILTHY SCOUNDREL! WHAT KIND OF THIEF WOULD STEAL FROM HIS OWN PARTNERS?
YOU MUST HAVE KNOWN WE'D CATCH UP TO YOU!
YAHH!
2.

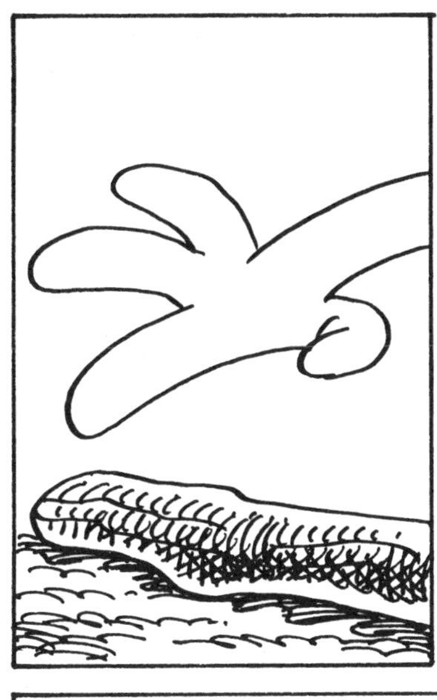

GYAHH!
HA!

THOK!
UHH--!

WHACK!
WHACK!
WHACK!
WHACK!
WHACK!
AHHH!

UH... HE GOT ME GOOD, THAT ROTTEN SCUM.
UH...

LOOK AT ALL THE BLOOD. I WON'T GET FAR... NOT WITH THIS WOUND.

BUT I'LL SHOW THEM! THEY'LL NEVER GET THEIR HANDS ON MY JADE. I'LL THROW IT IN THE RIVER, RATHER THAN LET THEM HAVE IT!
3

RUSTLE!
SHAKE!
SHAKE!
HA HA HA HA HA!

HA! HA! HA!

CALM DOWN, MAYUMI. HERE, HAVE A *TAKOYAKI*.
HA HA! I'M HAVING SO MUCH FUN, USAGI!

THEN YOU WOULD BE HAPPY IN THIS TOWN.
OH, I'M HAPPY BECAUSE I'M WITH YOU.

WE AGREED THAT I WOULD TAKE YOU TO THE NEXT TOWN--AND THIS IS IT!
HMM--?!
4.

YOU'RE NOT JUST GOING TO LEAVE ME HERE, ARE YOU?

I'VE GOT TO LEAVE YOU SOMEWHERE.
YOU'RE MEAN!

MY LIFE AS A WANDERER IS TOO DANGEROUS.
AND I'VE BEEN FEELING UNEASY LATELY.

I CAN'T BE BURDENED WITH YOU.
A BURDEN, AM I? DON'T YOU LIKE MY COMPANY?

NO. I DON'T LIKE YOU AT ALL!

OH, YOU'RE JOKING! YOU'RE SUCH A JESTER!
5.

I GUESS WE'LL STAY IN TOWN TONIGHT, AND DECIDE WHAT TO DO IN THE MORNING.
THERE HE IS!
PANT! PANT! GASP!

HEY-- WATCH WHERE YOU'RE WALKING!
UH--!

HE'S HURT! HE WON'T GET FAR!
WE'LL TEACH HIM TO STEAL FROM US!

ARE YOU ALL RIGHT?
YEAH, LOOK AT HIM STAGGERING! HE'S SO DRUNK HE CAN HARDLY WALK STRAIGHT.
6.

HEY! LOOK OUT!
YOW!
GET HIM!

ARE YOU OKAY?
YEAH, I THINK SO. I'M JUST SHAKEN UP A BIT.
THEY STEPPED ON MY TAKOYAKI.

HE DUCKED INTO THAT ALLEY.
COUGH! COUGH!

UH...

FOOL!
YOU SHOULD HAVE KNOWN YOU COULD NOT ESCAPE US!
.....

HE'S DEAD, BUT HE DOESN'T HAVE THE JADE!
WHAT?!

WHERE IS IT, YOU GREEDY SCUM?!
KICK!

HE MUST HAVE HIDDEN IT... OR PASSED IT ON TO SOMEONE.
HE BUMPED INTO THAT WOMAN! SHE MUST BE HIS ACCOMPLICE!

COME ON! DO YOU REMEMBER WHAT SHE LOOKS LIKE?
YEAH. I DO!

SHE COULDN'T HAVE GOTTEN TOO FAR AWAY!
OUT OF OUR WAY!

THERE SHE IS-- BY THE RIVER!
YEAH, BUT SHE'S WITH SOMEONE.
A SINGLE *SAMURAI*? HE DOESN'T LOOK THAT TOUGH. BESIDES, IT'S FOUR AGAINST ONE.
8.

IT'S GETTING DARK... AND A BIT CHILLY.
THE STREETS ARE ALREADY DESERTED.
I GUESS WE SHOULD FIND AN INN FOR THE NIGHT.

GET THEM!
HUH?

I'LL GRAB THE GIRL! YOU THREE TAKE CARE OF HIM!
GET BEHIND ME, MAYUMI!

YAHHHH!
WHAT DO YOU WANT WITH US?
9

RUN, MAYUMI!
THAT'S ONE OF THEM!
GLUB!
SPLASH!

OOF!

SPLASH!
TWO DOWN!

SWITT!

GURK!
THREE!

AND NOW--
HOLD IT, SAMURAI!
10.

LET HER GO!
STAY BACK, SAMURAI, OR I'LL KILL HER!
USAGI!
KEEP QUIET, GIRL!

ALL I'M AFTER IS THE JADE!
I DON'T KNOW WHAT YOU'RE TALKING ABOUT!

DON'T MOVE, SAMURAI, OR I'LL SLIT HER THROAT! THROW YOUR SWORD INTO THE RIVER!

OKAY, OKAY! YOU WIN!

HA! GOOD!
SPLASH!

NOW GIVE ME MY JADE!
WHAT ARE YOU LOOKING AT, GIRL?
11.

A SAMURAI CARRIES TWO SWORDS--
--IDIOT!
BONK!
OW!
USAGI!

OH, USAGI--!

I-I WAS SO SCARED!

12

POLICE! WHAT'S GOING ON HERE?
THERE ARE A COUPLE OF GUYS IN THE RIVER!
!

I RECOGNIZE THOSE FOUR! THEY'RE WANTED CRIMINALS!
WE JUST ARRIVED IN TOWN, AND THEY ATTACKED US.

NO DOUBT THEY INTENDED TO ROB YOU. IT'S A GOOD THING WE WERE PATROLLING THE AREA, LOOKING FOR THIEVES WHO STOLE A PRICELESS ARTIFACT!

I'LL GIVE YOU A RECEIPT FOR THESE CRIMINALS. BRING IT TO THE POLICE STATION TOMORROW TO CLAIM YOUR REWARD.
THANK YOU.

WHILE YOU'RE DOWN THERE, COULD YOU FISH OUT MY SWORD?
?
13

山田

MMM... THIS IS DELICIOUS.
WITH THE REWARD MONEY WE'LL GET TOMORROW WE CAN AFFORD A NIGHT AT A DECENT PLACE.

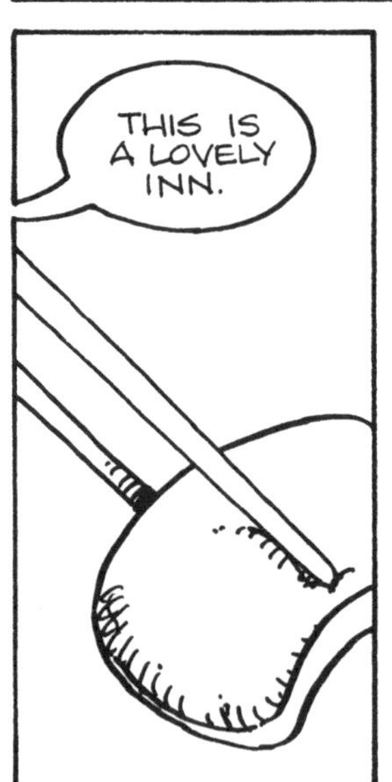
THIS IS A LOVELY INN.

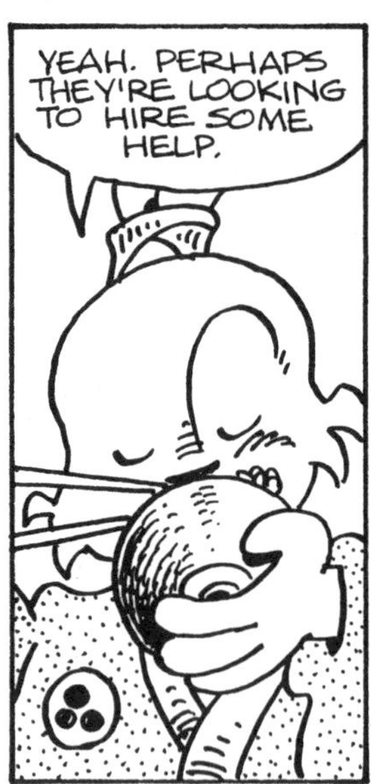
YEAH. PERHAPS THEY'RE LOOKING TO HIRE SOME HELP.

OH--?

YOU USED TO WORK AT AN INN, DIDN'T YOU? YOU CAN GET A JOB HERE.

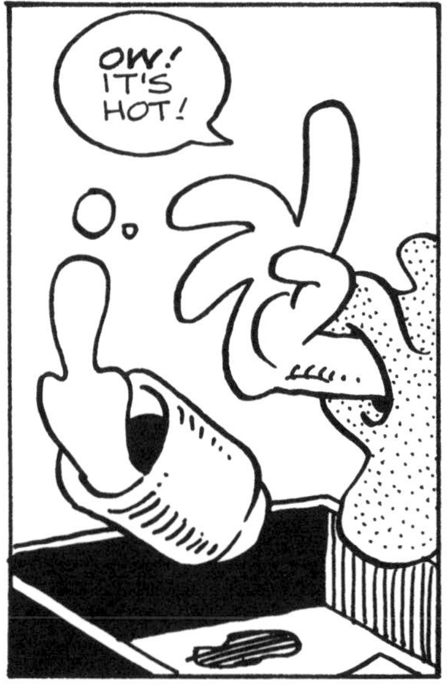
OW! IT'S HOT!

THAT'S A *BACHI**! YOU DESERVED IT FOR BEING SO MEAN TO ME!

BUT I FORGIVE YOU. I HAVE A SMALL TOWEL WITH WHICH YOU CAN WIPE UP THE SPILL.
14.

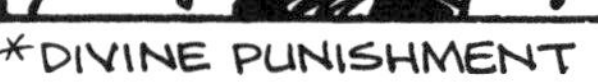
*DIVINE PUNISHMENT

OH--! WHAT'S THIS?
A **JADE DRAGON**?

I HAD IT AFTER ALL!
THAT MUST BE WHAT THE POLICE WERE SEARCHING FOR.

BUT HOW DID I GET IT?
THAT GUY WHO BUMPED INTO YOU MUST HAVE SLIPPED IT INTO YOUR SLEEVE.

I'LL TURN IT IN TOMORROW MORNING. I'VE GOT TO GO TO THE POLICE STATION ANYWAY. MAYBE THERE'S A REWARD FOR THE JADE AS WELL.

IT'S GETTING LATE. WE WALKED A LOT. YOU SHOULD GET SOME REST.
WHAT ABOUT YOU?

I'M GOING OUT ON THE BALCONY. I NEED SOME NIGHT AIR TO CLEAR MY HEAD.
OH?
15.

IT WAS JUST LUCK THAT MAYUMI WAS NOT HURT.
I DRAW DANGER TO ME WHEREVER I TRAVEL.

AND THE DANGER EXTENDS TO ANYONE WHO IS WITH ME.
IT'S ONLY A MATTER OF TIME BEFORE MAYUMI GETS HURT...
...OR WORSE.

THIS LOOKS LIKE A NICE TOWN, AS GOOD A PLACE AS ANY TO LEAVE HER.
I'LL GIVE MAYUMI THE REWARD MONEY. THAT WILL SUPPORT HER UNTIL SHE GETS SETTLED IN.
BUT KNOWING HER, SHE WON'T GO ALONG WITH THIS PLAN.

SO I HAVE GOT TO **ABANDON** HER HERE.

IT CAN'T BE HELPED. IT'S FOR HER OWN GOOD.
I'LL REALLY MISS HER, THOUGH.
BUT I CAN'T SHAKE THIS FEELING OF DANGER.
16.

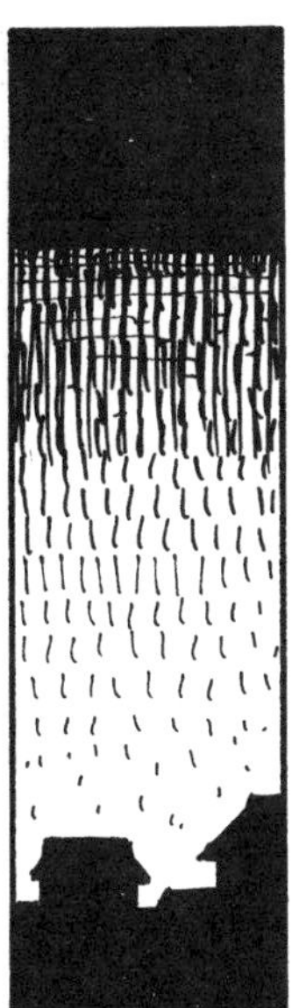

MMM...?

OH--!
USAGI!

USAGI--!
WHERE ARE--?

OH...

I--
I HAD A DREAM THAT YOU HAD DEPARTED DURING THE NIGHT. I SHOULD HAVE KNOWN YOU WOULDN'T JUST LEAVE ME HERE.

HAVE YOU BEEN OUT HERE ALL NIGHT?
I LIKE TO WATCH THE SUNRISE.

THEN LET'S WATCH IT TOGETHER.
17

I'M GOING TO THE POLICE STATION TO CLAIM OUR REWARD.
WAIT-- I'LL GO WITH YOU.

NO NEED TO. WHY DON'T YOU CHANGE, AND HAVE SOME BREAKFAST? I SHOULDN'T BE GONE TOO LONG.
OH--?

I'LL MEET YOU ON THAT BRIDGE IN TWO HOURS. THEN WE CAN GET A QUICK START ON THE ROAD.
TWO HOURS, THEN.

YOU **WILL** BE BACK, WON'T YOU?
UH... YEAH.
PROMISE, ON YOUR HONOR?

OF COURSE. WOULD I LIE TO YOU?
18

GOOD... UH...MORNING, SAMURAI.
GOOD MORNING. PLEASE SEND UP BREAKFAST FOR MY COMPANION-- THE BEST YOU'VE GOT.
A MEAL FOR TWO?
NO. I'M GOING OUT FOR A WHILE.

I'LL BE BACK SOON.

USAGI-SAN!
EH--?

I'LL SEE YOU IN TWO HOURS!
UH... YEAH. THAT'S RIGHT.
I'M SUCH A CAD!

SIGH! WHAT A BEAUTIFUL DAY!
19.

LATER...
THANK YOU, INNKEEPER. I'M LEAVING NOW.
UH... I HAVE UH... SOMETHING FOR YOU... UH... MISS.

UH...THE SAMURAI RETURNED SOON AFTER HE LEFT, AND...UH... ASKED ME TO GIVE THIS TO YOU...UH...WHEN YOU CAME DOWN. UH...THERE'S A NOTE ATTACHED.
OH--?

WHERE IS USAGI NOW?
UH...I DON'T KNOW. HE...UH...LEFT AGAIN, AND...UH...I HAVE NOT SEEN...UH...SEEN HIM SINCE.

I WONDER WHAT THIS COULD BE.
A GIFT, NO DOUBT.
HE'S SO EXTRAVAGANT TO SPEND THE REWARD MONEY ON ME.
LET'S SEE WHAT THE NOTE SAYS.

"FORGIVE ME."
WHAT--?!

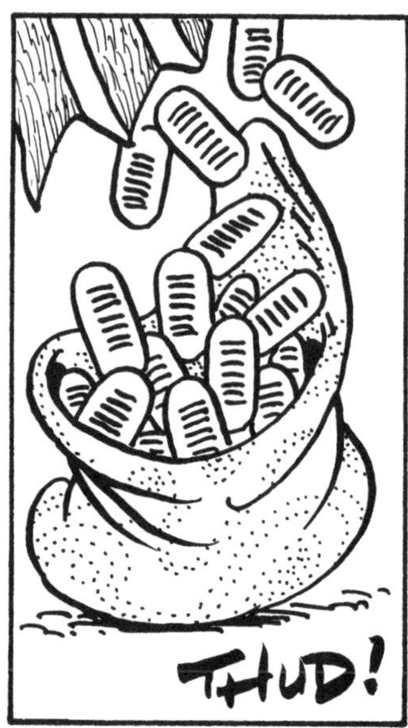
THUD!

NO!
?
20.

IT'S JUST A CRUEL JOKE! HE'S WAITING ON THE BRIDGE!
I KNOW HE IS!
UH... MISS? MISS!
YOU DROPPED YOUR MONEY!

USAGI!

USAGI!

USAGI!

.....
21

USAGI--?

USAGI--?!

HERE YOU ARE! I'VE BEEN LOOKING FOR YOU!

OH, USAGI, I WAS SO WORRIED! I--

YOU...UH...LEFT YOUR MONEY AND... UH...SANDALS AT THE INN, MISS.
OH--!

THERE'S...UH... QUITE A LOT HERE... UH...EVEN ENOUGH TO... UH... START A SMALL BUSINESS.
NO! NO!

NO...
SOB! SOB!

I...UH...I'VE GOT TO GET BACK TO...UH... THE INN. I'LL...UH...JUST LEAVE YOUR THINGS HERE...UH... NEXT TO YOU...UH... OKAY?
SOB!
22

BUT YOU PROMISED...

23

YOU SHOULDN'T LEAVE YOUR MONEY LYING AROUND.

EH--?

OH--!

EXCUSE ME, BUT WHO ARE YOU?

I AM SHIZUKIRI, A FRIEND OF USAGI'S.
HE ASKED ME TO BRING YOU TO HIM.

THE END

EPILOGUE
HOW COULD I HAVE BEEN SO HEARTLESS?

I EVEN GAVE HER MY WORD OF HONOR!

I CAN'T BELIEVE THAT I LEFT WITHOUT HER!

I PRAY SHE'S STILL THERE!

MAYUMI!

MAYUMI!
MAYUMI!
WHERE ARE YOU, MAYUMI?

.....

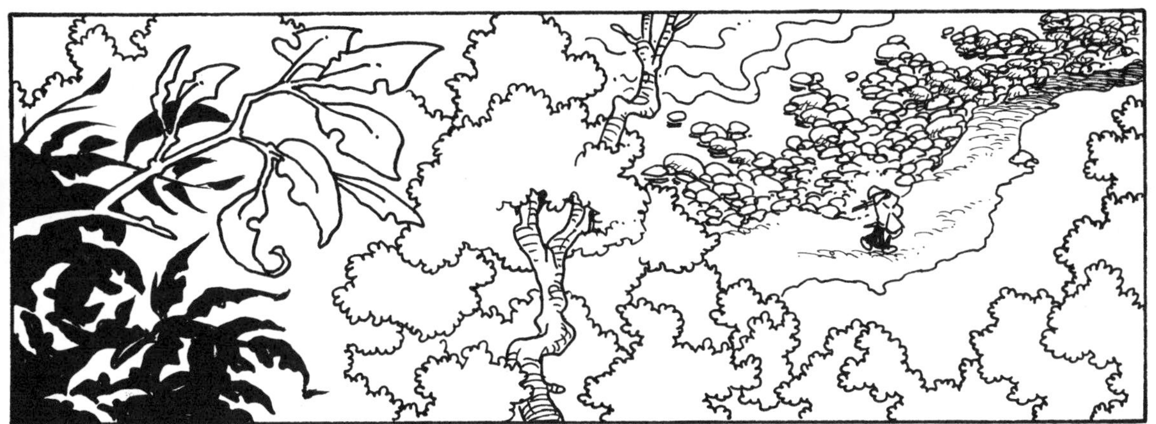

FEVER DREAM

MAYUMI WAS COUNTING ON ME TO WATCH OVER HER, BUT I JUST HAD TO LEAVE HER BEHIND.

IT'S JUST TOO DANGEROUS FOR HER TO STAY WITH ME.

I DID GO BACK, BUT NO ONE I ASKED KNEW WHERE SHE HAD GONE.
WELL, I LEFT HER IN A SAFE TOWN, WITH SUFFICIENT FUNDS TO START A NEW LIFE.

I DID THE BEST THAT I COULD.
NOW HER DESTINY LIES WITH THE GODS.
EH--?

WHO--?

NO ONE...
BUT I KEEP GETTING THIS FEELING THAT I'M BEING FOLLOWED. IT STARTED EVEN BEFORE I MET MAYUMI. IT'S AS IF SOMEONE WERE WATCHING ME.

I'M PROBABLY JUST IMAGINING IT.

OR MAYBE NOT.
TANG!
TANG!
TANG!
TANG!
2.

TANG!

TWANGG!

SHHH!
TOK!

URK!
GURK!
I DON'T WANT TO FIGHT YOU, BROTHERS!
ERK!

I AM CHIZU, LEADER OF THE NEKO NINJA CLAN.
KAGEMARU IS OUR LEADER NOW... OR HE WILL BE AFTER YOUR DEATH!
YOUR DEATH TONIGHT.
KILL HER!
3.

KAGEMARU IS A PAWN OF THE EVIL LORD HIKIJI!

HE WILL LEAD OUR CLAN TO RUIN!
URK!

CHUK!
UHH!

GLURK!

GYAHH!
CHOK!
4.

HOLD ON, CHIZU! I'M HERE!
USAGI!

IT PAINS ME TO HAVE TO SLAY THOSE OF MY OWN CLAN!

YOU HAVE NO CHOICE, IF YOU WANT TO LIVE!
TANG!

JUST ONE MORE!

I'VE GOT HIM!
TANG!

FLOO--!

OW!

TAK!
TAK! TAK!
TAK! TAK!
TAK!

UH...

COUGH! COUGH! GAG!
6.

.....
GURK!

USAGI!

HE'S BEEN POISONED. FORTUNATELY, HE WAS HIT BY A SINGLE NEEDLE.

BUT IF HE DOES NOT GET THE ANTIDOTE SOON, HE'LL BE DEAD IN A FEW HOURS.

THERE ARE MORE OF MY FORMER COMRADES AROUND. I'VE GOT TO GET USAGI TO SAFETY!
I'D BETTER GATHER OUR SWORDS.
7.

HE CAME TO MY RESCUE. HE MUST NOT DIE BECAUSE OF ME.
I PASSED A PEASANT'S HUT NOT FAR FROM HERE.

UGH... I THINK HE'S PUT ON WEIGHT SINCE THE LAST TIME I SAW HIM.

THERE IT IS. IT LOOKS LIKE THERE WAS A FIRE HERE A SHORT TIME AGO.

GOOD. IT'S ABANDONED.

THIS STRAW RAINCOAT WILL MAKE GOOD BEDDING. IT'S CHARRED AND BUG-RIDDEN, BUT I SUSPECT USAGI HAS SLEPT ON WORSE.
8.

GLUG! GLUG!

THE WOUND ON HIS NECK LOOKS FIERCE.
UHH...

WHAT A FEVER HE HAS. HIS FOREHEAD FEELS LIKE IT'S ON FIRE.

THE HERBS FOR THE ANTIDOTE SHOULDN'T BE TOO HARD TO FIND.
USAGI **HAS** TO HOLD ON UNTIL I RETURN.
9.

.....

UHHN...

NNNGHH--!

WE'VE GOT TO STOP HIM BEFORE HE GETS FURTHER INTO THE CASTLE!

URK!
SWIT!

GYAH!
FWIK!

ACH!
SLIT!
10.

HURRY-- THE DEMON IS IN THE EAST WING!

GYAHH!
SWIT!
HE'S HERE! HE'S HERE!

I'LL GET HIM!

ARRH--!

Heh, heh, heh, heh.
11.

SLAY THE FIEND!
HE CAN'T GET PAST US!

Heh, heh, heh.
OOG!
GLUK!
FLOOK!

GAHH!
Hyaahhh!
YAHHH!
IT BURNS LIKE FIRE!

Hyaaah!!
AHH--!
WE CAN'T STOP HIM!
12

Heh, heh, heh, heh, heh. You can never hide from one who is sent by the Gods.
Fighting me is futile.
SSS---
USAGI! YOU ARE THE DEMON WHO HAS INVADED THE GEISHU CASTLE?!
I go where the Gods direct me...
...and the Gods direct me to destroy the evil that lurks within this castle.
No one defeats the Blade of the Gods. Not even you, Lady Tomoe.
STAY BEHIND ME, LORD NORIYUKI!
13

HER TRAIL LEADS HERE.
WHO IS THAT?
A LONG-EARED *RONIN*-- CHIZU HAS HAD DEALINGS WITH HIM IN THE PAST.
NGGHH...

THEN HE'S HER FRIEND.

IT LOOKS LIKE HE'S BEEN POISONED.

UHHGH!

JUST KILL HIM, AND WE'LL CONTINUE OUR SEARCH FOR CHIZU.

14.

HIYAHH!
ULK!
ZWIP!
?
UHH...

IT LOOKS LIKE I GOT BACK JUST IN TIME.
GLUK!
NNGH...

KIAII!
GLNN...

THUNK!
URK!
.....
15

HIS FEVER SEEMS WORSE.

I HOPE I WAS ABLE TO GATHER ENOUGH HERBS.

CHEW! CHEW! CHEW!

SWISH! SWISH!

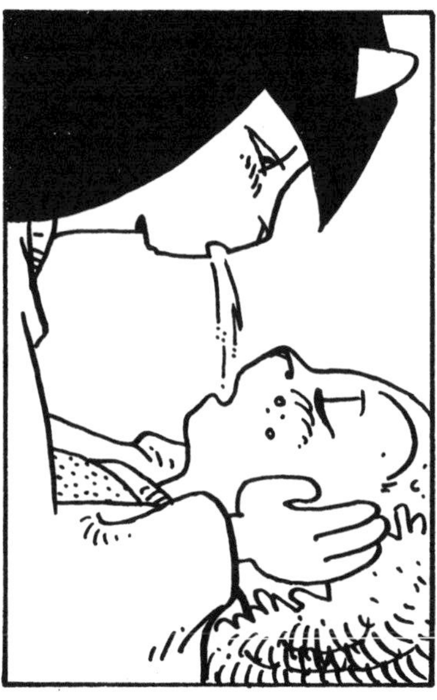

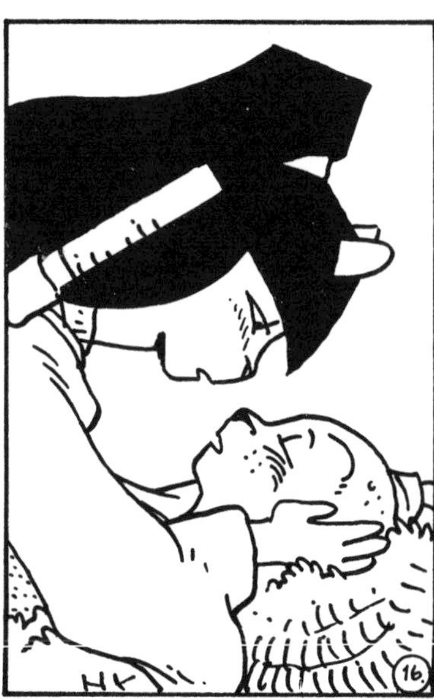
16

THESE CHEWED HERBS WILL TAKE CARE OF YOUR WOUND.

I'LL NEED TO TIE THEM INTO PLACE.

THERE'S NOT MUCH MORE THAT I CAN DO.
NGGH...
THE FEVER MUST RUN ITS COURSE.

HIS HEAD IS EVEN HOTTER THAN BEFORE. WHAT AGONY HE MUST BE GOING THROUGH.

IYAHHHHH!!
17

AAAAAAAAHHHHH
YOU WERE OUR FRIEND, USAGI-- WHY DO YOU NOW SEEK MY LORD'S DEATH?

The Gods have sent me to destroy all the evil in the world.

SLICE!
YOU ARE THE GREATEST EVIL HERE!
Uhh--!

Heh, heh, heh, heh...

Ryahh!
18.

UH--!
SCHAK
WHY, USAGI?

Don't call me "Usagi"... call me "Jei"!
"JEI"? THE DEMON BLADE OF THE GODS?

WHOEVER YOU ARE-- YOU WON'T GET PAST ME!

Hauk!
YAHHHH!
DIE, YOU MONSTER!

Grr...
OW--! LET GO!

STOP, USAGI! YOU'RE POSSESSED BY AN EVIL SPIRIT! FIGHT HIM, USAGI! YOU'VE GOT TO FIGHT HIM!
19.

KIYAHH!
AHH--!
SHOONK!

U-
USAGI...

uh...
uh...
uh...

uhhh...
I-- I...
UH...

I-IT'S LIKE I'M STEPPING OUT OF THE FOG...
T-TOMOE...?
USAGI...

.....
20.

SIGH...

USAGI...?

HIS FEVER HAS BROKEN, THANK THE GODS!

HE SHOULD BE AWAKE BY SUNRISE.
BUT HE IS STILL IN DANGER.
21.

THE LONGER I STAY HERE, THE GREATER THE THREAT FOR HIM.

THEN I'LL HAVE TO LEAD MY PURSUERS AWAY FROM HERE.

GOOD-BYE, USAGI.

MMM...

22.

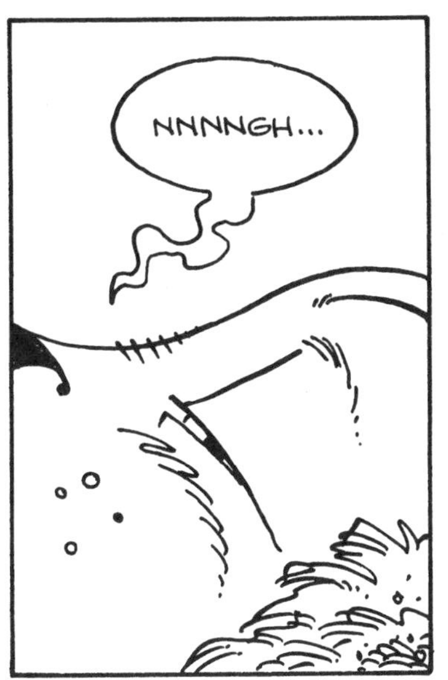
NNNNGH...

WHERE AM I? ALL I REMEMBER IS AN EVIL DREAM...

I HOPE IT WAS NOT A PREMONITION.

A DEAD NEKO NINJA--?
CHIZU! I REMEMBER CHIZU!
THE DARTS-- I WAS POISONED.

CHIZU-- ARE YOU STILL HERE?
UHH... I'M STILL GROGGY.
I'M IN NO SHAPE TO BE TRAVELING YET.
CHIZU?!
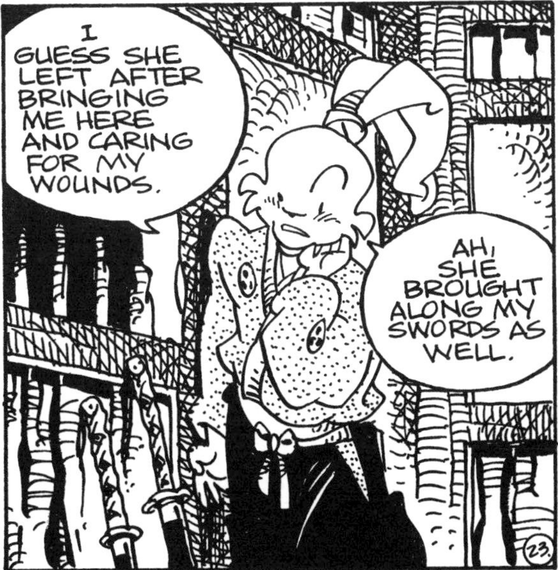
I GUESS SHE LEFT AFTER BRINGING ME HERE AND CARING FOR MY WOUNDS.
AH, SHE BROUGHT ALONG MY SWORDS AS WELL.
23

USAGI! IT'S ME--MAYUMI! PLEASE STEP OUTSIDE!
EH?

MAYUMI! SHE MUST HAVE FOLLOWED ME AFTER ALL! IT WILL BE SUCH A RELIEF TO KNOW SHE IS SAFE!
UH... I'M STILL UNSTEADY.

MAYUMI, HOW DID YOU FIND ME?

!
I'VE BEEN AFTER YOU A LONG TIME, USAGI.
I AM CALLED SHIZUKIRI, AND I AM HERE TO KILL YOU.
USAGI!

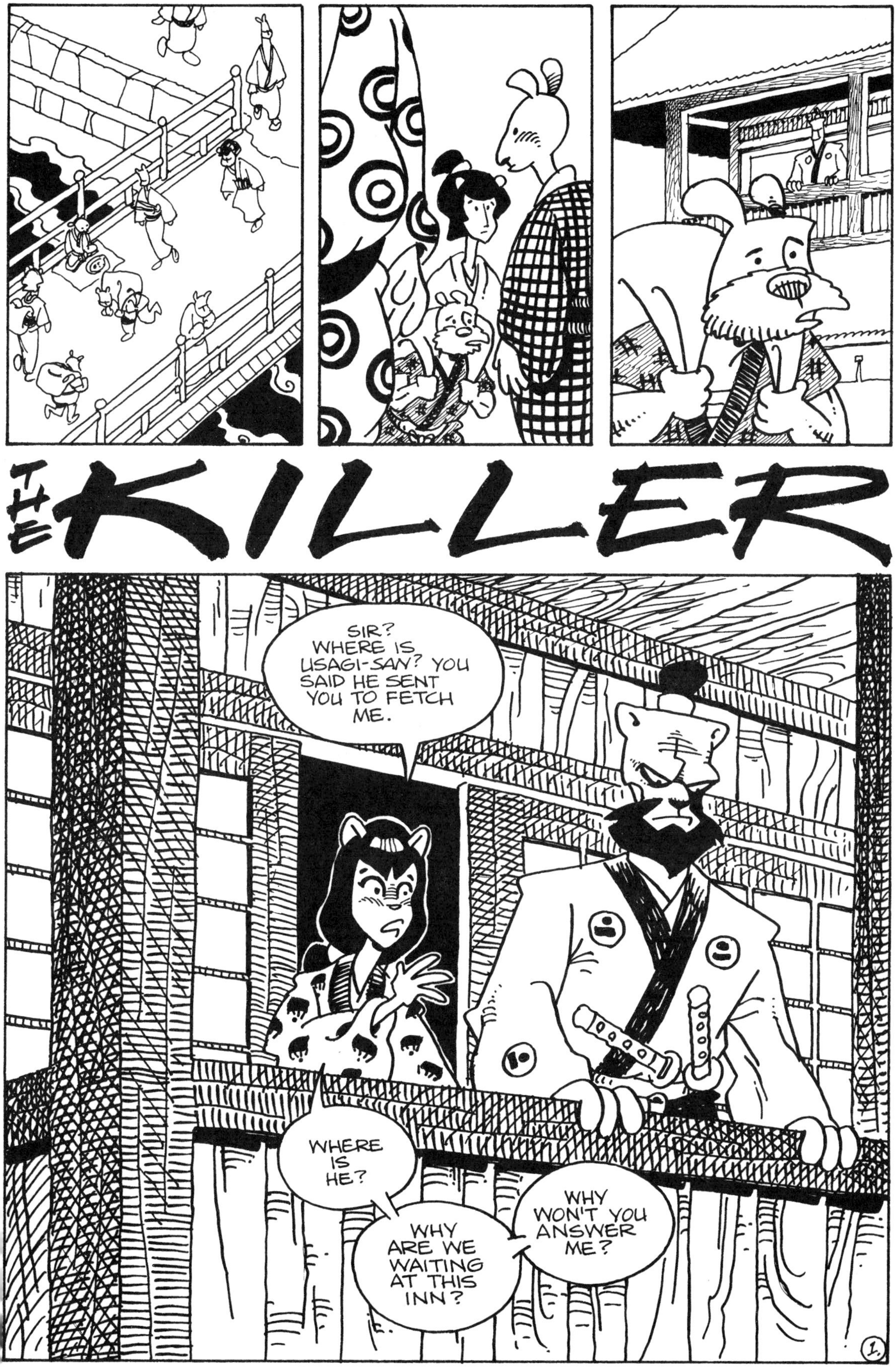

THE KILLER

SIR? WHERE IS USAGI-SAN? YOU SAID HE SENT YOU TO FETCH ME.

WHERE IS HE?

WHY ARE WE WAITING AT THIS INN?

WHY WON'T YOU ANSWER ME?

1.

I WAS SO DISAPPOINTED WHEN HE LEFT ME ON THAT BRIDGE, AFTER HE PROMISED TO MEET ME THERE.
I WAITED FOR SO LONG.

IS HE COMING HERE? IS THAT WHAT WE'RE WAITING FOR?
HE *IS* COMING HERE, RIGHT?
WHY ELSE ARE WE WAITING?

TOK! TOK! TOK!
TOK! TOK! TOK!
OH! THAT MUST BE HIM!

I'M COMING, USAGI-SAN!

WE'VE BEEN WAITING SO LONG FOR YOU, I--
OH!

HEH, HEH, HEH!

PRETTY. VERY PRETTY. VERY NICE.

DON'T TOUCH ME!
MMM... VERY, VERY NICE.
IT'S ABOUT TIME YOU GOT HERE. DO YOU HAVE THE INFORMATION?

YES, YES! I FOUND HIM! I FOUND HIM!
ARE YOU SURE IT'S HIM?

LONG EARS. SCAR OVER LEFT EYE. YEAH, IT'S HIM.
USAGI?
WHERE IS HE?

HE WENT TO THE EAST BRIDGE, THEN HEADED WEST OUT OF TOWN.
THE BRIDGE?

THEN... HE DID RETURN FOR ME! I SHOULD HAVE WAITED A BIT LONGER! WHY DIDN'T I HAVE MORE FAITH IN HIM?
3

B-BUT IF USAGI SENT YOU, YOU WOULD HAVE KNOWN HE WOULD COME BACK FOR ME!
NOW TO FINISH UP OUR BUSINESS.

COME ON, PAY ME! PAY ME NOW!
I'LL PAY YOU WHAT WE AGREED, THEN I WANT YOU OUT OF HERE. YOU DISGUST ME!

DISGUST YOU, DO I? THAT'S OKAY. I DISGUST EVERYBODY. BUT I GIVE YOU WORD OF ADVICE. HE LOOKS TOUGH, THAT ONE. HE'LL BE HARD TO... KILL!
WHAT?

"KILL"? WHAT DOES HE MEAN BY THAT?
OH, DID I SAY SOMETHING I SHOULD NOT HAVE?

ANSWER ME-- WHY DID HE SAY THAT?
YOU'VE GOT YOUR MONEY. NOW GET OUT OF MY SIGHT, BEFORE I KILL YOU.
OH, I'LL LEAVE, MASTER...

...BUT YOU CAN'T KILL SOMEONE AS DISGUSTING AS ME. THAT WOULD ONLY FOUL YOUR BLADE. HEH, HEH, HEH.
THANKS FOR THE COINS.
HEH, HEH.
4.

TELL THE TRUTH--
WHO ARE YOU? DO YOU
INTEND TO KILL
USAGI?

I AM SHIZUKIRI--AN ASSASSIN.
I'VE BEEN AFTER YOUR BOYFRIEND
FOR A WEEK.
!

YOU CAN'T KILL
HIM! AS THAT DIRTY
INFORMANT SAID--
USAGI IS TOO
SKILLED A
SWORDSMAN
FOR YOU.
YES,
HE IS
GOOD, ALL
RIGHT...

...THAT IS WHY
I HAVE YOU--FOR
LEVERAGE.
DO YOU
THINK HE WILL
GIVE UP HIS
LIFE FOR
YOURS?
"L-LEVERAGE"?

HA, HA,
HA! COME
BACK HERE,
YOU
FOOL!
NO!
NO!
USAGI!!

YOU'RE CRAZY IF YOU THINK YOU CAN USE ME TO MURDER USA--
UHH--!
DO YOU THINK YOU HAVE A CHOICE?!
SLAP!

NOW LET'S GO--
--AND KEEP YOUR MOUTH SHUT!

HELP! HELP! HE'S A KILLER! HE'S GOING TO MURDER SOMEONE!

WHAT'S GOING ON HERE?
MY SISTER IS DELUSIONAL. I AM TAKING HER TO THE PRIEST TO EXORCISE HER DEMONS.

DEMONS, HUH? I DON'T KNOW. MAYBE I SHOULD CALL THE AUTHORITIES TO BE SURE.
THIS IS NOT YOUR BUSINESS. STEP ASIDE, AND LET US PASS.
6.

YOU CAN'T SPEAK TO ME LIKE THAT!

.....
COME ALONG, **SISTER**!
OH--!

PICK UP YOUR SANDALS. YOU CAN TIE THEM ON LATER.
OW! YOU'RE HURTING ME!

CRY OUT AGAIN, AND I'LL KILL YOU AND WHOEVER COMES TO YOUR AID.
UNDER-STAND?
Y-YES.
7.

I'VE RELEASED YOUR HAND...

...BUT IF YOU TRY TO RUN, I'LL CUT YOU DOWN BEFORE YOU TAKE FIVE STEPS.

BUT DON'T DAWDLE. IF WE DON'T CATCH UP TO HIM BY NIGHTFALL, YOU'LL BE OF NO USE TO ME ALIVE.

I'LL BE GLAD WHEN USAGI KILLS YOU!
AND HE WILL! HE IS A GREAT SWORDS-MAN!
HA, HA, HA!

COOPERATE WITH ME, AND YOU'LL GET OUT OF THIS ALIVE.
THE ONLY REASON I'M COOPERATING IS BECAUSE I KNOW USAGI IS TOO SKILLED A SWORDSMAN FOR THE LIKES OF YOU!

!
8.

USAGI! USAGI!
!

USA--MMMPH!

MMMPH!

QUIET! I'M NOT READY TO LET HIM KNOW I'M AFTER HIM!

BUT DOES HE SUSPECT SOMETHING?

NO. HE PROBABLY JUST THINKS IT'S HIS IMAGINATION.
MMPH!
9.

THE FOOL IS TOTALLY OBLIVIOUS TO US.
AS FOR YOU--

I'VE BEEN AS PATIENT AS I'M GOING TO BE WITH YOU!
WAK!

GET UP, AND LET'S GO.

STAND UP, I SAID...
...OR I'LL HIT YOU AGAIN!

GIVEN THE CHANCE, I WOULD KILL YOU MYSELF!

HA HA HA HA HA! I'D BETTER NOT TURN MY BACK TO YOU, THEN!
10.

DON'T TRY TO RUN AWAY. YOU KNOW YOU WON'T GET FAR.
HA HA!
DON'T TOUCH ME!

WHY DO YOU HUNT USAGI? WHAT HAS HE DONE TO YOU?
NOTHING.

I MET HIM JUST ONCE, AND ONLY FOR A FEW SECONDS.
THEN WHY--?

FOR MONEY. WHY ELSE WOULD I KILL?

USAGI WOULD NEVER FIGHT FOR MONEY. HE HAS HONOR. HE IS A TRUE *SAMURAI*--
QUIET.

WHAT IS IT?
HE LEFT THE ROAD IN A HURRY. HE DID NOT COVER HIS TRACKS, SO HE MUST STILL BE UNAWARE OF US.
11.

SOMETHING LURED HIM INTO THE TREES. COME ON, BUT KEEP SILENT.

HIS TRAIL IS EASY ENOUGH TO FOLLOW.
THEN HE'LL KILL YOU ALL THE MORE QUICKLY.

CAN'T YOU SEE THAT YOU CAN NEVER BEAT USAGI?
YOU MAY AS WELL ABANDON YOUR SEARCH FOR HIM NOW.
HE DID THIS? HE IS EVEN MORE FORMIDABLE THAN I THOUGHT. I'M GLAD I BROUGHT YOU ALONG.

NO... THESE CUTS WERE MADE BY TWO DIFFERENT BLADES.

HE MUST HAVE HAD AN ACCOMPLICE.
BUT WHERE ARE THEY?
12.

HMM... JUST ONE SET OF FOOTPRINTS LEAVING THE CLEARING. THEY ARE SMALLER THAN USAGI'S, BUT MUCH HEAVIER.

WHOEVER IT WAS MUST HAVE BEEN CARRYING HIM. I BET USAGI WAS INJURED IN THAT FIGHT... TOO INJURED TO WALK AWAY ON HIS OWN.

HE MIGHT EVEN BE DEAD BY THE TIME WE CATCH UP TO THEM...
...BUT WHO CAN THAT OTHER PERSON BE?
YOU SHOULD NOT HAVE TURNED YOUR BACK TO ME.

I SAID I WOULD KILL YOU IF I HAD THE CHANCE.
WHO IS HE?
HE MUST ALSO BE A SKILLED FIGHTER.

IT COMPLICATES THINGS.
13.

HA! DID YOU THINK YOU COULD TAKE ME UNAWARES?
OH--!

BUT I'M IMPRESSED. I DID NOT BELIEVE YOU ACTUALLY HAD THE NERVE TO ATTACK ME.
UHN--!

I WON'T UNDERESTIMATE YOU AGAIN.

WOK!

.....
14

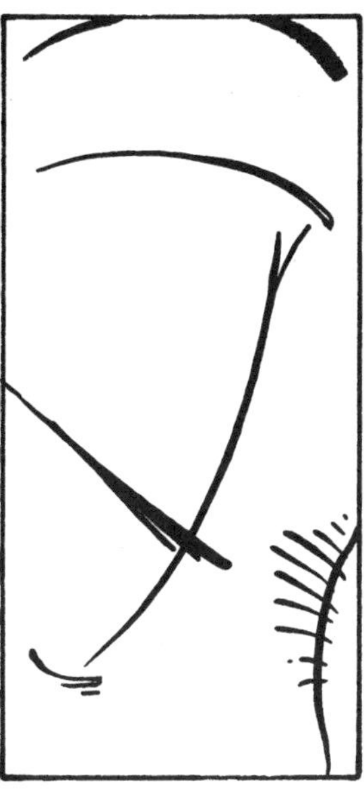

.....

UHN...

?

SO YOU'RE AWAKE, ARE YOU? I TIED YOU UP WITH THE SASHES OF THE DEAD *NINJA*. YOU WON'T BE ANY MORE OF A PROBLEM NOW. I'LL UNDO YOUR GAG WHEN I NEED YOUR VOICE.
MMMPH!

I FOLLOWED THE FOOTPRINTS TO THAT ABANDONED HUT. IT WASN'T EASY. I LOST THE TRAIL A COUPLE OF TIMES. I STILL DO NOT KNOW WHO IS WITH USAGI.

WHAT'S THIS NOW?
NEKO NINJA?
I'M GLAD I HELD BACK ENTERING THE HUT.
WHAT IS GOING ON HERE?
15

A WOMAN NOW--AS IF THINGS WERE NOT MYSTERIOUS ENOUGH.

SLASH!
HACK!
CUT!
ULK!
UH--GAK!
SLIT!

IT SOUNDS LIKE A BATTLE IN THERE.
WHAT DOES USAGI HAVE TO DO WITH THE NEKO NINJA?

NOW SHE'S LEAVING... FOR GOOD, OR WILL SHE RETURN?
ARE THOSE THREE *NINJA* DEAD? WHAT ABOUT USAGI?
THERE'S NOTHING TO DO BUT WAIT.
16.

HOURS LATER...

UHH...

OHH... I FEEL TERRIBLE.
WHERE AM I?

DEAD NEKO NINJA...?
I REMEMBER NOW... CHIZU!

I WAS HIT BY A POISON NINJA DART. CHIZU MUST HAVE BROUGHT ME HERE.

CHIZU-- ARE YOU HERE?
I GUESS NOT.
AT LEAST SHE LEFT MY SWORDS.

USAGI! IT'S ME--MAYUMI! PLEASE STEP OUTSIDE!
EH?
17.

UH...
I'M STILL
UNSTEADY.

MAYUMI,
HOW DID
YOU FIND
ME?

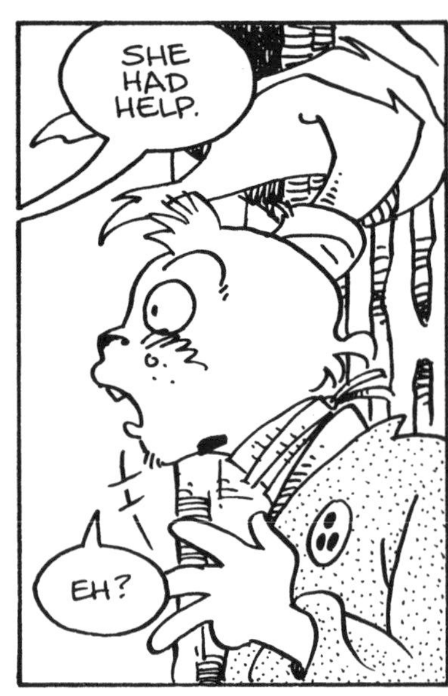
SHE
HAD
HELP.
EH?

I AM CALLED
SHIZUKIRI, AND I
AM HERE TO KILL
YOU.
I'VE
BEEN AFTER
YOU A LONG
TIME,
USAGI.
USAGI!

I KNOW YOU--
YOU'RE A SWORD
FOR SALE... AN
ASSASSIN.

YOU HAVE BEEN A THORN IN THE
HAND OF KOROSHI, THE LEAGUE OF
ASSASSINS. I HAVE BEEN
ASSIGNED TO PLUCK
THAT THORN.

CAN'T
YOU SEE
HE'S
HURT?
GOOD. THAT WILL
MAKE IT EASIER TO
KILL HIM!
18.

REMOVE YOUR SWORDS, AND TOSS THEM AWAY, USAGI.

BUT THAT'S NOT FAIR!
HE WON'T STAND A CHANCE AGAINST YOU!

YOU MISTAKE ME FOR AN HONORABLE SAMURAI. I AM AN ASSASSIN.

NOW THROW OUT YOUR SWORDS OR I'LL KILL HER, USAGI!
NO, USAGI! DON'T

I WARNED YOU TO BE SILENT!
UH--!
SMAK!

LOSE YOUR SWORDS OR SHE DIES, USAGI!

STOP IT! STOP IT! I'M REMOVING MY SWORDS!
BUT RELEASE HER BEFORE I THROW THEM AWAY!
19.

VERY WELL.
SWIT!
OH!

NO!

CALM DOWN, RONIN.
GET UP, GIRL.
WHIMPER!
GET UP!

OKAY. NOW TOSS AWAY YOUR SWORDS, AND I'LL LET HER GO.
!

ALL RIGHT. I'M DISCARDING MY BLADES.
NOW GET OUT OF HERE, MAYUMI. RUN!

B-BUT IT'S MY FAULT HE FOUND YOU!

THERE IS NOTHING YOU CAN DO. I CAN TAKE CARE OF MYSELF. I'LL CATCH UP TO YOU SOON. I PROMISE.

YOU PROMISED TO MEET ME AT THE BRIDGE, AND I WAITED SO LONG...
20

I'M SORRY I LET YOU DOWN, BUT I DID RETURN, MAYUMI... EVENTUALLY. IT TOOK ME THAT LONG TO REALIZE WHAT YOU MEAN TO ME. I *DID* RETURN...

YES, I KNOW. BUT BY THEN IT WAS TOO LATE. IF I'D ONLY HAD MORE FAITH, I WOULD HAVE WAITED LONGER.
HAVE FAITH IN ME NOW, MAYUMI. I'LL SEE YOU VERY SOON.

BUT, USAGI, YOU'RE HURT--AND UNARMED!

ENOUGH OF THIS PRATTLE! YOU'LL SOON MEET ALL RIGHT--*IN HELL*!

STAY OUT OF THE WAY, MAYUMI!

HIIYAAAAAA

21.

WHAT?
NO!

USAGI--
RUN!

MAYUMI--
LET HIM
GO!
THUK!

I'VE
GOT HIM,
USAGI!
RUN!
LET--

--GO!
ZWIT!

RYAAA
22.

RYAAAAAAAA

.....

B-BUT... HOW DID YOU GET THE...
...SWORD...

MAYUMI!
23.

I'M SORRY, MAYUMI. YOU WERE LOOKING FOR A BETTER LIFE, BUT I JUST BROUGHT YOU DEATH.

DON'T FEEL GUILTY, USAGI. IT WAS MY FAULT. I SHOULD HAVE HAD MORE FAITH.

BUT I'LL DIE KNOWING THAT YOU RETURNED...

...TO...
...THE...

...BRIDGE...

MAYUMI...?
MAYUMI...?

SOB.

THE END

RETURN OF THE BLACK SOUL

TWENTY-SIX YEARS AGO, a rabbit in samurai costume entered a lonely hut seeking shelter from a blizzard, announced, "I am called Miyamoto Usagi"—and began one of the most remarkable sustained narratives in the history of the comics.

Although his name comes from the warrior-hero Miyamoto Musashi, Usagi is a fusion of Japanese and American elements, from Akira Kurosawa and George Stevens to Tsukioka Yoshitoshi and Will Eisner. Stan Sakai took the title for his comic from Kurosawa's classic *Yojimbo*. A *ronin* (masterless samurai), Usagi began as a bodyguard for hire, but he quickly turned into a wanderer, following the *musha shugyo* (warrior's path) to perfect his spiritual and martial skills.

Usagi owes as much to Alan Ladd in *Shane* as he does to Toshiro Mifune in *Yojimbo* or *Sanjuro*. He's the stranger who wanders into town, rights a wrong, tosses out a tin-horn bully, solves a mystery, and maybe breaks a heart. The townspeople, a feudal lord, or a beautiful girl ask Usagi to stay, but he moves on. He may long for a peaceful, settled life, but the backroads and byways are his only real home.

Stan set *Usagi Yojimbo* in a country that resembles Japan in the early seventeenth century, shortly after the establishment of the Tokugawa shogunate ended an era of civil wars. His careful research helps to bring his imaginary world to life. The buildings, tools, weapons, and costumes evoke the early Edo era, giving Usagi a believable stage for his adventures.

Usagi has a more complex personality than the standard comic book hero. An honorable and highly disciplined practitioner of Bushido, the warrior's code, he despises bullies. He'll help anyone in trouble, and his propensity for sticking his nose in others' business often lands him in trouble. His mischievous sense of humor balances his volatile temper. Usagi prefers not to kill, but when he's forced to unsheathe his weapon, his consummate swordsmanship (swordsrabbitship?) enables him to dispatch enemies swiftly and decisively, leaving one of Stan's delightfully weird skulls floating over the victim's body.

The adventures that follow focus on Jei, the demon who believes he's a divine emissary of justice. Usagi destroyed the previous form of this murderous foe with the Kusanagi, the sacred sword of the sun goddess Amaterasu, in *Usagi Yojimbo Saga* Book 2, *Grasscutter*. But Jei requires a lot of killing. Taking possession of one body after another, he spreads death and terror wherever he appears. Stan leavens these dark tales with impish humor. Jei's name is a pun: when the standard Japanese honorific *san* is appended, it becomes "Jei-*san*"—or "Jason," the villain from the *Friday the 13th* horror movies. And like Jason, Jei will be back.

Demons often appear in Japanese folktales. So do *tengu* (forest goblins) and *kappa* (water demons), whom Usagi has also fought. The more the reader knows about these traditions, the more he can appreciate the richness of Stan's narrative. The supernatural attack of the monstrous spider in "The Doors" (*Saga* Book 5, *Tomoe's Story*) is a great ghost story. But it's also an evocation of Yoshitoshi's famous print *Minamoto no Yorimitsu Striking at the Ground Spider* and of the Kabuki plays that feature spider monsters.

That "Doors" works as both a straightforward tale and a modern retelling of a classic fable highlights Stan's greatest skills: he's a storyteller par excellence and a master of the comic book form. The crisp, calligraphic drawings and immaculately lettered words in *Usagi Yojimbo* present those stories more powerfully than words or images could alone. I was introduced to Stan and his work several years ago by our mutual friend, comics packager Lee Nordling. I've been a fan ever since, and I continue to admire the apparently effortless way Stan fuses words and pictures into a seamless, timeless tale. Happily, the story continues, taking Usagi and the reader to new adventures that lie beyond the next bend in the road.

During the last twenty-six years, Usagi has survived countless sword fights, pitched battles, attacks by Jei and other monsters—and the equally violent ups and downs of the American comic book industry. Yet readership for the series has never flagged. Gen X fans who enjoyed *Usagi Yojimbo* as teenagers have begun passing old, dog-eared books on to their kids, creating a second generation of readers.

Not bad for a rabbit who came in from the cold.

Charles Solomon

2010

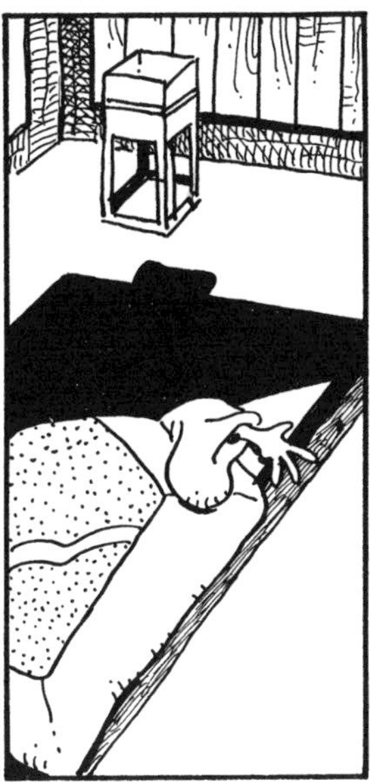

The Darkness and the Soul

1.

KIIII-AH!

TWILL!

HIYAHH!

KLAK!

KLAK!
KLAK!
KLAK!
KLAK!
KLAK!
KLAK!

KYAAAA
2.

KLAK!
UH--!

OW!
THUD!

HYAAAA

HA HA HA HA HA!

THAT WAS A GOOD MATCH, KIN-SAN.

I'M JUST A POOR OPPONENT FOR YOU, PRIEST JIZONOBU.

YOU ARE AS SKILLED AS ANY OF THE WARRIOR-MONKS OF MOUNT HIEI.

BUT THEY PRACTICE THE SPEAR TO INTIMIDATE.
FOR ME, THE SPEAR IS AN EXERCISE IN DISCIPLINE.

I MAY HAVE BEEN A *SAMURAI* YEARS AGO, BUT NOW THE SIMPLE LIFE OF A PRIEST SUITS ME.
4.

NO ONE CAN QUESTION YOUR DEVOTION...
...AND YOU ARE KNOWN THROUGHOUT THE AREA AS A SKILLED HEALER.

I TRY TO ATONE FOR MY PAST LIFE.
BUT NOW I MUST MAKE MY ROUNDS TO THE SMALLER VILLAGES.

HERE IS YOUR MEDICAL BAG, HEAD PRIEST JIZONOBU.
THANK YOU, BUNJI.

WOULD YOU LIKE ME TO ACCOMPANY YOU, PRIEST JIZONOBU?
THANK YOU, BUT NOT TODAY, KIN.
BE CAREFUL. IT LOOKS LIKE IT WILL RAIN TODAY.

SUCH A DEVOTED PERSON.
IT IS FITTING THAT HE IS NAMED AFTER JIZO THE COMPASSIONATE.

5.

PRIEST JI IS COMING!

*GRANDPA

HAHAHA! THAT'S OKAY. I ENJOY THE SOUND OF THEIR LAUGHTER.
YOU ARE MUCH TOO TOLERANT OF THESE RASCALS!
WHAT DID I DO?

LOOK, PRIEST JI, I GREW THIS MYSELF! THIS IS FOR YOU!

AH, A FINE PUMPKIN, KEI-CHAN. IT WILL MAKE A FINE MEAL.

AND YOU, ICHIRO, HOW IS YOUR LEG TODAY?

MUCH BETTER, PRIEST JI! SEE?
HA HA HA! I HOPE THAT WILL TEACH YOU NOT TO JUMP OFF THE ROOF ANYMORE, ICHIRO.
HOP!
HOP!
7.

LET ME SEE... AH, YES. IT IS COMING ALONG VERY NICELY.

YOU HAVE THE GIFT OF HEALING, PRIEST JIZONOBU. IF ONLY YOU CAN HELP YOUNG JUBEI.

JUBEI? WHAT'S WRONG WITH HIM? IS HE INJURED?
IT'S THE STRANGEST THING!

HE BECAME TERRIBLY SICK LAST NIGHT, AND IS DECLINING RAPIDLY.
I'VE NEVER SEEN ANYTHING LIKE IT.

LEAD ME TO HIM.
IF THERE IS ANYONE WHO CAN HELP HIM, IT IS YOU, PRIEST JIZONOBU.
8.

I'VE NEVER FELT A FEVER SO HOT!
HOW LONG HAS HE HAD THIS FEVER?

HE WAS FINE YESTERDAY, THEN HE JUST COLLAPSED, AND WE HAVE NOT BEEN ABLE TO ROUSE HIM.
HE WON'T EAT, AND HE SPITS OUT WATER AS IF IT WERE POISON.

WHAT AILS HIM?
I DON'T KNOW.
CAN YOU CURE HIM?

I'VE NEVER SEEN SUCH SEVERE SYMPTOMS.

IT COULD BE A NEW SICKNESS, BROUGHT HERE BY FOREIGNERS.
THEN THERE IS NO HOPE FOR HIM? H-HE WILL DIE?
WHAT KIND OF ILLNESS IS THIS?
9.

THOSE FOREIGN DEVILS-- I HEAR THEY ARE NOT HUMAN, AS WE ARE!

NOW, NOW, DON'T JUDGE THEM TOO HARSHLY. I IMAGINE A FEW OF THEM MIGHT BE QUITE DECENT.

THERE IS NOTHING MUCH MORE I CAN DO, EXCEPT PRAY TO MERCIFUL BUDDHA.

I HAVE TWO OTHER CHILDREN. D-DO YOU THINK JUBEI MIGHT BE CONTAGIOUS?
I DON'T KNOW. IT MIGHT BE WISE IF YOUR OTHER CHILDREN SPEND A FEW DAYS AT A NEIGHBOR'S HOME.

PERHAPS THERE IS SOMETHING I CAN FIND IN THE TEMPLE INFIRMARY.
I WILL BE BACK SOON. I PROMISE.
THANK YOU, PRIEST JIZONOBU! THANK YOU!
10.

LATER...

JUBEI'S ILLNESS IS TRULY A MYSTERY.

ARE YOU TROUBLED, PRIEST JIZONOBU?
EH--?

HEH HEH HEH.

WHAT DO YOU WANT, IBARAKI?
NOTHING. NOTHING. I AM JUST WANDERING, AS YOU DO.

WE ARE ***NOTHING*** ALIKE. YOU PRAY TO THE ***DARK GODS***. BUDDHA IS ABOUT COMPASSION.
YOUR WORDS HURT ME, JIZONOBU.

YOU AND I-- WE WANT TO ELIMINATE THE EVILS IN THIS WORLD.
BUT WHAT MAY BE EVIL TO YOUR GODS MIGHT NOT BE EVIL TO MINE.
11.

EVIL IS EVIL, AND I WILL HAVE NOTHING TO DO WITH YOU.

I JUST OFFER YOU MY FRIENDSHIP, GOOD PRIEST.

I WILL TAKE **NOTHING** FROM YOU. YOUR GODS ALWAYS DEMAND A TERRIBLE PAYMENT.
HEH HEH. BUT I TAKE NO MORE THAN WHAT ONE IS WILLING TO GIVE.

THE PEOPLE ARE AWARE OF YOUR LIES. YOU WILL GET NO MORE SUPPORT AROUND HERE.
I HAVE ALL THE SUPPORT I NEED.

THAT'S ENOUGH! I CAN'T TAKE ANY MORE OF YOU! CRAWL BACK INTO THE CAVE YOU CAME OUT OF!

OKAY, OKAY, I'M GOING, BUT I'LL SEE YOU SOON ENOUGH, JIZONOBU. IN FACT, **YOU** WILL SEEK **ME** OUT!
12.

THAT CHARLATAN INFURIATES ME!
THERE IS NOTHING I CAN DO, EXCEPT SHOW HIM UP AS THE EVIL HE IS!
HEH HEH HEH.

!

CRUNCH!

THE INTERIOR IS FILLED WITH VERMIN AND FILTH.
BZZZZZZZ
BZZZZZZZZZ
BZZZZZZZZZ
SCAMPER!
SCAMPER!

TOO BAD. IT LOOKED SO GOOD ON THE OUTSIDE.
13

BAM! BAM! BAM! BAM! BAM! BAM!
OPEN UP! LET US IN!

HURRY AND OPEN THIS GATE!
HOLD ON! WE'RE COMING!
BAM! BAM! BAM!

WHAT IS SO IMPORTANT THAT YOU HAVE TO COME TO THE TEMPLE AT THIS HOUR OF THE NIGHT?

I GO WHERE I PLEASE, WHENEVER I PLEASE.
GULP! LORD GOYO!

PLEASE COME IN, LORD GOYO!

PRIEST JIZONOBU! PRIEST JIZONOBU!
14.

WELCOME, LORD GOYO. HOW MAY OUR HUMBLE TEMPLE BE OF ASSISTANCE TO YOU?
I COME ON BEHALF OF MY DAUGHTER, KEIFUMI.
SHE HAS FALLEN ILL SUDDENLY-- AND VERY SEVERELY.

MY OWN DOCTORS ARE UNABLE TO CURE HER. IT IS SAID THAT YOU ARE THE MOST SKILLED PHYSICIAN IN THIS AREA, SO I TURN TO YOU, PRIEST JIZONOBU.

D-DOES SHE HAVE AN INTENSE FEVER, AND WILL NOT DRINK OR EAT?

AH, I SEE YOU ARE FAMILIAR WITH HER SYMPTOMS, SO I KNOW KEIFUMI WILL BE IN GOOD HANDS.

I PLACE HER LIFE IN YOUR CAPABLE HANDS, HEAD PRIEST JIZONOBU. SAVE HER, AND I WILL BECOME A PATRON OF THIS TEMPLE...

...BUT IF SHE DIES--!
I-- I WILL DO MY BEST, LORD GOYO.
15

SHE HAS THE SAME SYMPTOMS AS JUBEI.
WILL SHE DIE?
WE WILL DO OUR BEST TO MAKE HER WELL.
BUT IF SHE DIES, WILL LORD GOYO REALLY BLAME THE TEMPLE?
DO NOT CONCERN YOURSELF WITH THAT.
CONCENTRATE ON HELPING THIS POOR CHILD.
PRIEST JIZONOBU, WE HAVE FOUND ACCOMMODATIONS FOR LORD GOYO AND HIS MEN OVER IN THE OTHER BUILDING.
THANK YOU. SEE TO IT THAT THEY ARE WELL TAKEN CARE OF.
WE HAVE MUCH TO DO TONIGHT, KIN.
16.

MORNING...

SHE IS GETTING WORSE! WHAT KIND OF HEALER ARE YOU?
I ASSURE YOU, WE ARE DOING EVERYTHING WE CAN.

THAT IS NOT ENOUGH! IF SHE DIES, I SWEAR THAT THIS TEMPLE WILL BE RAZED, THE GROUNDS SALTED, AND EVERYONE WITHIN WILL BE BEHEADED!

NO! YOU CAN'T DO THAT! THAT IS...IS... EVIL!
KIN! SHOW RESPECT TO LORD GOYO!

YOU DARE CRITICIZE ME?!

GRR...
CURE HER, OR I WILL KEEP MY PROMISE!
17.

NGGH...!
KIN, ARE YOU ALL RIGHT?

THIS IS ALL YOUR FAULT! WHY DON'T YOU GET WELL?!
STOP IT, KIN!

SHE IS BLAMELESS--AND THE TRUE VICTIM HERE. SHE IS AN INNOCENT IN THIS. IT IS HER FATHER WHO HARBORS EVIL.

WE HAVE DONE ALL WE CAN. NOW IT IS UP TO MERCIFUL BUDDHA.
YOU ARE RIGHT. I APOLOGIZE.

I MUST NOT NEGLECT MY OTHER PATIENTS. JUBEI HAS AS MUCH RIGHT TO MY CARE AS THE DAUGHTER OF A LORD, AND I HAVE ALREADY LEFT HIM MUCH TOO LONG.
I WILL WATCH OVER THE GIRL.
I WILL LEAVE HER IN YOUR CARE, THEN.

I WILL RETURN IN A COUPLE OF HOURS.
YES, HEAD PRIEST.
18.

LORD GOYO IS SERIOUS. HE WILL DESTROY THE TEMPLE AND EXECUTE US ALL.

HE IS A HARSH PERSON, AND HIS DAUGHTER'S ILLNESS HAS MADE HIM UNREASONABLE.
WE MUST SAVE KEIFUMI.

BUT NOW I SHOULD THINK OF JUBEI. I FEAR I WILL HAVE TO RECITE PRAYERS FOR THE DEAD WHEN I SEE HIM. I HOPE HIS MOTHER IS NOT TOO DISTRAUGHT.

I GOT HERE JUST BEFORE THE RAIN.
I HOPE IT HOLDS OFF UNTIL I'M BACK AT THE TEMPLE.

HELLO! I'M SORRY I DID NOT COME EARLIER.
AH, PRIEST JIZONOBU! WELCOME!
19.

EH--? JUBEI?!
HI, PRIEST JI!

Y-YOU'RE ALL RIGHT?!
YEAH! NEVER BETTER!
BUT HOW--?

PRIEST IBARAKI CAME BY SOON AFTER YOU LEFT, AND OFFERED POTIONS AND PRAYERS.
I TOLD YOU NOT TO HAVE ANYTHING TO DO WITH HIM!

BUT YOU COULD NOT HELP MY SON, AND HE DID.
I WAS AS GOOD AS NEW A FEW HOURS LATER.

WHAT ABOUT PAYMENT?
OH, HE ASKED FOR NOTHING IN RETURN.

"NOTHING"?
HE MUST HAVE FELT GENEROUS...BUT I WOULD HAVE PAID ANYTHING FOR MY JUBEI'S LIFE.
20.

NOW STAY UNTIL THE RAIN LETS UP. JUBEI, LET'S SERVE PRIEST JIZONOBU SOME OF OUR GRUEL.
YES, MAMA.

MMM... IT SMELLS GOOD!

AH, IT'S STILL NICE AND HOT. MY, SUCH A FIERCE STORM. AREN'T YOU GLAD TO BE WARM AND DRY IN OUR LITTLE HUT, PRIEST JIZONOBU?

PRIEST JIZONOBU?
HUH? WHY WOULD HE LEAVE NOW?
MY COOKING IS NOT **THAT** BAD.
IS IT?
21

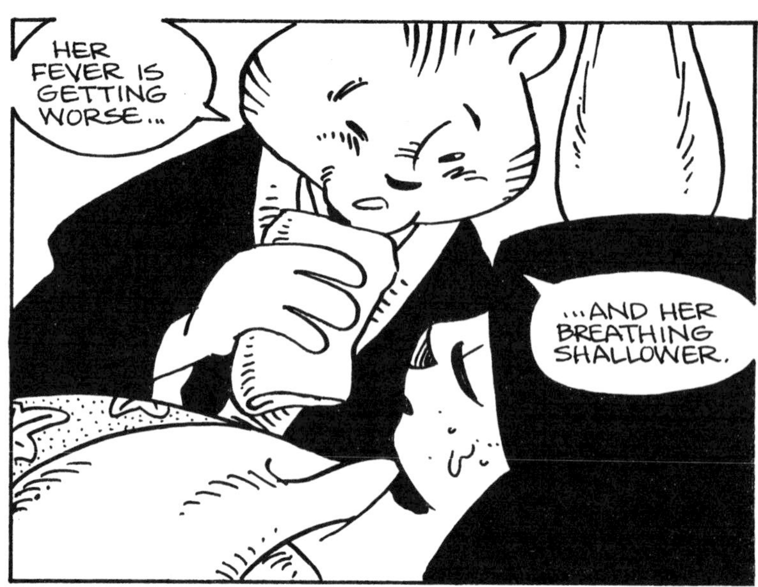
HER FEVER IS GETTING WORSE...
...AND HER BREATHING SHALLOWER.

SHE CAN'T POSSIBLY LIVE MUCH LONGER.

WHERE ARE YOU, PRIEST JIZONOBU? IT HAS BEEN HOURS SINCE YOU LEFT.

22

KRAK!
BOOM!

STATUES! THEY ARE JUST STATUES.

23.

WELCOME.
.....

PRIEST JIZONOBU... YOU MUST HURRY BACK!

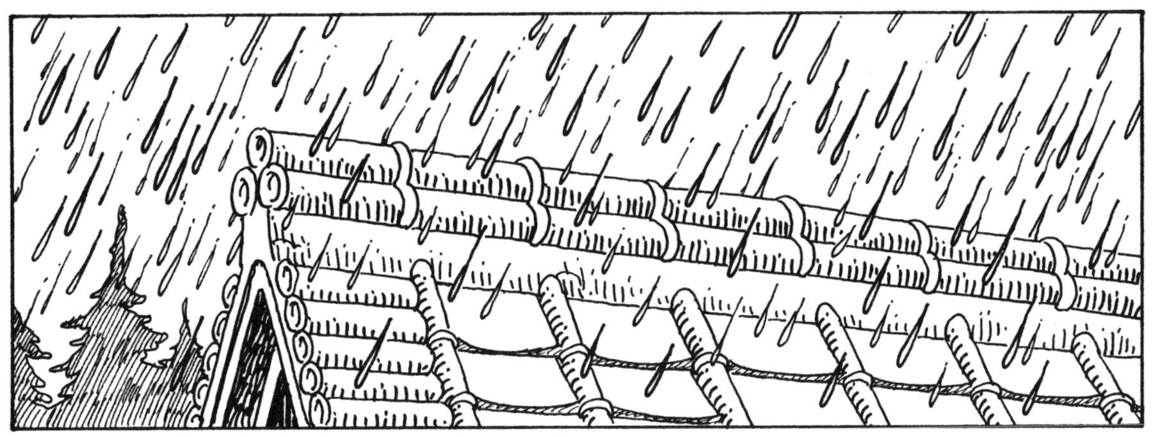

OH, PRIEST JIZONOBU... WHERE ARE YOU?

WELL, PRIEST, HOW IS MY DAUGHTER?!
GASP! L-LORD GOYO!

THERE IS NO CHANGE IN HER CONDITION, BUT I'M SURE SHE WILL GET BETTER SOON.
YOU HAD BETTER HOPE SO.

HER BREATHING IS EVEN SHALLOWER.
SHE'S IN EVEN WORSE CONDITION THAN BEFORE.
1.

WHERE IS PRIEST JIZONOBU?

THE HEAD PRIEST? I-- I DON'T KNOW. HE COULD HAVE BEEN CAUGHT OUT IN THE STORM.
BUT HE DID ALL HE COULD, SIR.

WELL, HE DIDN'T DO ENOUGH! THE SECOND AFTER SHE BREATHES HER LAST, YOU AND THE OTHERS IN THIS TEMPLE WILL AS WELL. UNDERSTAND?

;GULP!; Y-YES, LORD GOYO! I UNDERSTAND.

WE NEED YOU, PRIEST JI! PLEASE HURRY BACK!
2.

UH--!

TANG! TANG! TANG! TANG!

TANG! TANG! TANG! TANG!

TANG! TANG! TANG!

AH, PRIEST JIZONOBU...
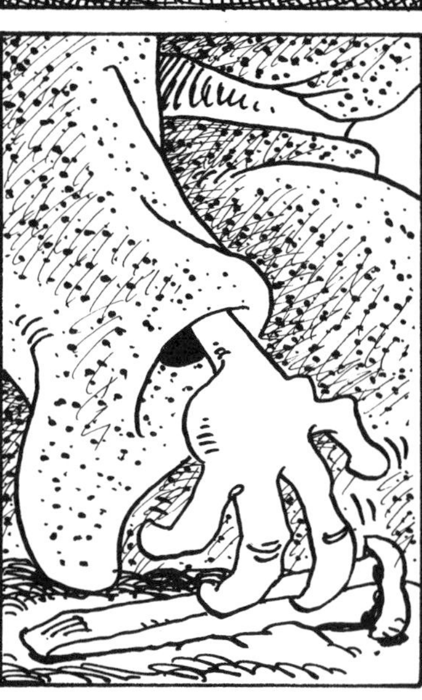

WELCOME. I HAVE BEEN EXPECTING YOU.

!
4.

SO, HEAD PRIEST, HAVE YOU FINALLY COME TO YOUR SENSES AND ENTERED MY TEMPLE TO PRAY TO THE TRUE GODS?

LORD GOYO'S DAUGHTER IS DYING, AND IT IS BEYOND MY POWER TO SAVE HER!

SO YOU TURN TO MY GODS WHERE YOURS HAVE FAILED?

IT IS I WHO HAVE FAILED.
THEN WHAT ARE YOU DOING HERE?

YOU CURED THE BOY, JUBEI--HE HAD THE SAME SYMPTOMS.
AH, YES. IT WAS A SIMPLE TASK.

THEN-- THEN YOU CAN SAVE HER?
OF COURSE.
BUT...
5.

UNLIKE YOURS, MY GODS DEMAND A HEAVY PAYMENT.

WH-WHAT PAYMENT DO THEY WANT FROM ME?

YOU.

B-BUT YOU ASKED NOTHING OF JUBEI.

JUBEI IS NOT THE HEAD PRIEST OF A TEMPLE, NOR THE CHILD OF LORD GOYO.

ACCEPT MY CONDITION, OR SHE WILL DIE.

AND ALL THOSE IN THE TEMPLE AS WELL.
WELL?

I--I ACCEPT.

HEH. HEH. HEH. GOOD.
6.

NOW ENTER DEEP INTO THE CAVE, AND MEET THOSE GODS OF WHOM YOU WOULD ASK A FAVOR.

.....
WELL? GO ON. WHY DO YOU HESITATE? DO YOU WANT THE GIRL TO DIE?

HURRY! THE GODS WILL NOT WAIT FOREVER, YOU KNOW.

I...I'M GOING.
HURRY-- THEY'RE WAITING FOR YOU! HA HA HAAA--!

HAHAHAHAHAHAHA

HAHAHAHAHAHA

HAHAHAHAHAHA

HAHAHAHAHAH
EYAHH!
7.

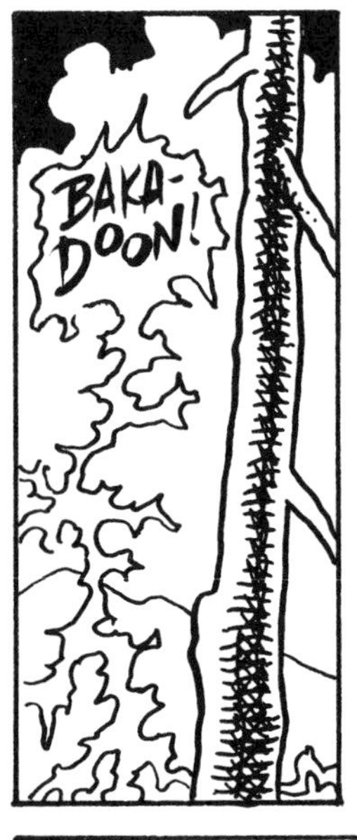
BAKA-DOON!

SHAAAA!!

.....

AHH--!
PAPA! PAPA!

SHE'S AWAKE!
AND HER FEVER IS GONE!
IT'S A MIRACLE!
SOB! SOB! SOB! OH, PAPA!
8.

MORNING...

WHAT A MESS.
IT LOOKS LIKE ANOTHER STORM MAY HIT US TONIGHT.
THE GIRL IS RECOVERING NICELY...

...BUT PRIEST JIZONOBU DID NOT RETURN LAST NIGHT.
OH? HE PROBABLY SOUGHT REFUGE FROM THE RAINS.

WELL, I'M WORRIED ABOUT HIM.
IF HE IS NOT BACK SOON, WE SHOULD GO OUT AND LOOK FOR HIM.

PRIEST JIZONOBU!
9.

LATER...
YOUR DAUGHTER IS RECOVERING QUICKLY, LORD GOYO. SHE WILL BE STRONG ENOUGH TO TRAVEL HOME TOMORROW.

MY ESCORTS AND I WILL SPEND ONE MORE NIGHT AT YOUR TEMPLE THEN.

PLEASE FORGIVE MY EARLIER THREATS TO THIS TEMPLE. THEY WERE MADE IN FRUSTRATION AND ANGER.
OF COURSE, LORD GOYO.

I PROMISE TO BECOME THIS TEMPLE'S LARGEST PATRON. YOU CAN COUNT ON MY SUPPORT.
YOU ARE VERY GENEROUS, MY LORD.

BUT WHAT CAN I DO FOR **YOU?** AFTER ALL, IT WAS YOU WHO SAVED MY LITTLE GIRL.
IT WAS NOT ME. IT IS PRIEST JIZONOBU YOU SHOULD THANK.

THEN WHERE IS HE? I WOULD LIKE TO THANK HIM PERSONALLY, PRIEST KIN.
ALAS, THAT IS NOT POSSIBLE.
WHY IS THAT?
10

PRIEST JI HAS SUCCUMBED TO THE SAME ILLNESS THAT ALMOST KILLED YOUR DAUGHTER.
BUT I FEAR THAT HE WILL NOT RECOVER AS SHE DID.
I AM SORRY TO HEAR THAT.
YOU HAVE MY SYMPATHIES.

BUT I KNOW THERE IS NOTHING I CAN DO FOR HIM. YOU MAY GO NOW.
ER... YES, LORD GOYO. THANK YOU.

11.

PRIEST KIN.
HOW IS PRIEST JIZONOBU?

HE GETS WORSE EVERY MOMENT. I DON'T KNOW HOW HE MADE IT BACK TO THE TEMPLE.
HIS FEVER BURNS SO HOT, I'M AMAZED HIS BEDDING DOESN'T CATCH ON FIRE.

YOU'RE RIGHT. HE'S EVEN WORSE THAN LORD GOYO'S DAUGHTER WAS.

GO AND GET SOME REST. I'LL SIT WITH JI FOR A WHILE.
BUT, KIN, YOU DIDN'T SLEEP AT ALL LAST NIGHT,

IT'S ALL RIGHT. I WON'T BE ABLE TO SLEEP TONIGHT EITHER.
WELL, IF YOU INSIST.
12.

SHAAAAAA!!

WE WERE ABLE TO SAVE THE GIRL, PRIEST JI--

--I PRAY THAT WE WILL SAVE YOU AS WELL.

YOUR FEVER HAS GOTTEN EVEN HOTTER, THOUGH I WOULD NOT HAVE BELIEVED IT POSSIBLE.

.....

Nnnghh...

EH...?
13

Unghh--!

Nggh!
PRIEST JI--YOU'RE WAKING UP! PRAISE THE GODS!

Uhuk! Uhuk! Heee--!
JI! JI!

Heee!

!

Heeeeee--!
GULK!

JI--STOP! Y-YOU'RE ⁝GASP⁝ CHOKING ME! JI--⁝GASP⁝ J-J-JIII--! JIII!
14

JIII--!
GASP! CHOKE!
JIIIII...
UH--!
Heh heh heh heh!

J--
J--J-- URK!
JEI--!
URK!
GURGLE!

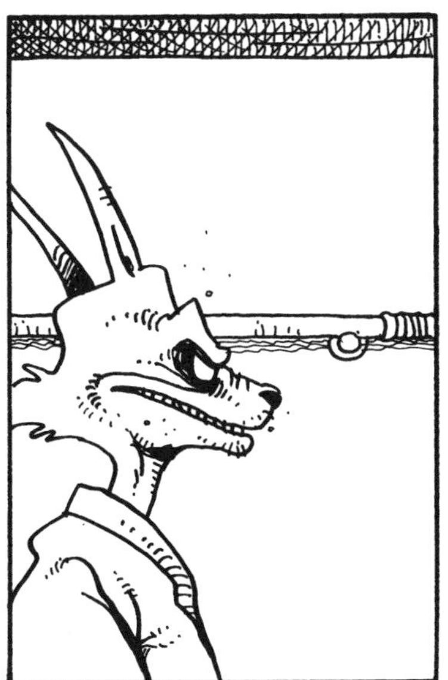

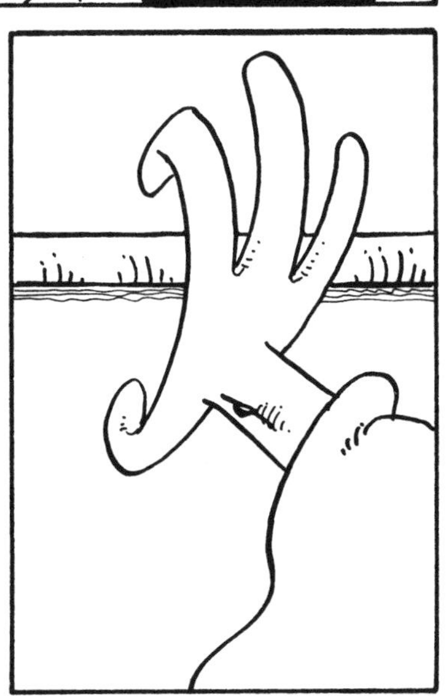

Heh heh heh.

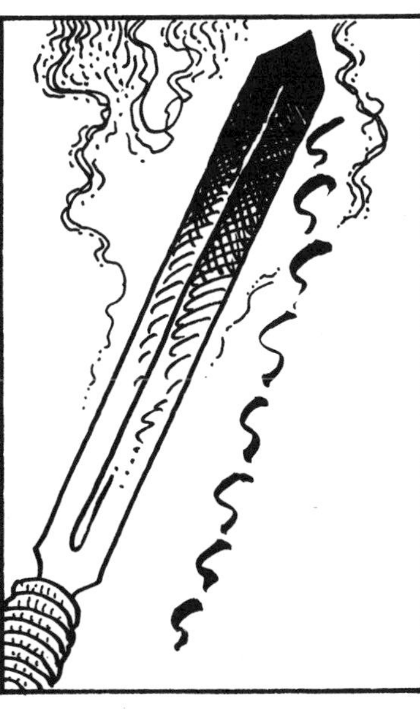

15.

AH, PRIEST JI-- IT'S GOOD TO SEE YOU UP AND AROUND.
IT'S ME--HAMA. I'M NEW HERE.

H-hama...? Yes... yes... Hama...

Gyaahh!
!
SHOONK!

Heh! Heh, heh, heh, heh.

Haaah!!
SPLURT!

Hama...
UH... UH... UH...
16.

GYAHH!
ULK!

EEYAGH!
AHHH!
NO! NO! NO!

UHHK!
GAAHH!

YAHHK!
EYAHH!
AHHK!
EEEEE!

PRIEST JI--STOP IT! ARE YOU **CRAZY**?
Ha ha ha ha ha haaa!
GAAH!

PRIEST JI-- **NO!**
FLOOK!

WHO IS OUT THERE?
17

Ahhh... I would have overlooked you completely if you had not called out--
--little princess.
.....
Grrr--!
18.

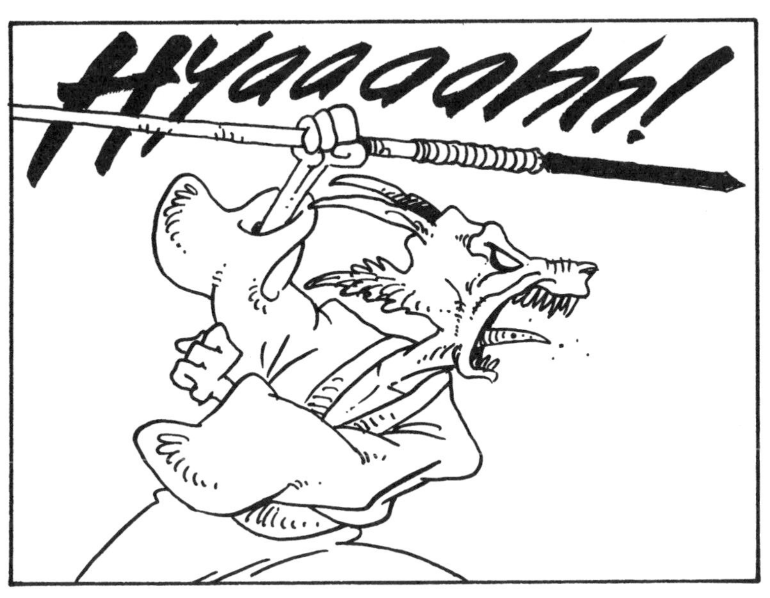
Hyaaaahh!

Haaahhh-!
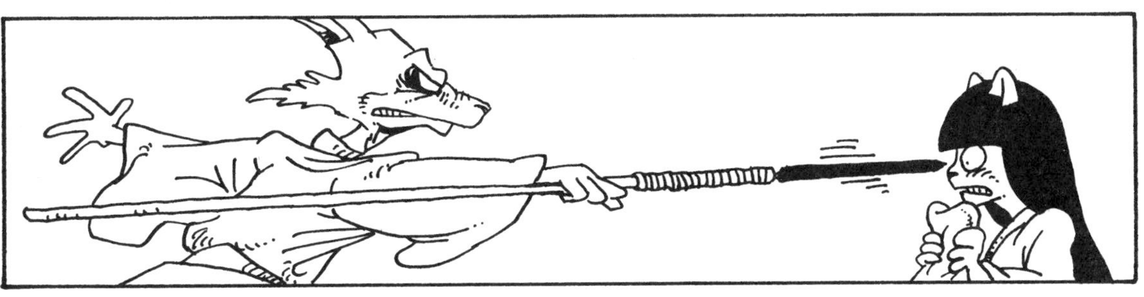

No... not you. You are an innocent in all this.

You are not mine to hurt.

It is the evil that I must search out.
19.

HELP! HELP!

GYAHH--!
SLIT!

WHAT'S GOING ON?
PRIEST JI! HE'S AWAKE!
BUT THE FEVER HAS DRIVEN HIM INSANE!

Kyaahh!

ALERT! LORD GOYO'S SAMURAI-- ALERT!
GAK!
OOF!
GAHH!
20.

THE TEMPLE IS BEING ATTACKED!
ONE OF THE PRIESTS IS ON A RAMPAGE!
HE MUST BE AN ASSASSIN AFTER LORD GOYO!
GYAHH! THE SPEAR BURNS! IT BURNS!

KILL HIM!

GYAK!
AHK!
PROTECT LORD GOYO!
OOK!
ULK!
AHH!
HE WON'T GET THROUGH US!
21.

AHHK!

YAHH! IT BURNS!

YAHH!

UH--!
Hee hee hee!

GURK!
Hyahh!
22.

IF HE GETS PAST US, THE LORD WILL BE UNPROTEC-- URK!
Ha ha ha ha ha!
GULK!
Heh heh heh heh heh!
YAHH!!
And so the Gods have led me to you-- the evil in your soul.
23.

PRIEST JIZONOBU--
WHY ARE YOU DOING THIS?

"Jizonobu"...? Who is this "Jizonobu"?

THEN... WHO ARE YOU?

My name?
My name is... JIII--! ;GASP! CHOKE!; JIIIII...

UH--! J--J-- URK!

Jei--! URK!
Jei.

Call me--
--Jei!

YAHHHHHH--!

SHOONK!
24.

AHHHHHH!

SENZO-- ARE YOU ALL RIGHT?

I-IT WAS ANOTHER NIGHTMARE, PRIEST SANSHOBO. IT WAS SO...SO... **REAL.**

YOU'VE BEEN GETTING MANY OF THOSE SINCE THE MASSACRE AT OUR TEMPLE*. THEY WILL END ONCE THE KILLER IS CAUGHT.

YES... THEY WILL END.
THEY WILL ALL END.

*UY BOOK 12: GRASSCUTTER

THE END

THREE WEEKS AGO...
...ONE HUNDRED RYO FROM THE FORTUNATE PLUM GAMBLING HOUSE...
...ONE HUNDRED FIFTY FROM THE CRESCENT MOON HOUSE...
...AND TWO HUNDRED FROM THE EIGHT PEARLS HOUSE.
WELL?
IS THAT ALL?
ER... YES, BOSS BAKUCHI.

WHAT OF THE LUCKY HERON HOUSE, OR THE CRYING BADGER?
SLURP!
UH...IT SEEMS THEY REFUSED TO PAY THIS MONTH, BAKUCHI-SAMA.
SPLURT!
WHAT?!
1.

THEY ARE NOT THE ONLY ONES. THREE OTHER GAMBLING HOUSES ALSO REFUSED TO PAY TRIBUTE.

I AM THE HEAD OF THE GAMBLERS' ASSOCIATION! **I** AM THE ONE WHO DECIDES WHO CAN AND WHO CANNOT SET UP A GAMBLING HOUSE IN THIS AREA!
HOW DARE THOSE FIVE HOUSES DEFY ME?!
ARE THEY TRYING TO USURP MY AUTHORITY?!

BURN DOWN THOSE HOUSES! RAZE THEM TO THE GROUND! LET THEM BE AN EXAMPLE TO ANY OTHERS WHO WOULD EVEN THINK ABOUT REBELLING AGAINST ME!

THAT WILL TEACH THEM TO FEAR AND RESPECT ME!
BUT, BAKUCHI-SAMA--

DESTROYING THE GAMBLING DENS WILL **NOT** WIN THEIR OWNERS' RESPECT, AND IT **WILL** REDUCE THE TRIBUTE THAT IS PAID TO YOU!
THEN WHAT DO YOU SUGGEST?

YOUR SON WAS MURDERED YEARS AGO-- BY A WOMAN, NO LESS--AND YOU HAVE YET TO AVENGE HIS DEATH.

2.

PEOPLE SNICKER AND SAY YOU ARE TOO OLD, TOO SENILE, AND THAT YOUR POWER IS GONE... THAT YOU CANNOT EVEN KILL THE FEMALE WHO WRONGED YOU!
YOU MUST SHOW THEM YOU ARE STILL STRONG! YOU MUST SLAY THIS WOMAN.

I HAVE ALREADY OFFERED A SIGNIFICANT REWARD FOR HER HEAD.

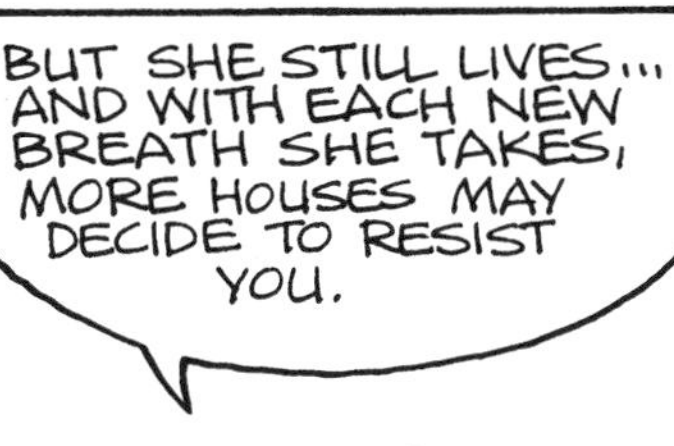
BUT SHE STILL LIVES... AND WITH EACH NEW BREATH SHE TAKES, MORE HOUSES MAY DECIDE TO RESIST YOU.

THEN I WANT HER DEAD BY MONTH'S END!
TRIPLE THE REWARD FOR HER HEAD!
THAT WILL GET THE REAL KILLERS AFTER HER!

TAKE CARE OF IT.
YES, BAKUCHI-SAMA.

ONE MORE THING-- KILL THE OWNERS OF THOSE FIVE HOUSES--
--AND THEIR FAMILIES.
3

SPARROWS
CHAPTER 1
THE PRESENT.
DEPART, UNCLEAN VERMIN FROM HELL!
RELEASE HIM!
I COMMAND YOU!
4.

BEGONE, I SAID!

¡WHIMPER...¡

ARE YOU CERTAIN JIRO'S AILMENTS ARE CAUSED BY DEMON POSSESSION, PRIEST SANSHOBO?
IT MIGHT JUST BE INDIGESTION.
THERE IS AN EVIL IN HIS SOUL, PRIEST HAMA.

BUT YOU ARE GUESTS IN OUR TEMPLE--NO NEED TO GET INVOLVED. A FEW HERBS WILL CURE JIRO.

HERBS WILL NOT CURE THIS PEASANT. HIS SOUL MUST BE EXPUNGED!
NO... PLEASE...

I--I DON'T KNOW ABOUT THIS, SANSHOBO,
BUT I DO.

RELEASE HIM, DEMON!

WHINE! PLEASE, PRIEST HAMA! DON'T LET HIM DO ANYTHING MORE TO ME!

THAT'S ENOUGH! STAND BACK, SANSHOBO!
UNTIE HIM!
YES, PRIEST HAMA.
WHIMPER!

ARE YOU ALL RIGHT, JIRO?
SOB! SOB! NO MORE! PLEASE! NO MORE!

DON'T LET THAT PRIEST ABUSE ME ANYMORE! PLEASE! PLEASE!
DON'T WORRY! YOU WILL BE WELL TAKEN CARE OF!
6

TAKE HIM TO THE INFIRMARY, AND TREAT HIM WELL.
YES, PRIEST HAMA.

AS FOR YOU-- HOW COULD YOU BE SO CALLOUS, SANSHOBO?!
HEY, LOOK AT ME WHEN I'M REPRIMANDING YOU!

Heh, heh, heh, heh heh...
!

UH... PRIEST HAMA?
Heh, heh, heh, heh, heee--!

¡GULK!
Haha ha haa!
7.

STOP!
LET GO OF HIM!
Hahaha hahaa--!
GASP! CHOKE!

UGH!
CHOKE! GASP!

OW!

So, Sanshobo, did you really think you could eliminate me so easily?
I'll kill you! I'll kill you all!
8.

JIRO--WHAT IS WRONG WITH YOU? WHY ARE YOU ATTACKING US?!

Heh, heh, heh. You refuse even to believe your own eyes, Hama.

Gyaahhh!

LOOK OUT, SANSHOBO!
OOF!
SENZO!

Graa!

Graahh!
YAHH!
GREAT BUDDHA, SAVE ME!

YAHH!
9.

Whimper! Whimper!
WHAT?

Whimper!
No! No!

GET OUT, FOUL DEMON! I COMMAND YOU TO RELEASE HIM!
Gyaahh!

Don't let him torture me any-more, Priest Hama!
Please!
ENOUGH OF THAT!

HE WILL NOT LISTEN TO ANY MORE OF YOUR LIES!
ABANDON THIS PEASANT'S BODY NOW!
10.

RELEASE HIM!
GYAAHHH!

uh--!
uh--!
uh--!

JIRO!
SANSHOBO!
UH...
.....
I-IT'S DONE.

PRIEST SANSHOBO-- ARE YOU ALL RIGHT?
UH... YEAH, SENZO, THAT DRAINED ME. I'LL BE BETTER AFTER I'VE RESTED A BIT.

YOU'RE OKAY NOW, JIRO.
UH... PRIEST HAMA? WHAT HAPPENED? EVERYTHING IS A BLUR.
11.

TAKE HIM TO THE INFIRMARY. THERE SHOULDN'T BE ANY MORE TROUBLE.
YES, PRIEST HAMA.
WHY DID HE PAUSE WHEN HE HAD ME AT HIS MERCY, PRIEST SANSHOBO?
CLEARLY IT WAS BECAUSE YOU INVOKED THE NAME OF MERCIFUL BUDDHA.

I OWE YOU AN APOLOGY, SANSHOBO.
NONSENSE. YOUR SKEPTICISM WAS UNDERSTANDABLE. FORTUNATELY, IT WAS A LESSER DEMON.

BUT I SHOULD HAVE KNOWN EVIL COULD BEFALL THIS TEMPLE. IT HAS HAPPENED ONCE BEFORE.
OH?

IT WAS YEARS AGO, JUST AFTER I CAME TO THIS TEMPLE.

"THE HEAD PRIEST AT THAT TIME--JIZONOBU--WENT BERSERK--

"--AND MURDERED ALMOST EVERYONE WITHIN.
12.

"HE ATTACKED ME, BUT I RECOVERED. ONLY A LITTLE GIRL AND I LIVED THROUGH THAT NIGHT. I HAD NEVER SEEN SUCH HORROR.

"THE WORST SIGHT WAS THE DEAD... THEY ALL HAD SUCH AN EXPRESSION OF SHEER TERROR."

IT WAS THE MOST TRAGIC EVENT IN THIS TEMPLE'S HISTORY...
...AND THE MOST TERRIBLE THING I HAVE EVER SEEN.

WHAT BECAME OF PRIEST JIZONOBU?

NO ONE KNOWS. PERHAPS HE TRAVELS THE ROADS STILL.
NOW EXCUSE ME. I HAD BETTER LOOK TO OUR PATIENT IN THE INFIRMARY.
OF COURSE.

THE ONLY TREATMENT HE WILL REQUIRE IS MUCH REST.
SANSHOBO--HIS STORY IS ALMOST EXACTLY LIKE WHAT OCCURRED AT OUR TEMPLE.
COULD THERE BE A CONNECTION?

YES.
13.

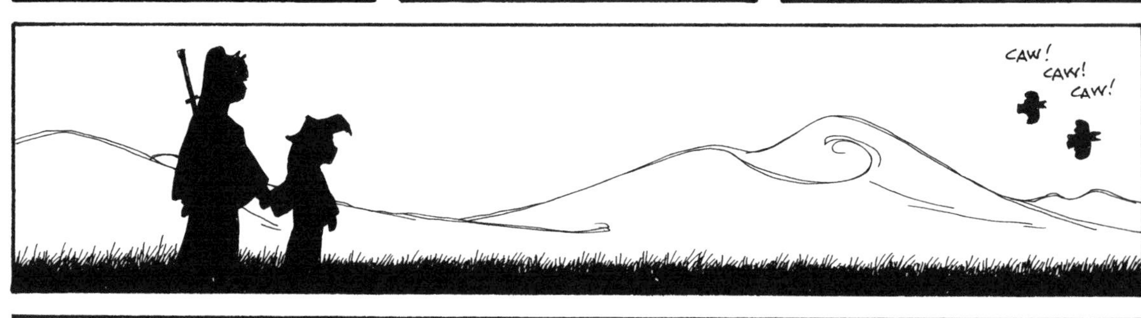
CAW!
CAW!
CAW!

ZWIP!
14.

SHWIGG!
THUK!

GAHH!

WE'RE DISCOVERED!

OUR AMBUSH FAILED!

THEN JUST KILL HER!

Keiko-- stay out of the way.
YES, AUNTY.
15.

HHYAAAHHHHH

URK!

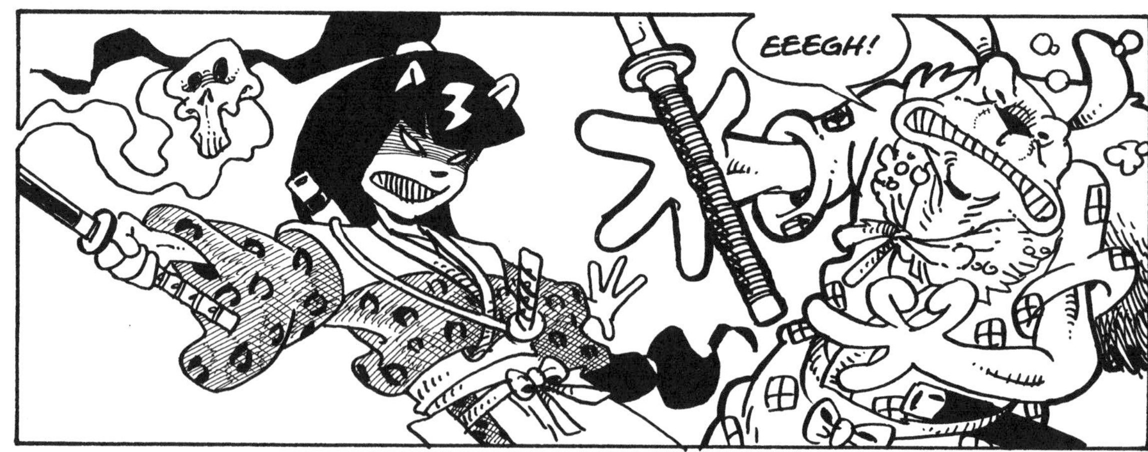
EEEGH!

HAHH

SHAK!
16.

SWIP!
CHOP!

TANG!!

HYAH!

HAH!
Hauk!

I--I DON'T BELIEVE IT! I DID IT! I KILLED HER! I'M RICH! I'M RICH!

I'M RICH! I'M RICH! I'M RI--
17.

AUNTY--! YOU'RE HURT!

Hmm...?

Why, yes. So I am.

But it's merely a flesh wound.

Now come along, my innocent. We must continue on.
YES, AUNTY.

18.

YOU AND YOUR STUPID SHORT CUTS!

IT TOOK US **TWICE** AS LONG TO GET HERE.
IDIOT.
THE IMPORTANT THING IS THAT WE'RE HERE, RIGHT?

A LOT OF GOOD THAT DOES US! SHE'S PROBABLY LONG GONE BY NOW.
DON'T WORRY. WE'LL PICK UP HER TRAIL AGAIN REAL SOON.

WHAT MAKES YOU SO SURE?
PEOPLE TEND TO NOTICE SOMEONE LIKE INAZUMA.

I CAN'T ARGUE WITH YOU ABOUT THAT.
HEY--WHAT'S THAT OVER THERE?
19.

?

IT LOOKS LIKE THEY WERE ALL KILLED BY BLADES.
HEY-- WHAT ARE YOU DOING?
ROBBING THEM?

THEY WON'T NEED ANYTHING WHERE THEY ARE NOW.
BESIDES, LOOK AT THEM. DO THEY LOOK LIKE THEY CAME ACROSS ANYTHING HONESTLY?

BUT DON'T WORRY. EVEN I'M NOT LOW ENOUGH TO STEAL FROM THE DEAD.
AH, THIS IS WHAT I WAS LOOKING FOR.
WHAT IS IT?

A BOUNTY FLYER.
20.

SO, THEY WERE BOUNTY HUNTERS AFTER INAZUMA.
EVERY HUNTER IN THE COUNTRY MUST BE AFTER HER NOW.

I BET THESE FOUR WERE KILLED BY OTHERS AFTER THE BIG REWARD.
WELL, I'VE HANDLED TOUGH COMPETITION BEFORE. SO HAVE YOU, I BET.

IT DOESN'T SEEM THEY'VE BEEN DEAD LONG. IF WE HAD GOTTEN HERE EARLIER, WE PROBABLY WOULD HAVE BEEN INVOLVED IN THIS.

THEN I GUESS IT'S LUCKY WE TOOK THE **LONG WAY**, HUH?

YOU'RE SUCH AN IDIOT.
COME ON. WE'VE GOT TO REACH THE NEXT TOWN BEFORE DARK.
IDIOT.
21.

CAW! CAW! CAW!

HMM... CROWS.
SOMETHING IS OVER THERE.

I CAN SMELL THE STINK OF DEATH FROM HERE.

22

I WONDER WHO THAT IS.
CAW!
CAW!
CAW!

WHOEVER HE IS, HE DOESN'T LOOK LIKE SOMEONE I'D LIKE TO GET INVOLVED WITH.
CAW!
CAW!
GOOD. HE'S LEAVING.

23

EH--?

WHAT'S THIS?

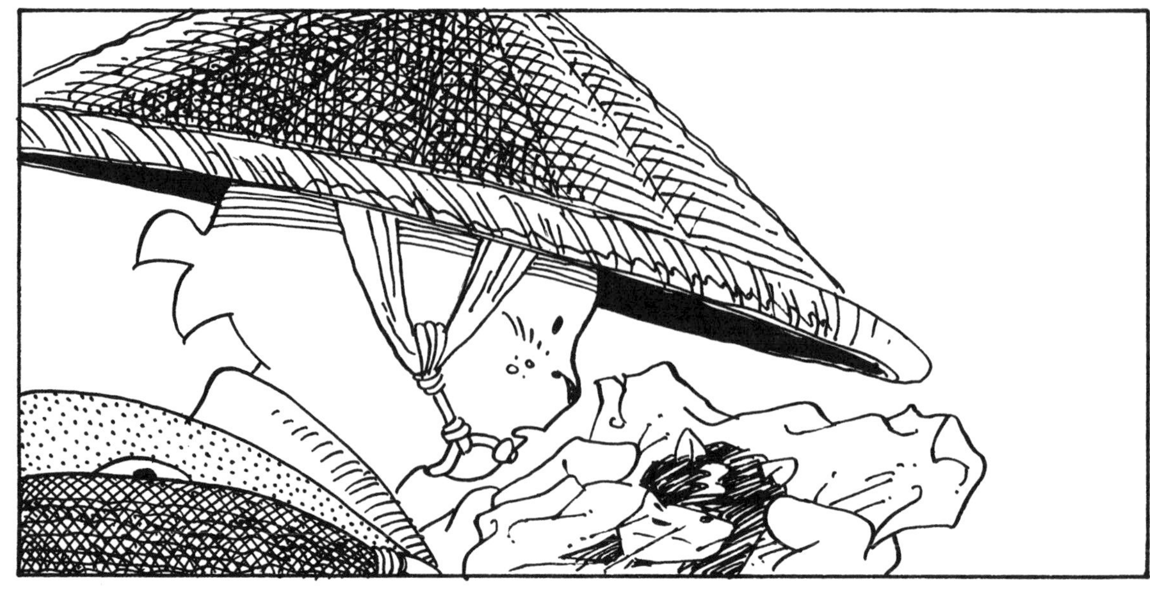

SPARROWS 雀

CHAPTER TWO

EEP?

1.

HA HA HA HA HA HA
MY CANE!
GIVE ME BACK MY CANE!
HA HA HA HA HA!
HA HA HA HA HA

IT'S PATHETIC TO BULLY A BLIND PERSON!
HA HA HA!
HA HA HA!

PLEASE!
WHERE ARE YOU?
HA HA HA HA!
POKE! POKE!

HA HA HA HA HA!

WHERE ARE YOU?
HA HA HA!
HA!
HA!
POKE! POKE!
HA!

HA! HA!
HA!
HA!
HA!

MY CANE!
I NEED MY CANE!

GIVE HIM BACK HIS STICK.
EH?

WHY DO YOU HARASS SOMEONE WEAKER THAN YOU?
WHY DO YOU INTERFERE WITH OUR BUSINESS?
WHAT'S THIS BLIND GUY TO YOU?

RETURN HIS CANE.

ARE YOU CRAZY?! WE OUTNUMBER YOU!
GET OUT OF HERE, OR WE'LL COME AFTER **YOU** NEXT!
3.

WE'RE PROFESSIONAL SWORDSMEN! DO YOU THINK YOU CAN KILL ALL OF US?!

NO.

JUST YOU.
GULP!

YOU WANT THE CANE?!

THEN GO AND FETCH IT!
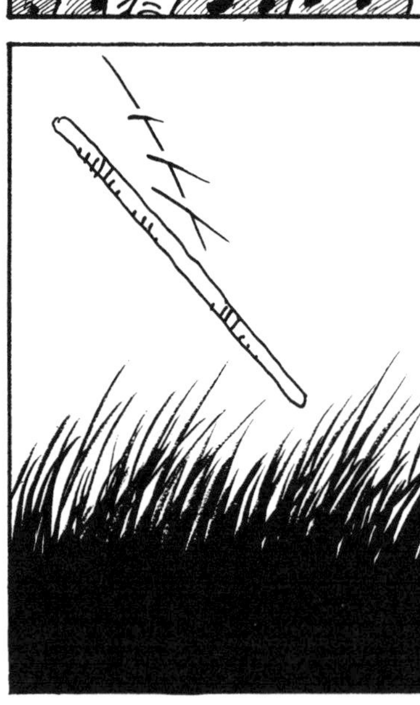

COME ON. WE'VE WASTED ENOUGH TIME HERE!
4.

WHY, THOSE--!
LET THEM GO. MY CANE IS NOT WORTH FIGHTING OVER.

¡GASP!¡
IT'S ORPHAN-MAKER!*
EH--? WHAT IS IT, SIR?
*UY BOOK 21: THE MOTHER OF MOUNTAINS

DO I KNOW YOU? BLINDNESS IS STILL NEW TO ME. IF I HAVE WRONGED YOU IN THE PAST, I APOLOGIZE.

UH... NO, WE HAVE NEVER MET.
GOOD.

WILL YOU HELP ME FIND MY CANE?
SURE. IT'S IN THE TALL GRASS.

I WAS A SAMURAI ONCE--AN ARROGANT BULLY.
I GUESS THAT IS WHY I DID NOT WANT YOU FIGHTING THOSE RUFFIANS. I WAS NO BETTER THAN THEM, JUST A SHORT TIME AGO.
5.

I WAS THE BULLY, BUT NOW IT IS I WHO AM ABUSED. IT IS KARMA, *NEH*?

THAT IS VERY UNDERSTANDING OF YOU.
NO, IT IS NOT.

I STILL WISH I HAD MY SIGHT, BUT THAT LONG-EARED *SAMURAI* WHO BLINDED ME MAY HAVE DONE ME A FAVOR.
OH?

I WAS ANGRY AT FIRST. I LOATHED HIM AND EVERYONE ELSE. I WALLOWED IN SELF-PITY AND HATRED, AND TOOK MY ANGER OUT ON ANYONE WITHIN REACH.

BUT I QUICKLY DISCOVERED THAT I COULD NOT SURVIVE ON MY OWN.
I WANDERED FOR A LONG TIME, UNTIL I WAS FILTHY AND NEARLY DEAD FROM STARVATION. THAT WAS WHEN A TEMPLE OFFERED ME SANCTUARY.
I'VE FOUND IT!
6.

I AM NOW A MENDICANT MONK, BEGGING FOR ALMS.
THANK YOU.

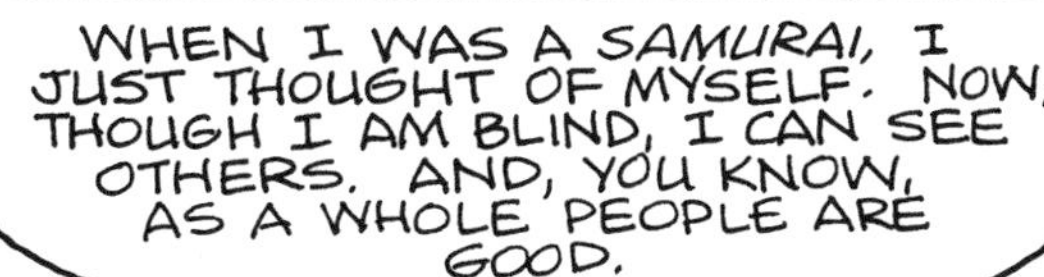
WHEN I WAS A *SAMURAI*, I JUST THOUGHT OF MYSELF. NOW, THOUGH I AM BLIND, I CAN SEE OTHERS. AND, YOU KNOW, AS A WHOLE PEOPLE ARE GOOD.

QUITE A DIFFERENCE FROM AN ARROGANT *SAMURAI*, EH?
I THINK IT IS A VAST IMPROVEMENT.

WHEN I RETURN IN MY NEXT LIFE, HOPEFULLY IT WILL BE AS A BETTER PERSON.

HERE ARE A FEW COINS...
...AND I HAVE A HAT YOU CAN HAVE.
THANK YOU, SIR, BUT I HAVE ONE QUESTION.

ARE YOU SURE WE'VE NEVER MET?
WHAT IS YOUR NAME?
I'M JUST A STRANGER.
7.

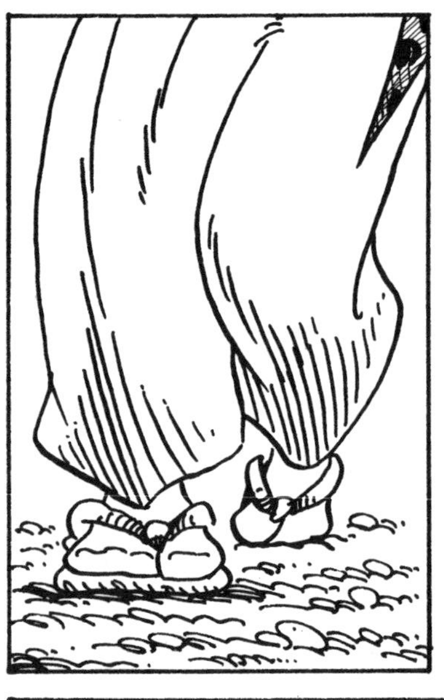

It is harder to sustain this body. It might be because of the injury.
WE'LL FIND SOMEWHERE WE CAN REST FOR A WHILE.
Yes. Rest will help this body to heal.

Uh...
ARE YOU OKAY, AUNTY?

She's fighting me, Keiko, as she's been fighting me for the past months.
LEAN ON ME FOR A WHILE, AUNTY.
8.

It is also harder to control this body. Its movements are sluggish.
Let us rest a while in that peasant's hovel.

HELLO! IS ANYONE HERE?
I GUESS NOT.

SIT HERE, AUNTY. I'LL FIND SOMETHING TO EAT.

BARLEY. NOT AS TASTY AS WORMS AND GRUBS, BUT IT WILL HAVE TO DO.

IT WON'T BE LONG BEFORE THE FOOD IS COOKED.
9.

DEM DUM DEM... OH, IT'S A HARD LIFE FOR A FERTILIZER HAULER...

EH? THERE'S SMOKE COMING OUT OF KOJI'S HOUSE.
BUT I JUST SAW HIM IN THE FIELDS!

THERE HAVE BEEN A LOT OF STRANGERS AROUND HERE. I'D BETTER BE CAREFUL.

IMAGINE-- SOMEONE BREAKING INTO KOJI'S HOUSE!

HEY--! I RECOGNIZE HER! SHE'S THE ONE EVERYBODY IS AFTER!
AND SHE LOOKS HURT.

I BET I WOULD SHARE IN THE REWARD IF I TOLD SOME BOUNTY HUNTERS THAT SHE'S IN KOJI'S HUT.
DO YOU SMELL SOMETHING AWFUL, AUNTY?
10.

HUFF!
HUFF! HUFF!
HUFF!

You are here at last. I have been waiting for you.

WHO ARE YOU? WHAT DO YOU WANT WITH ME?

11.

Heh, heh, heh, heh.

WH-WHO ARE YOU?

KRRRK!

FLOOOF!

GASP!

IT'S NO USE. I CAN'T SLEEP!
--NOT WITH THOSE DREAMS!
12

MAYBE A WALK OUTSIDE WILL CLEAR MY HEAD.

EH--? THE INFIRMARY? WHY DID I COME HERE?
ZNORE!

JIRO.
I SHOULD CHECK ON HIM.

JIRO.
UH...?

DON'T BE ALARMED. I JUST CAME TO SEE HOW YOU ARE DOING.
13

DO YOU KNOW WHO I AM?
YOU WERE WITH THE PRIEST WHO EXORCISED THE DEMON OUT OF ME.

YOU ATTACKED ME.
I DID? I-I DON'T REMEMBER.
THEN YOU RECOILED FROM ME IN FEAR. WHY?
I DON'T KNOW. I DON'T KNOW!

WAS IT BECAUSE I INVOKED THE NAME OF MERCIFUL BUDDHA?
...OR WAS IT SOMETHING ELSE?

WHAT WERE YOU AFRAID OF?
WHIMPER!
IT WASN'T YOU! IT WASN'T YOU! IT WAS HIM!

HIM? HIM, WHO? TELL ME!
STOP! YOU'RE HURTING ME!

I'LL DO MORE THAN THAT IF YOU DON'T ANSWER ME!
YAHHH!
14.

SHUU!
WHAT'S GOING ON?!
COUGH! CHOKE! GASP! GASP!
WHAT?
SENZO!

OH...UH... PRIEST HAMA! I-I COULD NOT SLEEP, SO I CAME TO... UH... CHECK ON THE PATIENT.

SANSHOBO TOLD ME YOU HAVE BEEN PLAGUED BY NIGHTMARES, AND HAVE BEEN GETTING VERY LITTLE SLEEP.
I CAN SYMPATHIZE. I WAS THUS AFFLICTED AFTER THE MURDERS AT THIS TEMPLE.

HE ATTACKED ME, PRIEST HAMA! HE'S CRAZY!
NO! NO! I CAN EXPLAIN!

RETURN TO YOUR ROOM AND STAY THERE, SENZO. I WILL DISCUSS THIS WITH PRIEST SANSHOBO IN THE MORNING.
Y-YES, PRIEST HAMA.

WHAT IS HAPPENING TO ME?
15.

HEY, PASS THAT SAKÉ OVER HERE!
TOO BAD. THE BOTTLE'S EMPTY.
WE'LL JUST GET SOME MORE.

HO-- INNKEEPER!

WE WANT SAKÉ! BRING LOTS OF SAKÉ!
ER... YES, SIR! RIGHT AWAY!

IT LOOKS LIKE WE'VE GOT MORE RIVALS FOR INAZUMA'S BOUNTY.
BAH! THEY'RE NOTHING MORE THAN A BUNCH OF DRUNKEN LOUTS!

WE WENT UP AGAINST INAZUMA A FEW WEEKS AGO, AND SHE BEAT US. DO YOU THINK THEY CAN TAKE HER ON?
16

FEH! THEY ARE A FLOCK OF SPARROWS INTENT ON BRINGING DOWN AN EAGLE.

WHAT ARE WE?
WE'RE DRAGONS! WE'LL GET HER, ALL RIGHT, AS LONG AS YOU DON'T FOUL IT UP LIKE YOU DID THE LAST TIME!

I TOLD YOU-- I HAD AN INJURY THAT WAS AGGRAVATED BY THE STORM. I'M FINE NOW.

I GUESS I'M JUST GETTING OLD, HEH, HEH!
IF IT HAPPENS AGAIN, YOU WON'T GET ANY OLDER. I'LL SEE TO THAT.

NOW, WHO'S THAT?
EH?

HE'S NO DRUNKEN LOUT.
17

THAT'S A BOUNTY HUNTER IF I EVER SAW ONE.
YEAH.
SLURP!

SLURP!

I'LL TAKE CARE OF HIM.
MY FRIEND SAID YOU LOOK LIKE A BOUNTY HUNTER. WELL, ARE YOU?

MY BUSINESS IS MY OWN.
IS THAT RIGHT, HUH?

SEE MY GANG OVER THERE? WE'RE AFTER INAZUMA, AS YOU ARE, I BET. BUT WE DON'T LIKE COMPETITION.

SO YOU'D BETTER LEAVE.
IF I DON'T?
18.

IF YOU DON'T GO, WE'LL HAVE TO **KILL YOU!**
NO! NO!

IF THERE IS A FIGHT, YOU'LL DESTROY MY INN! PLEASE DON'T!
PLEASE!

HEH, HEH, HEH, HEH, HEH!

COME ON. WE CAN HAVE FUN WITH THIS GUY.

COME ON.
IT LOOKS LIKE THERE'S GOING TO BE SOME EXCITEMENT.
19.

HEYHEYHEY! HOW DO WE KNOW YOU'RE REALLY GOING TO LEAVE THIS AREA? MAYBE YOU'RE STILL THINKING OF GOING AFTER INAZUMA.
WE'LL HAVE TO MAKE SURE THAT YOU DON'T.

DON'T WORRY. WE WON'T KILL YOU. WE'LL JUST LOP OFF A HAND OR SOMETHING.

I'LL BET YOU TEN *RYO* ON THE BIG GUY.
AND I TAKE THE SPARROWS? NO WAY!

20.

GET HIM!
HYAAHHHHHH

YAHH!
GAH!
YAK!

KIYAHH!!
UGH!
OOK!

URK!
21.

HE'S GOOD.
REAL GOOD.
HELP! POLICE! HELP!

SWIT!

THE AUTHORITIES WILL ARRIVE SOON. WE'D BETTER GET OUT OF HERE.
YEAH. COME ON.
22

IT'S THAT SAMURAI AGAIN!

HELP! HELP!

THE POLICE! WHAT'S GOING ON?

I SAW THE WHOLE THING! THEY ATTACKED A LONE *SAMURAI!* HE JUST DEFENDED HIMSELF!

THIS IS THE SECOND TIME I'VE SEEN THAT *SAMURAI,* AND THE SECOND TIME THERE IS DEATH.

IT WILL BE A LOT HARDER IF WE HAVE TO GO UP AGAINST THAT GUY AS WELL AS INAZUMA.
YEAH. WE'RE GOING TO NEED HELP.

Sparrows

CHAPTER 3

雀

USAGI!

1

THIS ONE IS STILL ALIVE!
USAGI! IT'S ME-- SANSHOBO!
USAGI!

WHAT IS THIS ASH--?
--AND THIS OLD SWORD*?
*UY BOOK 12: GRASSCUTTER

IT MAKES MY FINGERS TINGLE.

2

.....

FUMP!

RUB!
RUB!
RUB!
RUB!
GULP!
GULP!
GASP!

GASP!
GASP!
CHOKE!

HEH...
HEH...

HEH...
heh...
heh...

Heh...
heh...

Heh,
heh, heh
heh!

Heh,
heh, heh,
heh!

GYAHHH

GUAHHHHHH

WHAT WAS THAT?

IT CAME FROM THAT VISITING PRIEST'S ROOM!

IT SOUNDS LIKE HE'S BEING KILLED!

WHAT IS GOING ON? WHAT IS THE REASON FOR THIS COMMOTION?!
PRIEST HAMA! PRIEST SANSHOBO!
¡GASP! GASP!¡ I-- I'M OKAY NOW.

IT'S SENZO, PRIEST HAMA! HE SUFFERED SOME SORT OF FIT.

I-I HAD A NIGHTMARE, BUT I'M FINE NOW.
I APOLOGIZE FOR THE UPROAR I CAUSED.

I KNOW OF YOUR BAD DREAMS, SENZO.
HE HAS HAD THEM SINCE THE MASSACRE AT OUR TEMPLE.

I CAN SYMPATHIZE. IT TOOK ME A WHILE TO GET OVER THE SIMILAR EVIL THAT BEFELL THIS TEMPLE YEARS AGO.
5

I WILL PREPARE A SLEEP POTION TO HELP YOU REST SOUNDLY TONIGHT.

I HAVE A FAVOR TO ASK, HAMA.
YES, SANSHOBO? DO YOU STILL INTEND TO LEAVE IN THE MORNING?

YES, I MUST RETURN TO MY OWN TEMPLE, BUT SENZO IS IN NO CONDITION TO TRAVEL.

I AGREE. HE CAN STAY HERE UNDER OUR CARE. I CAN RELATE TO HIS DILEMMA.

THANK YOU. I APOLOGIZE FOR BEING SUCH A BOTHER.
IT IS NO TROUBLE, I ASSURE YOU.

I HOPE IT IS NOTHING MORE THAN A FEW BAD DREAMS.
I AM SURE IT IS NOT.
6.

THIS WAY! IT'S NOT FAR NOW!
YOU'LL REGRET IT IF YOU'RE WRONG!
IT WAS INAZUMA, ALL RIGHT! I RECOGNIZED THE LIGHTNING STREAK IN HER HAIR.
AND SHE'S BADLY HURT!
REMEMBER-- YOU SAID I WOULD SHARE IN THE REWARD!
OH, DON'T WORRY! WE'LL SHOW YOU OUR GRATITUDE!
7.

INAZUMA IS IN THERE--KOJI'S HUT. DON'T WORRY ABOUT HIM, THOUGH. I GAVE HIM A FEW COINS, AND HE WENT INTO TOWN. I FIGURED YOU WOULD COVER MY EXPENSES, RIGHT? IT WOULD BE A LOT CHEAPER THAN BRINGING KOJI IN AS ANOTHER PARTNER. AM I RIGHT?

YEAH. YOU'RE RIGHT.

I'LL GO CHECK IT OUT!

REST, AUNTY. THE FOOD WILL BE READY IN A FEW MINUTES.
8.

WELL?
IT'S INAZUMA, ALL RIGHT. I'D RECOGNIZE HER ANYWHERE!
AND SHE'S HURT BAD!

SEE? WHAT DID I TELL YOU? IT'S INAZUMA! DON'T FORGET MY REWARD!
YEAH. YOUR REWARD.

YOU'LL GET YOUR REWARD, ALL RIGHT.
WH-WHAT?!
NO...

.....
SLASH!

DID YOU REALLY BELIEVE WE WOULD SHARE THE BOUNTY WITH THE LIKES OF YOU?
BESIDES, YOU STINK.
9.

SLEEP A WHILE MORE, AUNTY. OUR MEAL WILL BE READY SOON.
.....

Nnnnhh...

...nngghh...

...Ngghhh...

UH...

WH-
WHERE AM I...?

UHN--!

!
10.

WHAT HAS HAPPENED TO ME?

UH--!

NGGHH--!

HERE IS YOUR FOOD, AUNTY!
AUNTY...? ARE YOU ALL RIGHT?
AUNTY?

ARE YOU OKAY?
Of course, my innocent. Why wouldn't I be?

HIYAHH!
KILL HER! ALL WE NEED IS HER HEAD!
11.

Hahahaha--!

12.

GYAHH!
UH--!

Ha!
AHHK!

HYAH!
KIYAH!

URK!

STAY BACK! STAY BACK!
Heh, heh, heh.

Ngghh...
13.

WH-
WHAT'S
GOING
ON?

HYAAHHH..!

GURK!

WHY IS THIS HAPPENING TO ME?

HEH, HEH!
Heh...heh... heh...heh... heh...

These foolish samurai will not stop me from doing the will of the Gods, will they, Keiko?

Keiko?
Keiko?

Where could she have gone?
14.

PAY THE INNKEEPER, STRAY DOG. IT'S ABOUT TIME WE WERE ON OUR WAY.
NOT ME, GEN. I PAID FOR YESTERDAY'S BREAKFAST. BESIDES, I'M LOW ON CASH.

YOU OWE ME FOR **THREE MEALS!**
WHAT?! THERE ARE ONLY THE **TWO** OF US!

THAT GUY OVER THERE SAID YOU WOULD BE HAPPY TO PAY FOR **HIS** MEAL AS WELL!

WHAT GUY?!

15.

YOU CAN'T BE SERIOUS!
WOULD I LIE?
ABOUT THIS, I MEAN?
I SWEAR IT, USAGI! SOMEHOW INAZUMA IS **JEI**!
IT CAN'T BE! I SAW HIM **DIE**!
I KNOW, I DID, TOO!
IT'S HIM, ALL RIGHT... OR **HER**!
WELL, IT'S SOMEBODY!
AND YOU'RE AFTER THE BOUNTY PLACED ON HER HEAD BY BOSS BAKUCHI.
YEAH, BUT HE JUST RAISED IT, SO THERE ARE A LOT MORE HUNTERS AROUND!
YOU WILL HAVE A LOT OF COMPETITION.
YEAH. THAT IS WHY WE COULD USE YOUR HELP!
16

SNIFF! SNIFF!
SMELL THAT?
WHAT?
I DON'T SMELL ANY-THING!

COME ON!
HEY-- WAIT FOR US!

HOW COULD YOU SMELL HIM FROM SO FAR AWAY?
YOU'VE GOT YOUR EARS. I'VE GOT MY NOSE.
GEN'S GOT NOTHING.

THIS DOESN'T LOOK LIKE INAZUMA'S HANDIWORK.

LOOK-- IN THE HUT!
SOMEONE IS IN THERE-- I SEE HIM THROUGH THE WINDOW!
17

WE KNOW YOU'RE INSIDE!
COME ON OUT!

AND GET CAUGHT IN AN AMBUSH? I HAVE MORE SENSE THAN THAT! MOVE AWAY FROM THE DOOR!
OKAY, WE'RE STEPPING BACK!

KEEP YOUR HANDS AWAY FROM YOUR SWORDS.

WHENEVER I SEE YOU, THERE IS DEATH!
I DO NOT GO LOOKING FOR IT!

DID YOU KILL THAT PEASANT OVER THERE?
WHY WOULD I KILL A PEASANT? BESIDES, HE WAS SLAIN BY A CLUMSY STROKE.
I SAY WE KILL THIS GUY NOW!

YOU CAN TRY.
KLIK!
18.

LEAVE YOUR SWORDS SHEATHED!
GEN'S RIGHT! WE'RE NOT HERE TO FIGHT!
BUT HE'S AFTER INAZUMA!

OF COURSE I'M AFTER INAZUMA-- AS ARE YOU.

THEN NO DOUBT WE WILL RUN INTO EACH OTHER AGAIN.

ABAYO*!
I DON'T LIKE HIM!
YOU DON'T LIKE ANYBODY!
WHAT WAS HE DOING IN THERE?
19.

*"SO LONG."

?

GET IN HERE, YOU TWO!

LOOK AT THEIR FACES! I'VE SEEN THIS BEFORE!

I MET THIS GROUP YESTERDAY, TAUNTING A BLIND MAN. STILL, THEY DID NOT DESERVE TO DIE LIKE THIS.

DO YOU BELIEVE ME NOW? JEI IS ALIVE-- AND LIVING IN INAZUMA!
HOW IS THAT POSSIBLE?

I WOULDN'T HAVE BELIEVED IT MYSELF, BUT WE RAN INTO HER A FEW WEEKS AGO.
WELL, THESE DEAD CONFIRM WHAT YOU SAY.
JEI IS STILL AROUND.
20.

GOOD. THAT MEANS WE'RE ON THE RIGHT TRAIL.

COME ON, BEFORE THAT OTHER GUY BEATS US TO THE REWARD.

THERE'S SOMEONE NEAR THAT DEAD PEASANT!
HOLD IT! I KNOW HIM!

SANSHOBO!
EH?
USAGI! GEN! I DID NOT EXPECT TO MEET UP WITH YOU!
WHAT ARE YOU DOING HERE, PRIEST?
SHOW HIM SOME RESPECT, STRAY DOG!
21.

I CAME ACROSS THIS POOR FELLOW AND STOPPED TO RECITE THE SUTRAS FOR HIS REPOSE!

THERE'S A LOT MORE PRAYING FOR YOU TO DO INSIDE, SANSHOBO.
OH?

AND...
MERCIFUL BUDDHA!

THEIR FACES--!
YES. TERRIBLE, ISN'T IT?

IT'S NOT THAT. I **KNOW** THESE EXPRESSIONS. I SAW THEM ON THE PRIESTS WHO WERE MURDERED AT MY TEMPLE!
WHAT?!

WHO DID THIS?
A DEVIL.
22.

WE ARE AFTER THE PERSON RESPONSIBLE FOR THIS-- INAZUMA.
INAZUMA?

SHE WAS IN THE TEMPLE WHEN MY PRIESTS WERE MURDERED...
...BUT SHE WAS IN NO CONDITION TO KILL ANYONE!

WELL...SHE MAY NOT REALLY BE ENTIRELY TO BLAME FOR THESE DEATHS.

NOW YOU'RE SPEAKING IN RIDDLES. DID SHE OR DID SHE NOT COMMIT THESE KILLINGS?

INAZUMA...UH... MAY BE POSSESSED BY THE SPIRIT OF THE DEMON, JEI.

YOU SAID JEI WAS KILLED BY THE SWORD OF THE GODS*!
HE GOT BETTER.
23

*UY BOOK 12: GRASSCUTTER

NOW YOU SAY THE SPIRIT OF JEI TORMENTS THE SOUL OF INAZUMA?

I'M JOINING YOU.
WHAT?!
!
O

NO!
I'M NOT SPLITTING THE REWARD UP ANY MORE!

IF YOU'RE GOING UP AGAINST DEMON POSSESSION, I THINK YOU'LL NEED ME!
UH... YEAH, YOU MIGHT BE RIGHT.

SPARROWS
CHAPTER 4
雀
:GLUG! GLUG!: WE'RE RUNNING LOW ON SAKÉ! LET'S GET SOME OF THE GOOD STUFF THIS TIME! :GLUG!:
YOU STUPID LITTLE VERMIN--I'LL TEACH YOU TO LOOK AT ME LIKE THAT!
YOU TOWNSFOLK THINK YOU CAN GET AWAY WITH ANYTHING!
NO! NO! PLEASE--!
HA! COME HERE, YOU--!
I LIKE IT WHEN THEY FIGHT BACK!
UH...
FEH! WHAT A MEAGER PURSE! IT'S HARDLY WORTH THE EFFORT IT TOOK TO BEAT HIM UP!
1.

SLAM!

BUUURPP!
YUCK! THAT LAST BOTTLE TASTED LIKE GUTTER WATER!
BURP!

COME ON, GUYS, LET'S GET OUT OF HERE!
LET'S FIND A PLACE WITH BETTER QUALITY *SAKE*!
B-BUT YOU HAVEN'T PAID FOR THE DRINKS YOU HAD HERE!

HA HA! DON'T WORRY. WE'RE GOOD FOR IT.

YOU'LL GET YOUR MONEY **AFTER** WE CLAIM THE REWARD FOR INAZUMA!
2

BUT--WHAT IF YOU DO NOT COLLECT THE REWARD?

WHAT?

ARE YOU QUESTIONING OUR ABILITIES?
NO! NO! NO!

DO YOU THINK WE'RE NOT GOOD ENOUGH TO KILL INAZUMA?!
UH--!
THUD!

YOU SHOULD BE GRATEFUL WE DRANK YOUR SAKE AT ALL! THIS IS ALL IT'S GOOD FOR!

LET'S GET OUT OF HERE. WE'LL FIND ANOTHER INN AND GET SOME REAL DRINKING DONE!
UH...
3

WHY, THAT--!
SIT DOWN, USAGI.
MIND YOUR OWN BUSINESS.
BUT THEY BULLIED THE INNKEEPER--!
THEY DID NOT PAY--!
SO HE LOST A FEW COINS, BUT, EXCEPT FOR HIS PRIDE, HE'S NOT HURT.
IS THAT WORTH STARTING A FIGHT OVER?
BESIDES, HIS INN WOULD GET WRECKED DURING A FIGHT, AND HE WOULD BE EVEN WORSE OFF THAN HE IS NOW.
SIP!
YEAH, I GUESS YOU'RE RIGHT.
IMAGINE-- GEN BEING THE VOICE OF REASON.
4

IT'S JUST THAT THEIR BEHAVIOR MAKES ME SO ANGRY!
BOUNTY HUNTERS HAVE BEEN POURING INTO THIS AREA EVER SINCE BOSS BAKUCHI **TRIPLED** THE REWARD FOR INAZUMA'S HEAD.

YEAH... AND THEY'RE NOT ALL AS HONORABLE AS WE ARE.

WHAT WILL HAPPEN WHEN INAZUMA IS FOUND?
SHE'LL BE KILLED...

...THEN ALL HELL WILL BREAK LOOSE WHEN **EVERYONE** TRIES TO CLAIM THE REWARD.

HOW IS HE, SANSHOBO?
HE'LL BE FINE--JUST A FEW BRUISES.
SLURP!

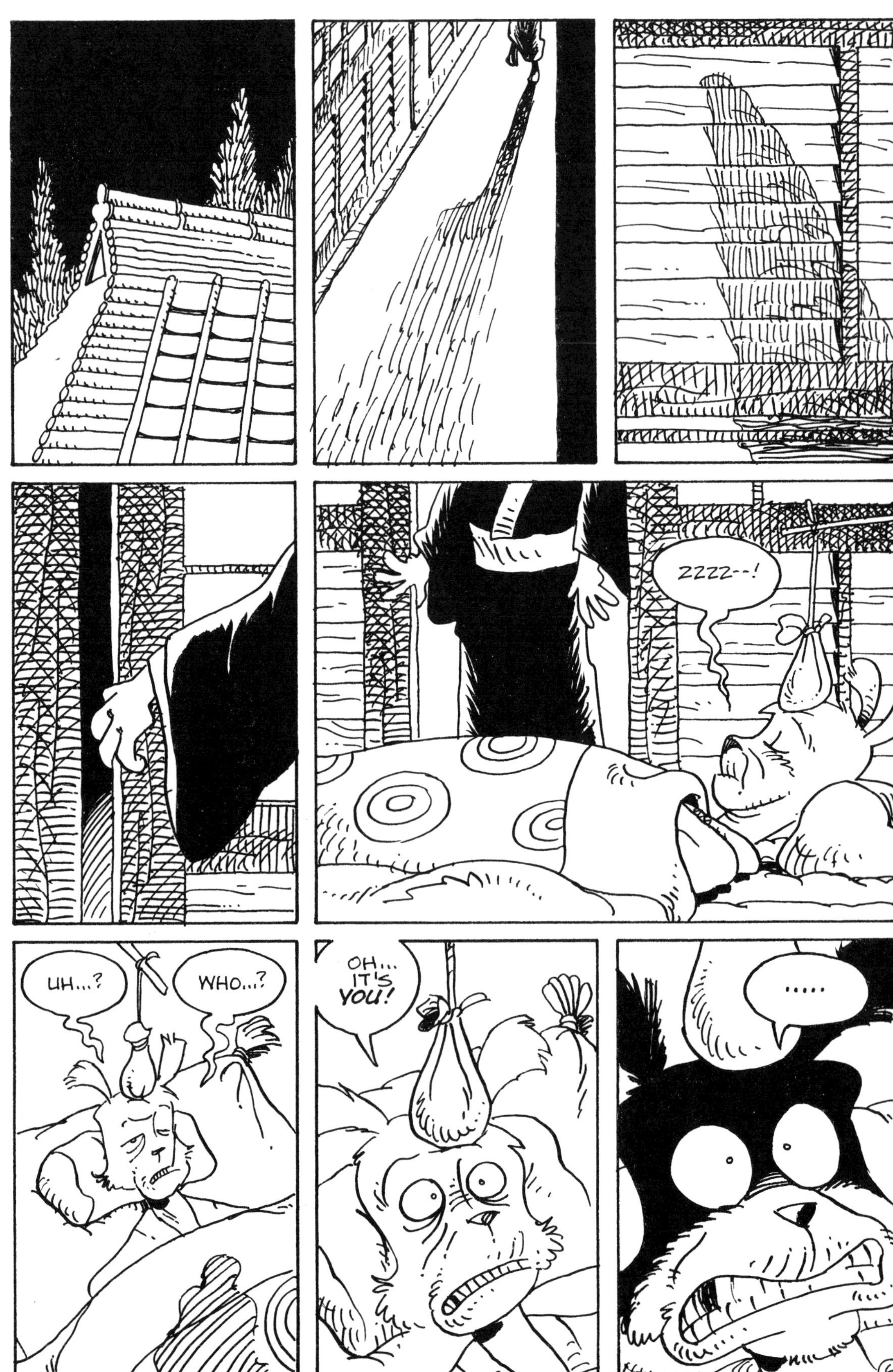
ZZZZ--!
UH...?
WHO...?
OH... IT'S YOU!
.....
6

COME ON!

YOU'VE GOT TO KEEP UP WITH ME IF YOU WANT TO BE MY ASSISTANT!
I'M NOT GOING TO HIRE YOU JUST BECAUSE YOU'RE MY SISTER'S HUSBAND.

COME ON! KEEP UP! YOU'RE SO LAZY!

I DIDN'T THINK BEING AN INFORMANT WAS SO MUCH WORK!
YOU'RE NOT ONLY LAZY, YOU'RE STUPID AS WELL!

THERE'S SOMEPLACE WE HAVEN'T CHECKED OUT YET--THAT OLD TEMPLE!
NOW YOU'RE THINKING! COME ON!

7.

IT'S HER! IT'S INAZUMA, AND SHE LOOKS DEAD!
DID YOU SEE ALL THAT BLOOD? WOW!

COME ON--LET'S FIND SOME BOUNTY HUNTERS AND SELL OUR INFORMATION.
HOLD IT!

TRUE, WE CAN SELL HER WHEREABOUTS AND COLLECT A SMALL INFORMER'S FEE...
YEAH.

...BUT IF WE TAKE HER HEAD AND DELIVER IT TO BOSS BAKUCHI OURSELVES, WE CAN CLAIM THE ENTIRE REWARD!
HUH?

HMM... I DON'T KNOW...

SHE'S DEAD, ISN'T SHE?
GO ON--CUT OFF HER HEAD!

HUH? WHY ME?
8.

GULP!
WHY SHOULD I BE THE ONE TO BEHEAD HER? WHY NOT YOU?
EVERYONE KNOWS THAT I'M THE BRAINS BETWEEN US, BUT YOU'RE THE BRAVE ONE!

OH, YEAH?
SURE... AND IF YOU TAKE HER HEAD, YOU CAN CLAIM HER SWORDS. THINK OF THE PRESTIGE THAT WILL GIVE YOU! YOU'LL BE AN IMPORTANT GUY!
YEAH!

OKAY, I'LL DO IT... BUT YOU'LL HAVE TO COME WITH ME!
SURE. LET'S GO!

ARE YOU SURE SHE'S DEAD?
OF COURSE!

LOOK AT HER EYES--LIKE THOSE OF A STEAMED FISH!

WELL, GO ON, GRAB HER SWORD AND DECAPITATE HER!
DON'T PUSH ME! DON'T PUSH ME!
9.

I'M GOING TO MAKE SURE SHE'S DEAD BEFORE I GET TOO CLOSE TO HER!

POKE! POKE! POKE!

POKE! POKE! POKE!

HA! SHE'S DEAD, ALL RIGHT!
I'LL TAKE HER HEAD!

Graahh!

!
SWIT!!
10

AH AH AH--!

AHHHH

AAAAAAHHHHHHHHHHHHHHHHHHHHHHHH

AAAAAAHHHHHHHHH
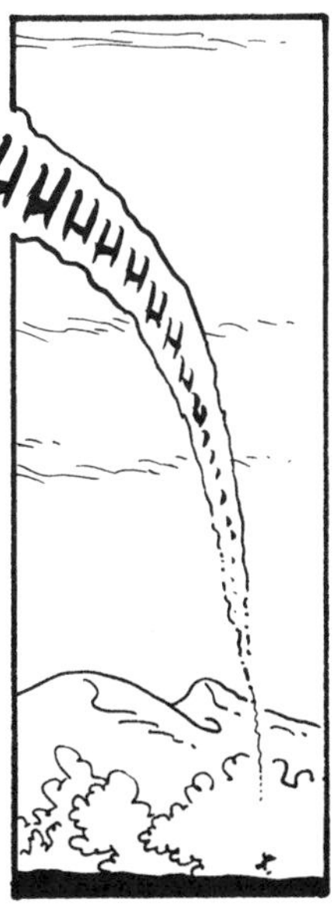

ONE HOUR LATER...
PANT! PANT! PANT! PANT! GASP!
POOR GUY...

WELL, IT'S NOT A TOTAL LOSS. I CAN STILL SELL HER LOCATION!
11.

PRIEST HAMA! PRIEST HAMA!
EH? WHAT IS IT, JUBEI?

IT'S JIRO! H-HE'S BEEN MURDERED!
WHAT?

HE WAS KILLED IN HIS SLEEP!
WHO COULD HAVE DONE IT?

I WALKED IN ON THE VISITING PRIEST SENZO AS HE ATTACKED JIRO TWO NIGHTS AGO!
HE'S THE ONE WHO'S BEEN PLAGUED BY THOSE NIGHTMARES!

THERE IS SOMETHING STRANGE ABOUT THAT PRIEST!
LET'S SEE WHAT HE KNOWS ABOUT THE DEATH.
12.

I KNOW NOTHING OF JIRO'S DEATH! I WAS ASLEEP!

YOU YOURSELF GAVE ME THE SLEEPING POTION!
TRUE...

...BUT IT IS NOT ALWAYS EFFECTIVE--IF ONE'S WILL IS STRONG ENOUGH.

I SHOULD HAVE INSISTED YOU LEAVE WITH YOUR MASTER, PRIEST SANSHOBO!

WE WILL CALL THE AUTHORITIES TO INVESTIGATE JIRO'S DEATH. JUST TO BE SAFE, THOUGH, YOU WILL BE LOCKED UP UNTIL THEY ARRIVE!

B-BUT I'M *INNOCENT*!
13.

YOU WILL HAVE TO STAY IN THIS EMPTY STORAGE ROOM.
WE ARE SORRY TO HAVE TO DO THIS, SENZO.
I'M SURE IT IS A MISTAKE, AND YOU WILL BE FREE BY TOMORROW.

DON'T WORRY. THE GODS ARE FAIR. IF YOU ARE INNOCENT AS YOU SAY, YOU WILL HAVE NOTHING TO FEAR.

AS A CHILD, I WAS NEAR DEATH. THE GODS LOOKED DOWN UPON ME WITH MERCY AND CURED ME. TO REPAY THEM, I BECAME A PRIEST.

THAT'S ENOUGH, JUBEI. LOCK HIM IN.

CLICK!

THEY THINK I MURDERED JIRO...

...AND MAYBE I **REALLY AM** GUILTY.
14

INAZUMA WILL BE FOUND SOONER OR LATER.
THEN THERE WILL BE A **BLOOD-BATH**.
HOLD IT.

WHAT'S THE MATTER?
WE'RE BEING WATCHED.

YOU'RE CRAZY! USAGI AND I CAN SENSE IF WE'RE BEING WATCHED AS WELL AS ANY--
LOOK!

WHAT'S **HE** DOING HERE?
WHO IS HE?
A SLIMY BOUNTY HUNTER!
THAT'S FUNNY COMING FROM **YOU!**
15.

WHAT DO YOU WANT?
TO JOIN YOU.
WHAT?!

I'M LOOKING FOR INAZUMA, SAME AS YOU ARE. I CAN'T COVER THE ENTIRE TERRITORY MYSELF, SO I NEED YOUR HELP.

WHY US?
YOU SEEM MORE TRUSTWORTHY THAN THE OTHER BOUNTY HUNTERS.

I SAY NO!
I'M NOT SPLITTING UP THE REWARD ANY MORE THAN I ALREADY AM!
NOT SO FAST, STRAY DOG!

WE'VE SEEN HIM FIGHT, AND IF IT COMES DOWN TO A BRAWL WITH SOME OTHER HUNTERS, I WANT HIM ON OUR SIDE!
OKAY, BUT HIS SPLIT COMES OUT OF YOUR SHARE OF THE REWARD!

THEN IT'S SETTLED!
CALL ME ISAMU.
16.

HEY, HEY, HEY! YOU LOOK LIKE BOUNTY HUNTERS!
I BET YOU'RE INTERESTED IN INFORMATION ABOUT INAZUMA!
WHAT CAN YOU KNOW?

HOW ABOUT WHERE SHE IS RIGHT NOW?
OKAY, TELL US!

HEY, HEY, HEY! I'M A BUSINESSMAN! I DON'T SAY A WORD UNLESS I'M PAID FOR IT!

I'LL MAKE HIM TELL US!

STOP IT! WE'LL PAY FOR HIS KNOWLEDGE.
17.

*1 RI = 3.9 KILOMETERS

HIS WORD IS NOT GOOD ENOUGH! I SAY WE KILL HIM TO MAKE SURE.
NO!
NO!
I SAY YES. WHAT ABOUT YOU, GEN?

WE'LL LET YOU GO--BUT IF YOU BETRAY US, I'LL HUNT YOU DOWN EVEN IF IT TAKES THE REST OF MY LIFE! UNDERSTAND?
YEAH! YEAH! SURE! I PROMISE!
GULP!

OH... ONE MORE THING...
WH-WHAT IS IT?

BONK!

HE'LL BE UNCONSCIOUS FOR A WHILE. THAT WILL BUY US A BIT MORE TIME.
THEN YOU DON'T BELIEVE HIS WORD?
HA! I WOULD BE DISAPPOINTED IF HE DIDN'T TELL OTHERS!
19.

WOULD YOU REALLY HAVE KILLED THAT SNITCH?
OF COURSE NOT! I JUST WANTED TO SCARE HIM INTO SILENCE.

GOOD. I DID NOT THINK YOU WERE AS COLD-HEARTED AS YOU APPEAR TO BE.
YOU WOULD BE SURPRISED AT HOW COLD-HEARTED I CAN BE.

THIS MUST BE THE PLACE.
LET'S SEE IF HE WAS TELLING THE TRUTH.

.....
GODS!

WHO'S THE OTHER GUY?
A BOUNTY HUNTER, NO DOUBT.
20

IS SHE STILL ALIVE?
SHE SHOULD NOT BE, BUT SHE IS! IT MUST BE BECAUSE OF THE SPIRIT OF JEI!

WHAT ARE YOU TALKING ABOUT?
SHE IS POSSESSED BY A DEMON. I'M GOING TO EXORCISE IT OUT OF HER BODY.

WHY BOTHER? JUST TAKE HER HEAD, AND LET'S GET OUT OF HERE!
NO! WE MUST GIVE HER PEACE BEFORE SHE DIES.

WE'VE NO TIME FOR THAT! OTHER HUNTERS WILL BE HERE SOON!

I'LL CUT IT OFF, IF YOU DON'T HAVE THE NERVE FOR IT.
NO.

LET THE PRIEST DO HIS WORK.
WHAT IS INAZUMA TO YOU?
THAT IS MY BUSINESS.
21.

WHO IS THAT GUY?
I DON'T KNOW. HE'S NO ORDINARY BOUNTY HUNTER. I DOUBT HE'S A HUNTER AT ALL!

I'M NOT AFRAID OF YOU!
YOU SHOULD BE.
THAT'S ENOUGH!

PUT YOUR SWORDS AWAY!
WE DON'T HAVE THE TIME TO FIGHT AMONG OUR-SELVES.
I SEE I'M OUT-VOTED.
YES, YOU ARE. GET ON WITH IT, PRIEST.
I'LL WAIT OUTSIDE UNTIL YOU'RE DONE.
MERCIFUL BUDDHA, I NEED YOUR HELP TO CLEANSE THIS BODY OF THE EVIL!

Heh, heh, heh, heh, heh...

WHAT?! HOW CAN SHE EVEN BE CONSCIOUS WITH THE AMOUNT OF BLOOD SHE'S LOST?!

Graahh--!
22.

UH--!

THIS IS GOING TO BE HARDER THAN I THOUGHT! JEI MUST BE A POWERFUL DEMON INDEED!
THE SPIRIT MAY BE STRONG, BUT THE PHYSICAL BODY MUST BE NEAR DEATH!

MERCIFUL GODS, AID ME IN DRIVING OUT THE EVIL FORCE FROM THIS INNOCENT!
Heh, heh, heh, heh, heh...

Gyahh..!

HYAHH!
BEGONE! BEGONE! FOUL DEMON!
LEAVE THIS ONE IN PEACE!
Aroughh--!
23.

TIME'S RUN OUT FOR US!
KEEP ON WITH YOUR WORK, SANSHOBO!
I THOUGHT FOR SURE IT WOULD HAVE TAKEN LONGER FOR THEM TO FIND US.
WHY, THAT MONEY-GRUBBING WEASEL--! HE WOULD STAKE HIS OWN LIFE TO GAIN A FEW MORE COINS.
YEAH. YOU'VE GOT TO ADMIRE HIM.
WHAT ARE YOU ALL DOING HERE? LEAVE US ALONE!
YOU KNOW WHAT WE'RE HERE FOR! HAND HER OVER!

WE KNOW YOU HAVE THE OUTLAW INAZUMA IN THAT TEMPLE!
GIVE HER TO US, AND WE'LL LET YOU GO.
SPARROWS
chapter 5 雀
THERE IS NO WAY YOU CAN DEFEAT ALL OF US!
1

AND IF WE GIVE HER UP, WHICH ONE OF YOU WILL CLAIM THE REWARD? OR DO YOU PLAN TO SPLIT IT BETWEEN ALL OF YOU?

WHAT?

WE'LL WORRY ABOUT DIVIDING THE REWARD LATER.
RIGHT NOW, ALL WE KNOW IS THAT YOU HAVE HER.

WE CAN'T GIVE HER UP.
WE HAVE NO INTENTION OF DOING SO.
WE WORKED TOO HARD FOR THIS.

SHE SAVED MY LIFE, AND I'M HONOR-BOUND TO PROTECT HER*.

SO THAT'S WHY YOU JOINED US! I KNEW IT WASN'T FOR BOSS BAKUCHI'S BOUNTY! YOU DECEIVED US!

CUT IT OUT! NOW IS NOT THE TIME TO ARGUE!
2

*UY: BOOK 10-THE BRINK of LIFE and DEATH

YOU'RE GEN AND STRAY DOG. YOU'VE GOT BIG REPUTATIONS.
IT WOULD BE A SHAME TO HAVE TO KILL YOU OVER A BOUNTY!
AND YOU'RE HIGASHI AND AKATSUKI--BOTH PROFESSIONAL HUNTERS AS WELL.
THE REST OF YOU ARE WET-EARED AMATEURS.
WE MAY BE INEXPERIENCED, BUT THERE ARE STILL MORE THAN ENOUGH OF US TO OVERRUN THE TEMPLE.
HE'S RIGHT, YOU KNOW.
HOW ARE PRIEST SANSHOBO AND ISAMU DOING IN THERE?
I'LL CHECK ON THEM!
SANSHOBO--WE'RE RUNNING OUT OF TIME!
OUT, FOUL DEMON!
Hisss--!
LEAVE HER IN PEACE!
3.

RELEASE HER!
Ughh--!

JEI IS SUCH A POWERFUL FORCE...

...FORTUNATELY HIS HOST BODY IS ALREADY IN A WEAKENED STATE, AND NEAR DEATH!
GET OUT!
Gyahhh--!

SHE'LL BE DEAD EVEN SOONER IF THOSE BOUNTY HUNTERS GET HER.

THEN IF SHE IS TO DIE, LET IT BE WITH HER SOUL INTACT!

MEANWHILE...

ZZZZ...!

¡GASP!

I-I CAN'T SLEEP. THAT IS WHEN THE DREAMS COME!

I KNOW I DID NOT MURDER JIRO!
OR DID I? I-- I JUST CAN'T REMEMBER!

WHEN THE AUTHORITIES ARRIVE, I'LL BE ARRESTED AND MAYBE PUT TO **DEATH**.

EH? THE DOOR IS AJAR! THEY MUST NOT HAVE LOCKED IT WELL!
IF I CAN GET TO SANSHOBO, I'M SURE HE CAN HELP ME!

5

THEY'VE WITHDRAWN, BUT THEY'RE NOT GOING TO LET US TAKE INAZUMA OUT OF HERE.
LOOK AT THEM-- HUDDLED AROUND LIKE PARASITES.
WE CAN'T FIGHT OUR WAY OUT--ESPECIALLY WITH AKATSUKI AND HIGASHI WITH THEM.
DO YOU WANT TO HAND HER OVER TO THEM?
YOU MEAN GIVE UP MY REWARD? YOU KNOW ME BETTER THAN THAT!
WE'RE BOTH OF THE SAME MIND, THEN.
YEAH.
DO YOU THINK SANSHOBO WILL EXORCISE THE DEMON OUT OF INAZUMA?
WHO CARES? I DON'T EVEN KNOW HOW SHE'S STILL ALIVE!
YEAH. SHE CAN'T BE LONG FOR THIS WORLD.
6.

WHAT DO YOU THINK IS GOING ON IN THERE?
ALL THAT YELLING? I DON'T KNOW.

THERE MUST ONLY BE A FEW OF THEM IN THE TEMPLE. WE MUST OUTNUMBER THEM AT LEAST FIVE TO ONE!

BUT GEN AND STRAY DOG ARE FORMIDABLE, AND THAT LONG-EARED SAMURAI LOOKS LIKE HE CAN ALSO HANDLE A SWORD.

WELL, WE'D BETTER DO SOMETHING REAL SOON. THAT SNITCH WHO TOLD US INAZUMA'S WHEREABOUTS IS PROBABLY SELLING THAT SAME INFORMATION TO OTHER HUNTERS RIGHT NOW.

YEAH. THERE ARE ALREADY TOO MANY OF US FIGHTING OVER HER.
WITH MORE ARRIVING EVERY MINUTE.

WHO WILL GET INAZUMA, ANYWAY?
YOU AND I ARE THE ONLY PROFESSIONAL HUNTERS HERE. WE SHOULD STICK TOGETHER.
7.

WE'LL HAVE THE OTHERS ATTACK THE TEMPLE. IF THEY KILL THEMSELVES OFF, I GUESS WE'LL HAVE TO SPLIT THE REWARD BETWEEN JUST THE TWO OF US.

I LIKE YOUR PLAN. LET'S GO.
PTOOEY!

WE'VE GIVEN YOU ENOUGH TIME! HAND HER OVER!
NO!

THEN WE'LL TAKE HER!
HIYAAHHH!
8.

GET THEM! GET THEM!
URK!
GHAA!
THEY CAN'T TAKE ON ALL OF US!
ULP!
OOP!
AHK!
GYUK!
GYAH!

HIGASHI AND AKATSUKI ARE HOLDING BACK!
THAT'S BECAUSE THEY'RE SMART!
YEAH. SIT BACK AND LET THE COMPETITION ELIMINATE EACH OTHER!
THAT'S WHAT I WOULD DO!
WE CAN'T HOLD THEM OFF FOREVER!
WHERE'S ISAMU? WE NEED HIS SWORDS!
10.

I KNOW YOUR NAME--JEI! RETURN TO HELL, PUTRID DEMON!
Gyahhh!

UH--!
I'll kill you, priest! Kill you!

Rwahhh--!

.....
11.

UH--!

TOMIKO!

.....

AHHH...!

TOMIKO!

UH...

I-ISAMU...? IT IS GOOD TO SEE YOU AGAIN...
...BIG BROTHER...

FATHER ORDERED ME TO BRING YOU HOME! HE FORGIVES YOU FOR RUNNING AWAY. HE WANTS YOU BACK WITH YOUR FAMILY!

THAT IS...
...GOOD.
THANK...

...YOU...

WILL YOU PERFORM THE SEGAKI RITES FOR HER, PRIEST? SHE'S DEAD.

BUT SHE DIED FREE.
13.

KYAH!
GAK!
!
FLOO..!
HIYAHH!

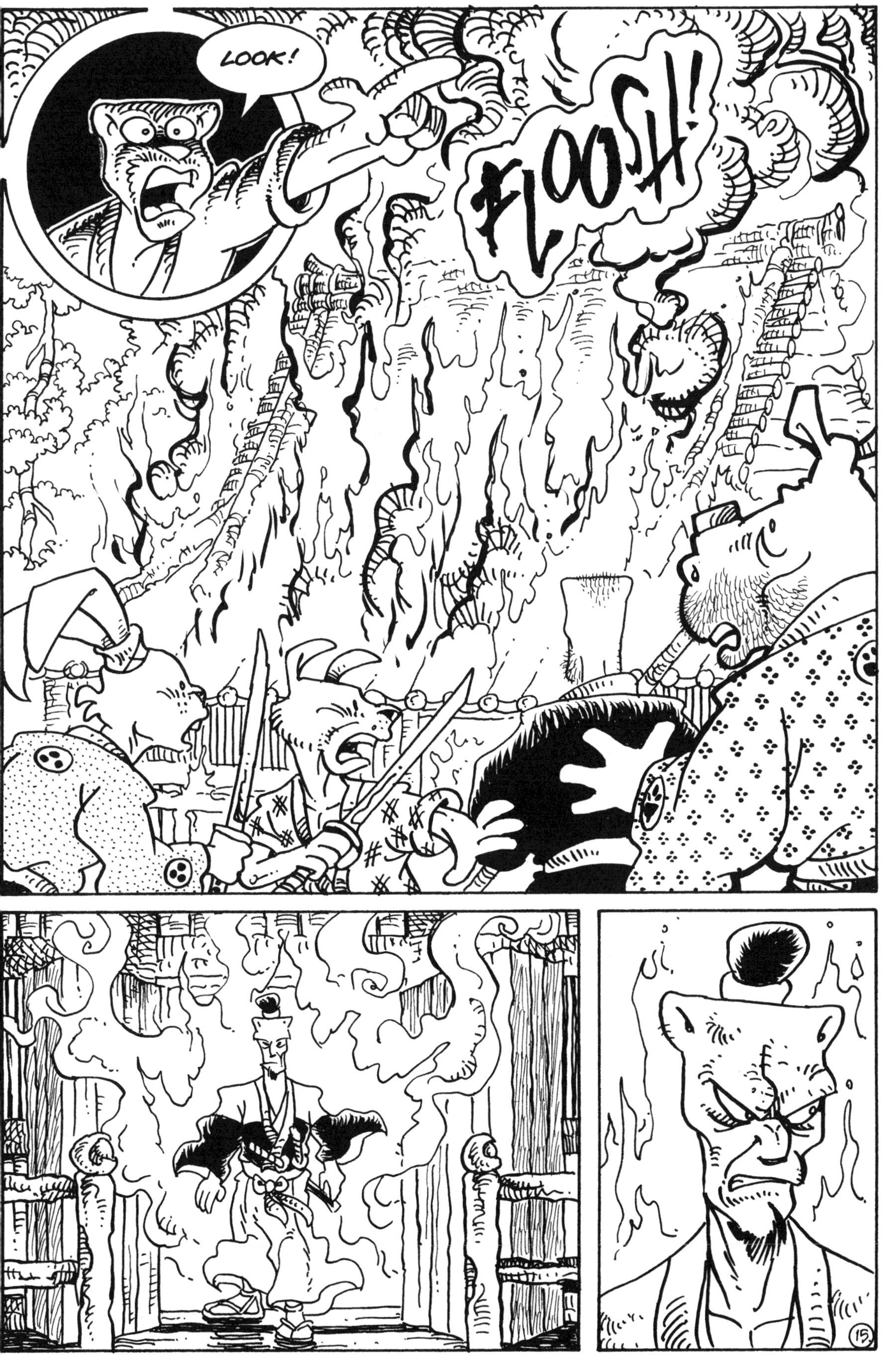

LOOK!

FLOOSH!

INAZUMA IS STILL IN THERE!

I'LL GET HER!

FLOOM!
UH--!

COUGH! COUGH! IT'S NO USE! NO ONE CAN GET IN THERE!

THERE WON'T BE ANYTHING LEFT IN THERE! NO ONE WILL GET THE REWARD!
COUGH! COUGH!

16.

LATER...
WE PAID A SNITCH FOR INFORMATION ON INAZUMA!
YOU TOO? HE'S THE ONLY ONE WHO MADE ANY MONEY TODAY!
THERE ARE TWO BODIES IN HERE--BOTH BURNED BEYOND RECOGNITION!
ONE OF THEM IS INAZUMA!

THEN THERE'S NOTHING WE CAN COLLECT THE REWARD ON.
COME ON. LET'S GO.
IT'S OVER? JUST LIKE THAT?

AS YOU SAID, WE'RE PROFESSIONALS. THERE'S NO PROFIT IN CONTINUING THIS.

SO LONG.
GOOD RIDDANCE.
17

YOU DID THIS, ISAMU! YOU CHEATED ME OUT OF MY REWARD!
HOLD IT, STRAY DOG!

IF HE HADN'T DONE WHAT HE DID, WE WOULD BE DEAD! THERE WAS NO WAY WE COULD HAVE BEATEN ALL THOSE HUNTERS! HE SAVED YOUR LIFE!

OKAY. I GUESS I OWE YOU SOMETHING FOR THAT. BUT GET OUT OF MY SIGHT NOW BEFORE I CHANGE MY MIND.
IT LOOKS LIKE OUR PARTNERSHIP IS OVER.

18.

I'VE HAD ENOUGH OF YOU GUYS AS WELL. BUT BEFORE I GO, TELL ME... WHAT'S ISAMU'S CONNECTION TO INAZUMA?
NONE.
WHAT?

HIS CONNECTION IS TO A WOMAN NAMED TOMIKO.
HE IS HER BROTHER!
HUH?

THAT EXPLAINS EVERYTHING.
YEAH. YOU CAN'T BLAME HIM FOR KEEPING THE REWARD FROM ALL OF US.
I CAN.

AT LEAST HE GOT TO SEE HIS SISTER DIE IN PEACE. YOU DID EXORCISE THE DEMON JEI OUT OF HER, DIDN'T YOU, SANSHOBO?

I DID NOT FORCE HIM OUT. IT WAS MORE LIKE HE... ESCAPED.

THEN WHERE IS JEI NOW?
WHEREVER HE IS, I HOPE WE DON'T RUN INTO HIM AGAIN!
LET'S GET OUT OF HERE!
17.

PANT! PANT! PANT! I'VE GOT TO FIND SANSHOBO! PANT!

PANT! GASP!
SLOSH! SLOSH!

I CAN'T LET THEM CAPTURE ME!

UH--!

I'M SO, SO TIRED.

SNAP!
HUH!

WH-WHO ARE YOU? COME ON OUT OF THE SHADOWS!

I'M LOOKING FOR MY UNCLE!
20.

YOU'RE MISTAKEN, YOUR UNCLE IS NOT HERE!
OH, YES HE IS.

HELLO...
...UNCLE.

EH?

HELLO, KEIKO.
PRIEST HAMA!

I TOLD YOU THAT YOU WERE NOT THE ONLY ONE PLAGUED WITH NIGHTMARES, SENZO. I HAVE HAD THEM EVER SINCE I LOOKED INTO PRIEST JIZONOBU'S EYES.

IT WAS YEARS AGO THAT HE MASSACRED ALL THE PRIESTS AT MY TEMPLE, BUT HE SPARED **ME** FOR A REASON.

I COULD FEEL THE SPIRIT OF JIZONOBU--JEI--REACHING OUT TO ME, AND NOW...

...now he's finally here.
Heh, heh, heh.
21

The peasant, Jiro, was also possessed and would have eventually recognized Jei. He had to die.

I needed a scapegoat, and you were perfectly suited for it.
STAY AWAY! STAY AWAY!

.....

SHOONK!

Come along, my innocent.
YES, UNCLE.

I MISSED YOU, UNCLE.
We have far to travel, my innocent.
22

WELL, KAMOGAWA, IT IS THE END OF THE MONTH.
WHY DON'T I HAVE INAZUMA'S HEAD BEFORE ME?
SHE HAS DISAPPEARED.

WE HAD REPORTS THAT BOUNTY HUNTERS HAD HER CORNERED, BUT THERE IS NO PROOF OF HER DEATH AND NO ONE HAS STEPPED FORWARD TO CLAIM THE REWARD.

WHAT?
THEN AS FAR AS ANYONE KNOWS, SHE'S STILL ALIVE AND OUT THERE--MOCKING ME!
23

WHAT ABOUT THE TRIBUTES FROM THE GAMBLING HOUSES?

ALL THE DENS HAVE REFUSED TO PAY! YOU ARE THROUGH AS THE CRIME BOSS OF THIS AREA!
BAH!

WHO COULD EVER TAKE MY PLACE?

.....
SWIT!

ME.

THE END

FOX HUNT

MY JOURNEY WITH *USAGI YOJIMBO*

SEVERAL YEARS AGO (I honestly don't remember how many years), I found myself on an exciting journey. An unexpected trek that provided adventure, danger, treachery, and even romance. Of course, it wasn't *my* journey. I was only a tagalong trying hard to keep up. I'll have to admit, the surroundings and countryside were not exactly familiar. Then again, this was not my homeland, nor was it my time. In spite of this, I quickened my pace. The journey was something I could hardly refuse. It was too intriguing, and I knew there was a good deal I would learn along the way. After all, how often does one get to accompany a samurai warrior on his travels?

Naturally, I was delighted to share these remarkable adventures. And it was an opportunity afforded me by a gifted artist and storyteller named Stan Sakai. I'm guessing you're already well aware of the samurai warrior, Miyamoto Usagi. However, if you're not acquainted with this unique character, you're in for a pleasant surprise. Like the master storytellers of comic book art, Stan Sakai breathes life into his animal characters and they become much more. They're not human, of course. They don't need to be. Stan's characters are *real*.

The integrity of Stan's storytelling is matched only by his art. Respectful of his medium, Stan crafts it all by hand. In an age of computers and digital shortcuts, every image on the page is meticulously penciled, inked, and drawn by the artist. Even the lettering is rendered by hand. As one who has also lettered comics in years past, I'm well aware of the discipline and skill required.

Another unexpected plus of *Usagi Yojimbo* is color—or, rather, the lack of it. While most comics stories rely on their graphics, Stan Sakai proves that a colorful story can be effectively told in black and white. Actually, once you've delved into an *Usagi* adventure, you're hardly aware the story is being told without color. Like the masters of Hollywood's golden age, Stan can be likened to cinematographers such as James Wong Howe or Gregg Toland for his mastery of the black-and-white medium. Finally, the stories have a visual richness. The Japanese patterns and textures that adorn the pages of *Usagi* are not purchased visual aids. Rather, they spring from the pencil, brush, and pen of a dedicated artist. Call it old school, if you will, but it represents the vision of an artist who will not compromise.

Finally, there's Stan Sakai the consummate storyteller, with his remarkable ability to engage the reader. As we follow the samurai on his adventures, Stan breathes life into his cast of unique characters. Like all of us, his characters are not immune from human frailty. They can be arrogant, vindictive, and selfish. Yet others demonstrate courage, sacrifice, and honor. Through it all, Miyamoto Usagi remains pretty much unchanged. Consistent with his samurai oath, he's the one constant in the series.

Of course, it gets even better. Our little group of cartoonists and writers happens to be lucky enough to join Stan Sakai for lunch each Friday. How many readers have this kind of access to the author? Should I have an *Usagi* question for Stan, he's usually sitting right next to me. How cool is that? Naturally, my questions are few. A consummate storyteller, Stan rarely is required to explain his stories.

All right, you've probably heard too much from me. It's time to discover *Usagi Yojimbo* for yourself. If you're a devoted reader of the series, you already know what I mean. If you're new to *Usagi*, I envy you because your journey is about to begin.

FLOYD NORMAN
2011

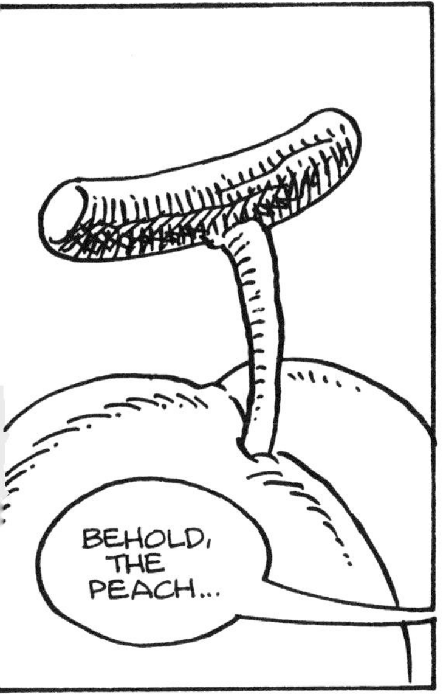
BEHOLD, THE PEACH...

...THE IMPERIAL FRUIT...

I COVER IT WITH THIS CLOTH...

...SLIP IT OFF...

...AND, SEE, IT'S NOT A PEACH AT ALL, BUT A *TOKAGE*!
EEP!

¡GASP!¡
WOW!
HA HA HA!
HUH?
1.

KITSUNEGARI

THANK YOU. THANK YOU.
EEP! EEP! EEP!
SHE'S PRETTY GOOD.
GOOD ENOUGH TO DO HER ACT IN THE CITY.
THEN I WONDER WHY SHE'S PERFORMING FOR SMALL CHANGE ON A COUNTRY ROAD.

*FOX HUNT

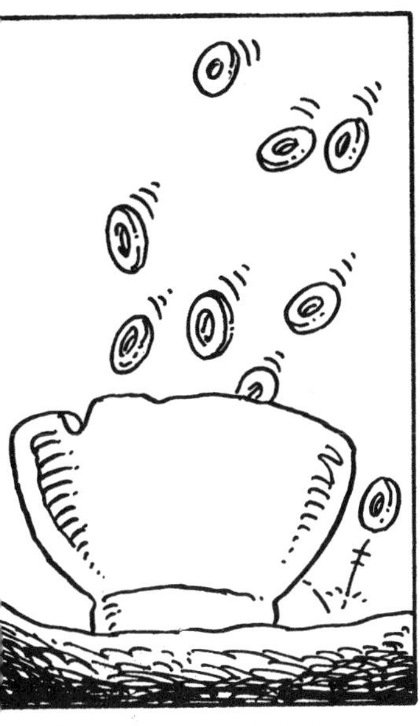

THANK YOU, SAMURAI! THAT IS MOST GENEROUS.
YOU WERE VERY GOOD.

?

WHAT?

DIDN'T YOU LIKE THE SHOW, GEN?
YEAH, BUT NOT ENOUGH TO SPEND MONEY ON IT.

I MISSED OUT ON THE REWARD FOR INAZUMA. I CAN'T AFFORD TO THROW MONEY AWAY.

NOW COME ON, USAGI! WE'VE GOT PRETTY FAR TO TRAVEL.

YOU COULD BE A BIT MORE GENEROUS. THAT'S ALL I'M SAYING, GEN.
HARUMPH! IT'S EASY FOR YOU TO SAY!

YOU GOT A BIG REWARD FROM LORD NORIYUKI FOR FINDING A **GOLD MINE**.*
MUNCH! MUNCH!

IN FACT, ***YOU'RE*** PAYING FOR ***EVERYTHING*** UNTIL WE SPLIT UP AGAIN.
4.

* UY BOOK 21: THE MOTHER of MOUNTAINS

SOON...
HMM... A CROSS-ROADS...

SO--WHICH WAY SHOULD WE GO?
HOW WOULD I KNOW?

HEY, FILTHY OLD MAN--WHERE DO THESE ROADS LEAD?

THEY LEAD TO THE SAME TOWN, BUT THIS WAY IS A SHORTCUT THROUGH THE KITSUNE WOODS.

A SHORTCUT I DON'T KNOW ABOUT? LET'S GO THAT WAY!
5

BUT BE CAREFUL NOT TO LEAVE THE TRAIL. THERE ARE **NINE-TAILED TRICKSTER FOXES** IN THOSE WOODS.

AND WOE TO YOU SHOULD YOU OFFEND THEM.

I DON'T LIKE THE THOUGHT OF FOXES. LET'S GO **AROUND** THE FOREST, GEN.

IT'S BEEN A LONG DAY, AND I'M TIRED...
...AND, AS HE SAID, WE'LL BE OKAY IF WE STICK TO THE TRAIL.

BESIDES, I DON'T KNOW ABOUT YOU, BUT **I** HAVEN'T OFFENDED ANYBODY.

COME ON, USAGI!
6

THIS WAY DOESN'T SOUND LIKE A GOOD IDEA.
WHAT'S LIFE WITHOUT TAKING A FEW RISKS?
I'D RATHER TAKE A SHORTCUT THAN GO THE LONG WAY ANY DAY.
I DON'T KNOW WHY YOU'RE SO CONCERNED. THE TRAIL IS PRETTY WELL MARKED.
IT ALWAYS IS, AT THE BEGINNING.
LATER...
WE'VE BEEN WALKING AWHILE, AND THE TRAIL STILL LOOKS GOOD TO ME.
MUCH LATER STILL...
OKAY, I TAKE IT BACK. IT'S A VERY GOOD PATH.
WE'LL GET THROUGH THE WOODS IN NO TIME.
7.

I DON'T LIKE THE LOOK OF THAT GORGE BRIDGE.
BUT WE'VE COME TOO FAR TO TURN BACK NOW.

HMM...YOU'D BETTER GO FIRST. IF IT'S SAFE, I'LL FOLLOW YOU ACROSS.
WHY SHOULD **I** CROSS FIRST?

IT MAKES SENSE, DOESN'T IT? YOU WEIGH LESS THAN I DO. IF YOU MAKE IT ACROSS, I'LL FOLLOW YOU!
AND IF I ***DON'T*** MAKE IT ACROSS?
WELL... UH...

FORGET IT. I'LL GO. WE CAN'T GO BACK, AND WE CAN'T SPEND THE WHOLE DAY ARGUING.

GULP!

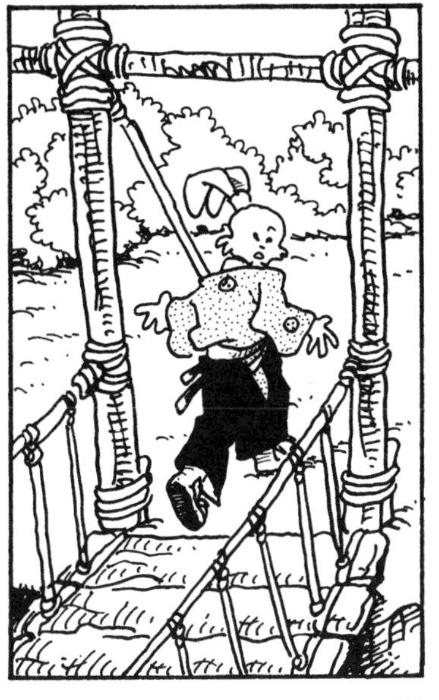

IT'S PERFECTLY SAFE, GEN! COME ON.

OKAY... IF YOU SAY SO...

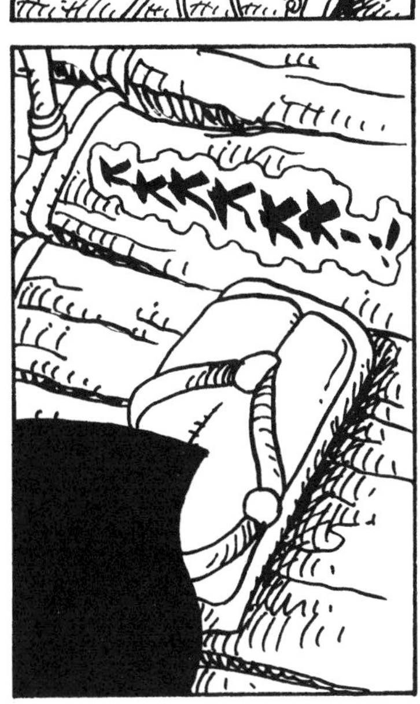
KKKKKK--!

!

YAHHH!
KKKKKKKKK

YOU IDIOT! DO YOU CALL THAT SAFE?!
HMM... IT'S A NARROW GORGE, BUT IT MAY AS WELL BE A MILE WIDE.
YOU'LL HAVE TO TURN BACK AND GO AROUND THE LONG WAY.
WHAT?! IT WILL TAKE ME HOURS TO CATCH UP TO YOU!
IT CAN'T BE HELPED. I'LL WAIT FOR YOU AT THE CROSSROADS, GEN.
TRY TO HURRY, OKAY?
YOU'RE JUST GOING TO ABANDON ME OUT HERE? SOME FRIEND YOU ARE!
I'LL SEE YOU LATER!
WHY WOULD SUCH A GOOD TRAIL LEAD TO SUCH A BAD BRIDGE?
10

EH--?

ANOTHER TRAIL. I DON'T REMEMBER THAT.

THIS COULD BE A SHORTCUT THROUGH THE GORGE.

I BET THIS IS THE REAL TRAIL. THE ONE WE TOOK WAS PROBABLY AN OLD ONE. THAT'S WHY IT LED TO THAT DILAPIDATED BRIDGE.

USAGI WILL BE SURPRISED WHEN I SHOW UP RIGHT BEHIND HIM!

IN FACT, IF I HURRY, I BET I CAN CATCH UP TO THAT LONG-EARED RUNT.
11.

SOON.
HEY, USAGI!
EH?
GEN?
WHAT'S THE MATTER, USAGI? IT'S ME!
NO! GEN WENT BACK THE WAY WE CAME! YOU MUST BE A TRICKSTER FOX IN DISGUISE!
WHAT ARE YOU TALKING ABOUT? DON'T YOU RECOGNIZE YOUR BEST FRIEND?
TURN AROUND. IF YOU HAVE NINE TAILS, YOU'RE DEAD!
THERE. SATISFIED?
I GUESS YOU MIGHT BE OKAY.
OF COURSE I AM. BESIDES, THE CURSE ONLY APPLIES IF YOU OFFEND THE FOXES. WE HAVEN'T OFFENDED ANYONE.
12

I FOUND A TRAIL THAT WE OVERLOOKED. IT WENT DOWN THE GORGE AND UP THE OTHER SIDE.
HOW FORTUNATE.

UH... YEAH.
COME ON.

USAGI IS USUALLY A REALLY CAUTIOUS GUY. HE WOULDN'T JUST TAKE MY WORD ON THIS.

THERE'S SOMETHING DIFFERENT ABOUT HIM. IT'S ALMOST AS IF--!

HE'S A TRICKSTER FOX!
QUIT DAWDLING.
UH... YEAH. I'M COMING.
13

IF I CONFRONT HIM, HE'LL JUST DENY IT. HE CAN LIE WITH HIS WORDS, BUT USAGI HAS A UNIQUE SWORD STYLE.

I'LL KNOW IF IT'S HIM OR NOT.

HIYAHHHHH

!

HAHH!
TANG!

SO-- YOU ARE A FOX!

YOU CAN'T CONFUSE ME! I'M NOT A FOX! YOU ARE!
14

ADMIT YOU'RE A FOX!

YOU'RE THE FOX!

YOU FIGHT PRETTY WELL FOR A *FOX!*
I WAS GOING TO SAY THE SAME ABOUT YOU!
15

STAND STILL, FOX!
YOU'RE JUST TOO SLOW--
--AND UGLY!
HA!
HA!
WOK!
I'LL KILL YOU FOR THAT!
NOW I KNOW YOU'RE NOT USAGI! THAT'S NOT SOMETHING HE WOULD SAY FOR A LITTLE WHACK ON THE JAW...
...FOX!
16.

HE'S THE TRICKSTER FOX, ALL RIGHT.
EH?

USAGI?
I'M NOT A FOX-- HE IS!

HE'S LYING. DON'T TAKE YOUR EYES OFF HIM!
DON'T WORRY. TWO OF US CAN EASILY TAKE CARE OF HIM!

WAIT A MINUTE--!

WHY WERE YOU BEHIND ME? USAGI SHOULD HAVE BEEN AHEAD!

HYAHH!
17

THEN YOU MUST BE THE REAL USAGI!
HYAHH!

HYAHHH!

UH--!

YOU'RE BOTH FAKES!
ONE FOX WAS BAD ENOUGH--BUT TWO OF THEM--!
THERE'S ONLY ONE THING I CAN DO--
18.

RUN!

WHAT'S THE USE OF RUNNING, BIG GUY?
YOU CAN'T GET AWAY FROM US!

HUFF! HUFF! HUFF!

HA HA HA HA HA HA HA

HUFF! HUFF! GASP! PANT!

HUFF! PANT! PANT!

19

HAHAHAHA

NNNGHH!

STOP RUNNING, SAMURAI!
IT WILL TOUGHEN UP YOUR FLESH AND MAKE YOU STRINGY!

HA HAHA HA HA HA HA!

NGGH~~! THEY'RE RIGHT ON MY HEELS, AND I CAN'T KEEP UP THIS PACE MUCH LONGER!
20.

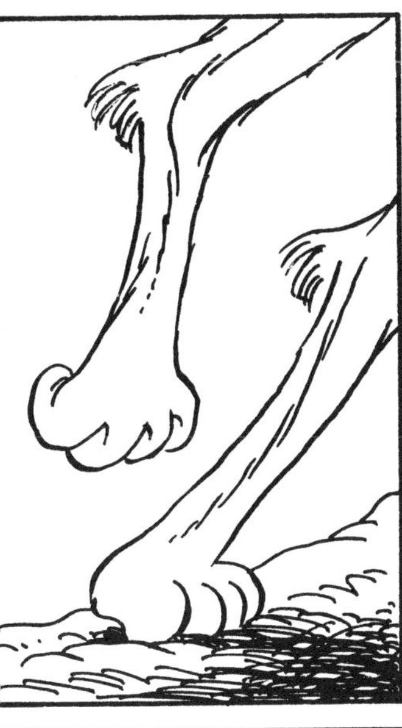

HA!
UH--!

WHOK!
GET OFF!

LET GO, YOU!
HA! HA! HA!

I SAID, LET--
--GO!
SLIT!

21.

PANT! PANT! GASP!

OOP--!

PANT! PANT! PANT!

GASP! PANT! PANT!

HUFF! PANT!
HUFF...
22

THEY'RE NOT COMING OUT OF THE FOREST.

YES! I BEAT THEM AFTER ALL! HA HA HA HA!

HEY, BIG GUY!
GULP!

DON'T BE SO ARROGANT!
AND NEXT TIME DON'T BE SO STINGY.

POOF!

DON'T EVER COME BACK INTO OUR FOREST!
HA HA HA HA HA HA!

TH-THEY WERE JUST TOYING WITH ME ALL ALONG.
23.

LATER...
WELL, YOU CERTAINLY TOOK YOUR SWEET TIME!
IT FEELS LIKE I'VE BEEN WAITING HERE FOREVER! WHAT DO YOU HAVE TO SAY FOR YOURSELF?
I'M THROUGH WITH SHORT-CUTS!

THE END

AND WHY DID YOU CUT YOUR OWN HAKAMA*?
I TOLD YOU--A MAGICAL FOX GOT A HOLD OF IT.
*BAGGY TROUSERS

WHY DIDN'T YOU USE YOUR SWORD ON THE FOX?

HE WAS ALREADY MAD AT ME. DO YOU THINK I WANTED HIM EVEN ANGRIER?!

IT SURE LOOKS FUNNY.
GRRR... I KNOW.

I'VE NEVER SEEN YOUR LEG BEFORE. IT LOOKS LIKE A BIG DAIKON RADISH.
OH, SHUT UP!
1.

SAKURA 桜 PART ONE

HEY, WHAT'S GOING ON DOWN THERE?
HEY, WAIT UP! DON'T WALK SO FAST!
EH?

A WOMAN TRAVELING ALL ALONE-- YOU'RE JUST ASKING FOR TROUBLE, HUH?
WE'D LIKE TO HAVE A GOOD TIME IN TOWN, BUT WE DON'T HAVE ANY MONEY, SEE?
JUST GIVE US ALL YOUR CASH, AND WE'LL LET YOU GO!

NOT SO FAST!
MY, YOU'RE A PRETTY ONE, AREN'T YOU?

IT WOULD BE A SHAME TO LET HER GO SO SOON.
YEAH!
3

COME ON! WE'VE GOT TO HELP HER!
WAIT!
HUH?
YOU'RE TOO IMPULSIVE-- ALWAYS WANTING TO BUTT IN BEFORE YOU GET ALL THE FACTS!
HOW CAN WE GET ALL THE FACTS?
LET'S WAIT AND SEE WHAT HAPPENS.
WHAT?!
BESIDES, THE TRAIL IS TOO LONG. WE'D NEVER GET TO HER IN TIME!
SHE'S A DEFENSELESS WOMAN! HOW CAN YOU BE SO HEARTLESS?!
GET OUT OF MY WAY!
I'VE GOT TO GET TO HER BEFORE IT'S TOO LATE!
THEN FORGET THE TRAIL! YOU HAD BETTER GO STRAIGHT DOWN THE MOUNTAIN!
GOOD IDEA!
4.

UH-OH!
MAYBE IT'S NOT SUCH A GREAT IDEA!
YAHHHH!!
AGH!
OO!
OUCH!
BOUNCE!
UGH!
POUND!
OW!
ACH!
OOK!
EYAG!
D'OH!
AUGH!
EEG!
OWIE OW OW!
OUCH!
RIP!
SHRED!
TEAR!
OUK!
AUGH!
OW!
ARR!
SPLAT!
UHH...
WELL, AT LEAST I'M DOWN.
NOW ON TO THE RESCUE...
OOHHH...
5

COME ON, CUTIE-- HAND OVER YOUR MONEY!
THEN WE CAN GET BETTER ACQUAINTED.
YOU CAN SHOW US A GOOD TIME!

MMM...YOUR SKIN IS SO SOFT. I CAN TELL YOU'RE A REAL LADY.

OOP!

WHAK!
FLOO!

WHY, YOU--!
6.

CHOP!
HA!

HA!
WHAP!

YOU DESTROYED MY WALKING STICK! NOW I'M UPSET!
ULP!

UH--!
SPASH!
7.

CRAK!
CRAK!
CRAK!
CRAK!
CRAK!
CRAK!
OW!
FLIP!
FLIP!
IS THIS THE GOOD TIME YOU WERE THINKING ABOUT?
OOO...
8.

NOW GET OUT OF HERE-- AND I NEVER WANT TO SEE ANY OF YOU AGAIN!
!
SNAP! CRAK!
YES, MA'AM!
YAHH!

EH--?

SO... THERE'S ANOTHER ONE OF YOU BRIGANDS, HUH?
YOU LOOK EVEN GRUBBIER THAN THE OTHERS! I DON'T KNOW WHY I DIDN'T NOTICE YOU BEFORE!
WHAT?

YOU HAD A CHANCE TO RUN AWAY WITH YOUR FRIENDS! I'M NOT AS CHARITABLE NOW!
NO--WAIT! THIS IS A MISTAKE!
CRAK!
9.

CRAK!
NO! STOP!

CRAK!
NOW IT'S GETTING SERIOUS!

WHIP! WHIP! WHIP!

I'VE HAD ENOUGH OF YOU BRIGANDS!
SSHH...!
ULP!

STOP! I DON'T WANT TO HURT YOU!

LEAVE HIM ALONE, SAKURA. HE'S WITH ME.
10.

USAGI CAN BE IRRITATING, BUT THAT'S NOT REASON ENOUGH TO KILL HIM!
GEN! IT'S BEEN A LONG TIME!
YOU KNOW EACH OTHER?

I HAVE A LIFE OUTSIDE OF YOU, YOU KNOW!
WHY DIDN'T YOU TELL ME SHE COULD HANDLE THOSE FOUR?

I COULD HAVE BROKEN MY NECK COMING DOWN THAT MOUNTAIN! AS IT IS, MY CLOTHES ARE SHREDDED!

OKAY, NOW WE'RE EVEN FOR YOU MAKING FUN OF MY HAKAMA!
11.

LATER...
THANK YOU FOR THIS MEAL, USAGI-SAN.
DON'T MENTION IT, SAKURA. USAGI'S RICH! HE FOUND A GOLD MINE*.
*UY BOOK 21: THE MOTHER OF MOUNTAINS

A GOLD MINE?

IT'S A LONG STORY, BUT THE GOLD BELONGS TO THE GEISHU CLAN.

I WAS JUST GIVEN A MODEST REWARD.

TOO BAD. I COULD ALWAYS USE A **RICH FRIEND**.

SO, SAKURA, ARE YOU STILL ON YOUR QUEST?
"QUEST"?

THOUGH WE'VE JUST MET, I CONSIDER YOU A FRIEND, USAGI. SO I WILL TELL YOU MY STORY.

12.

I WAS BORN INTO A PROMINENT *SAMURAI* FAMILY. UNFORTUNATELY, WE WERE ON THE LOSING SIDE OF THE GREAT WARS THAT INSTATED THIS *SHOGUN'S* REGIME.

MY FATHER WAS STRIPPED OF HIS VASSALS AND POSSESSIONS, AND WE WERE SOON DESTITUTE.

HE WAS FORCED TO SELL MY YOUNGER BROTHER TO AN UMBRELLA MAKER AS COMMON HELP.

MY FATHER AND HIS WIFE DIED, AND I WAS ALONE IN THE WORLD... EXCEPT FOR MY BROTHER. WHEN I WENT TO FIND HIM, THE SHOP HAD CLOSED. NO ONE KNEW WHAT HAD BECOME OF THE UMBRELLA MAKER OR MY BROTHER.
SLURP!

NOW YOU ARE SEARCHING FOR HIM.
HE IS ALL I HAVE LEFT IN THE WORLD!

I TRAVEL, EARNING MY LIVING AS A GAMBLER, BECAUSE THAT IS THE KIND OF PERSON WHO WOULD KNOW ABOUT MISSING PEOPLE!
13

ANYTHING ELSE, FOLKS?
A ROOM FOR TWO.
HOW ABOUT YOU, SAKURA? USAGI'S PAYING!
I AM?

ER... I MEAN, OF COURSE. YOU WILL NEED A ROOM FOR THE NIGHT.
THANK YOU FOR THE OFFER, USAGI-SAN, BUT I HAVE GOT TO CONTINUE MY SEARCH.

INNKEEPER-- WHERE IS THE TOWN'S GAMBLING DEN?
FEH! A GAMBLER, EH?

THEY HOLD THE TOWN IN A VISE. WHY, EVEN THE OFFICIALS CAN'T DO ANYTHING ABOUT THEM-- NOT THAT THEY WOULD WANT TO... THOSE CORRUPT SCUM.

HEY-- WE DON'T NEED A LECTURE.
GULP! Y-YES, SIR!
14.

BOSS KANEKO OWNS THE BLACK PEONY JUST DOWN THE ROAD.

KANEKO, HUH? I'VE HEARD OF HIM. HE HAS A REPUTATION AS A DESPICABLE, VILE PERSON!

BUT MONEY IS MONEY, WHETHER IT COMES FROM A NICE GUY OR A DESPICABLE ONE.
YOU'RE RIGHT.
THANK YOU FOR THE MEAL, USAGI.
IT WAS GOOD TO SEE YOU STILL ALIVE, GEN.

HEY, INNKEEPER-- ANOTHER BOWL OF RICE AND SOME PICKLED VEGETABLES!
LOTS OF PICKLES!
SO LONG.

A PECULIAR PERSON.
YEAH. THAT'S WHAT PEOPLE TELL ME ABOUT YOU.
15.

黒牡丹
BAM! BAM! BAM!
YEAH? WHAT DO YOU WANT?
I AM CALLED SAKURA. I CAN HANDLE DICE.
WE DON'T NEED ANYBODY.
THAT IS FOR BOSS KANEKO TO DECIDE.
HA! HA!
GIVE HER A CHANCE! MAYBE SHE'LL BRING ME SOME GOOD LUCK!
YOU WOULD NEED MORE THAN LUCK TO MAKE UP WHAT YOU'VE LOST!
16.

I'M BOSS KANEKO. I CAN ALWAYS USE A GOOD DICE HANDLER.
LET'S SEE HOW SKILLED YOU ARE.
THANK YOU FOR GIVING ME A CHANCE, BOSS KANEKO.
CHO*!
HAN**!
HAN!
HAN!
*EVEN
**ODD

NOW MAYBE MY LUCK WILL CHANGE.
THE ONLY LUCK YOU KNOW IS BAD LUCK!

FLUMP!

GASP!
WOW!
AHH...
17

WE SHALL BEGIN!
LOOK AT THOSE SAKURA*!
IT'S ALMOST AS IF THEY'RE GROWING ON HER SKIN!
*CHERRY BLOSSOMS

THE DICE ARE GOING IN!

FWITT!

GARA! GARA! GARA!

PLACE YOUR BETS!
THUMP!

HAN!
CHO!
CHO!

HAN!
18

HA! I WON!
RATS!
I KNEW I SHOULD HAVE BET HAN!
GRR!
THAT CLEANS ME OUT!
LOST AGAIN!

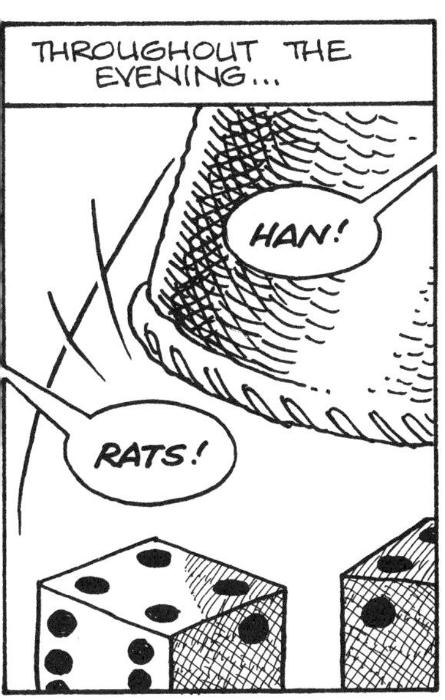
THROUGHOUT THE EVENING...
HAN!
RATS!

THEY'RE GOING IN!

CHO!
RATS!

CALL YOUR BETS.
HAN! CHO! HAN! HAN! CHO!
HAN! HAN! CHO!
THUMP!

GARA! GARA! GARA!

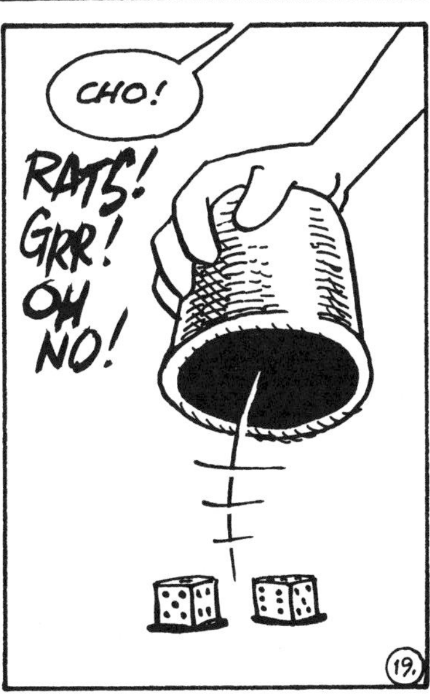
CHO!
RATS! GRR! OH NO!
19.

HERE'S YOUR CUT, SAKURA. YOU MADE ME A VERY NICE PROFIT TONIGHT.
THANK YOU, BOSS KANEKO.
HOW WOULD YOU LIKE TO WORK FOR ME PERMANENTLY?
ONE NIGHT WAS ENOUGH, THANK YOU.

THEN HAVE A DRINK TO CELEBRATE OUR PROFITABLE NIGHT.
MOMO!

SHE LOOKS SO SAD.
WHO IS SHE?
MOMO? SHE'S JUST A STUPID SERVING GIRL.
HER FATHER OWED ME A GAMBLING DEBT, BUT COULD NOT PAY. I TOOK HER INSTEAD.
A PITY-- HE DIED A WEEK LATER.
20.

HOW DID HER FATHER DIE?
HE RAN UP ANOTHER DEBT, BUT HAD NOTHING TO PAY WITH. I HAD A COUPLE OF MY MEN TEACH HIM A LESSON. I'M AFRAID THEY GOT A LITTLE... UH... CARRIED AWAY.
WHAT IS YOUR INTEREST IN MOMO?

A CHILD SHOULD NOT BE EXPOSED TO WHAT GOES ON IN OUR WORLD.
I'LL BUY HER FROM YOU.

IT WOULD TAKE MORE THAN A NIGHT'S PROFIT TO BUY HER FREEDOM.
WHAT WOULD YOU DO WITH HER, ANYWAY?

SHE HAS A **MOTHER,** DOESN'T SHE? I WILL RETURN HER TO HER FAMILY!
HA HA HA! YOU SURPRISE ME, SAKURA!

I WON'T SELL HER TO YOU, BUT IF YOU STAYED AND WORKED FOR ME, I'M SURE WE COULD STRIKE SOME SORT OF DEAL!
YOUR OFFER IS MOST GENEROUS, BOSS KANEKO, BUT I MUST KEEP TRAVELING, AS I AM SEARCHING FOR SOMEONE.

PERHAPS THERE IS SOME WAY I CAN PERSUADE YOU TO GIVE HER TO ME.
I WON'T SELL HER TO YOU-- WHY SHOULD I **GIVE** HER AWAY?
21.

IF YOU WON'T GIVE HER TO ME, I'LL TAKE HER!
UHH--!
WHAP!

YOU SCUM!
OOF!

KNOCK! KNOCK!
BOSS KANEKO!
UH-OH!
.....

WHAT IS IT?
WE CLOSED UP THE DEN FOR THE DAY AND COUNTED THE MONEY. I NEED TO REPORT OUR EARNINGS TO BOSS KANEKO.

BOSS KANEKO IS TIRED, AND ORDERED THAT HE NOT BE DISTURBED.
HE USUALLY LIKES TO BE TOLD RIGHT AWAY...
...ALL RIGHT. I'LL COME BACK LATER.

PHEW!
22

TOO MUCH RICE!

SEE--? THAT INNKEEPER GAVE US TOO MUCH RICE! I NEED MORE PICKLED VEGETABLES!
HE GAVE US ENOUGH. YOU JUST NEED TO PACE YOURSELF!

A BIT OF RICE, SOME PICKLES, A BIT OF FISH...

HE KNOWS I LIKE A LOT OF PICKLES.
I SAW HOW YOU ATE UP ALL YOUR PICKLES! YOU'RE JUST TOO MUCH OF A GLUTTON.

HEY, YOU'VE STILL GOT A LOT OF PICKLES.
YOU CAN'T EAT THEM ALL YOURSELF!

YES, I CAN! I PAID FOR THEM! I'M GOING TO EAT THEM!
23.

COME ON. JUST ONE PICKLE.
NO. ONE WILL BECOME TWO, THEN YOU'LL ASK FOR THREE!
SOON I WON'T HAVE ANY FOR MYSELF!
STOMP! STOMP! STOMP!
YUM!
WHAT'S THAT RACKET?
IT SOUNDS LIKE SOMEONE RUNNING UP THE STAIRS TO OUR ROOM!
IT'S *MUNCH* PROBABLY THE NEW CLOTHES WE *MUNCH!* ORDERED.
SLAM!
HIDE US!

SAKURA 桜 PART TWO

WHERE IS SHE?
WHERE IS THAT WOMAN?
WHERE IS SAKURA?!
WHAT--?

DO YOU THINK WE'LL JUST TAKE YOUR WORD FOR IT?
SEARCH THE ROOM!
STOP! HOW DARE YOU QUESTION MY WORD?
TAKE ONE MORE STEP, AND I WILL HAVE NO CHOICE BUT TO PUNISH YOU FOR YOUR INSOLENCE.

WHAT?
I PAID FOR THIS ROOM. THAT MAKES IT MY HOME UNTIL I LEAVE.
SO...?

SO I WILL NOT HAVE YOU BARGING INTO MY HOME.

AND WHAT ARE YOU GOING TO DO ABOUT IT, HUH?

KLIK!

GULP!
3

ER... UH... EVERYONE KNOWS A *SAMURAI* DOES NOT GIVE HIS WORD OF HONOR LIGHTLY.
BESIDES, WE CAN SEE THAT THERE IS NO ONE ELSE IN THIS ROOM.
IT'S JUST THAT THE INNKEEPER SAID THAT A WOMAN--
SHE WAS A ***DELIVERY*** WOMAN. SHE BROUGHT OUR NEW CLOTHES.
WELL... OKAY. WE'LL GO...
...BUT WE'LL KEEP AN EYE ON YOU TWO.
COME ON.
CLOSE THE DOOR.
FEH! GOOD RIDDANCE.
YEAH.
HEY!
MUNCH! MUNCH!
MMM...
4.

ARE YOU GOING TO EAT YOUR FISH?
HELP YOURSELF. YOU'VE ALREADY EATEN EVERYTHING ELSE.

THEY WEREN'T KID-DING. THERE ARE A LOT OF THUGS WATCHING THE INN.
THEY KNOW YOU LIED.

WELL... TECHNICALLY YOU WERE NOT *IN* THE ROOM.
NOW GET INSIDE.
BUT KEEP LOW, SO THEY CAN'T SEE YOU.
5.

I APOLOGIZE FOR BRINGING SO MUCH TROUBLE TO YOU, USAGI, BUT I KNEW OF NOWHERE ELSE TO GO.
I DID NOT THINK THEY WOULD BE AFTER US SO QUICKLY.
I WOULD HAVE STOOD UP TO THEM, BUT I DID NOT WANT MOMO TO GET HURT.
YES, I KNOW YOU ARE VERY CAPABLE WITH THE WHIP.
WELL, WHAT IS DONE IS DONE.

IMAGINE REFERRING TO SUCH A BEAUTIFUL CHILD AS "PROPERTY"!
BUT WHAT SHALL WE DO NOW?
I HAD PLANNED TO RETURN MOMO TO HER MOTHER, AND GIVE THEM THE MONEY I MADE LAST NIGHT SO THEY CAN LEAVE THIS AREA AND START A NEW LIFE.
SLURP! SLURP!

MOMO'S MOTHER LIVES AT THE OTHER END OF TOWN, BUT IT IS IMPOSSIBLE TO GET TO HER NOW.
BUT THE LONGER WE STAY HERE, THE MORE DIRE OUR SITUATION BECOMES.

WE'VE GOT TO FIND SOME WAY TO SNEAK OUT OF HERE. I DON'T WANT A BLOOD-BATH IN THIS TOWN.
6.

BURP!
AHH... THAT WAS GOOD.

WELL... SHALL WE GET GOING?
?
?
?

DIDN'T YOU HEAR ME? BOSS KANEKO'S THUGS ARE WATCHING THE INN. IT'S IMPOSSIBLE FOR US TO LEAVE UNNOTICED.

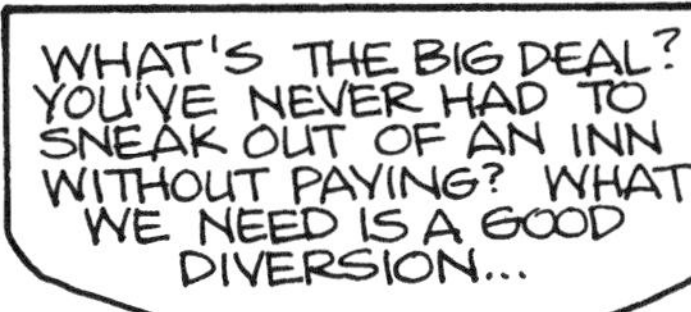
WHAT'S THE BIG DEAL? YOU'VE NEVER HAD TO SNEAK OUT OF AN INN WITHOUT PAYING? WHAT WE NEED IS A GOOD DIVERSION...

...AND IT WILL DEPEND ON HOW STUPID THOSE GAMBLER THUGS ARE.
7.

WHAT?!

YOU LET THEM SCARE YOU AWAY?! WHAT KIND OF THUGS ARE YOU? WHY AM I EVEN PAYING YOU?
GULP!

BUT THEY REALLY LOOKED LIKE THEY KNEW HOW TO HANDLE THEIR SWORDS-- BUT I KNOW THEY ARE HIDING THE GIRL!

MOMO IS MY PROPERTY! I WANT HER RETURNED!
DO YOU UNDERSTAND ME?
THUMP! THUMP! THUMP! THUMP!

AND I WANT SAKURA BROUGHT BACK TO ME, SO I CAN KILL HER MYSELF! I'LL TEACH HER TO ASSAULT ME!

AND WHAT MAKES YOU THINK THAT WOMAN AND MY PROPERTY EVEN KNOW THOSE RONIN, ANYWAY?
8.

WE ASKED AROUND, AND FOUND THAT SAKURA CAME TO TOWN WITH THOSE TWO LATE YESTERDAY.

SHE KNOWS NO ONE ELSE, SO SHE MUST HAVE GONE BACK TO THOSE TWO FOR HELP!
OUR MEN ARE WATCHING THE INN. THEY WON'T ESCAPE.

THERE *IS* SOMEWHERE ELSE SAKURA WOULD GO!

SHE TOLD ME SHE WANTED TO RETURN MOMO TO HER MOTHER.

HURRY TO MOMO'S MOTHER'S HOME. IF THE TWO WE ARE LOOKING FOR ARE NOT THERE, BRING THE MOTHER TO ME!

IF WE CAN'T FIND SAKURA, WE'LL MAKE HER COME TO ME!

HIRE AS MANY *RONIN** AS YOU CAN. IT SHOULD BE EASY, BECAUSE SO MANY OWE ME GAMBLING DEBTS.
WE'LL SET A TRAP FOR SAKURA AND HER FRIENDS!
*MASTERLESS SAMURAI WARRIORS
9.

ARE YOU READY?
YEAH.

HEY! THEY'RE ESCAPING!
THEY'RE CARRYING THE GIRL!

STOP!

THEY CAN'T OUTRUN US!

I'VE GOT THEM!
HIYAHH!

UH!
WOK!
10

SURROUND THEM!
DROP THE GIRL!
WHAT GIRL?
IN YOUR ARMS!

WE'RE JUST CARRYING OUR **OLD CLOTHES!**
WE'RE DONATING THEM TO A TEMPLE!

WHAT?
WE'VE BEEN **TRICKED!**

HURRY-- BACK TO THE INN!

THAT SHOULD HAVE GIVEN THEM ENOUGH TIME.
COME ON--LET'S MEET UP WITH THEM!
11.

ARE THEY FOLLOWING US?
NOPE.

THIS IS THE MEETING PLACE.
BUT WHERE ARE THEY?
THEY DON'T LOOK IT, BUT MAYBE THOSE GAMBLERS ARE SMARTER THAN WE THOUGHT!

YOU MEAN A COUPLE OF THEM COULD HAVE STAYED BEHIND INSTEAD OF FOLLOWING US, AND THEN SEEN SAKURA AND MOMO SNEAKING OUT OF THE INN?
YEAH, THE GIRLS SHOULD HAVE BEEN HERE BY NOW.

HEY!

WE THOUGHT IT WAS A GOOD IDEA TO STAY OUT OF SIGHT UNTIL YOU TWO GOT HERE.

BUT YOU WERE WORRIED ABOUT US.
HOW SWEET.
12

THERE IS MY MOTHER'S HOUSE!
ARE YOU SURE IT'S SAFE?
YEAH. WE SCOUTED THE AREA. THERE'S NO ONE ELSE AROUND.
INCLUDING MOMO'S MOTHER!

IT'S IN ***RUINS!***

IT LOOKS LIKE BOSS KANEKO GOT HERE BEFORE US.

THE FIRE PIT IS STILL WARM. THEY WERE HERE JUST A SHORT TIME AGO.

WHERE'S MY MAMA?

EH--?

DICE! IT'S A CHALLENGE FROM BOSS KANEKO.

YOU SHOULD HAVE LEFT ME AS A SLAVE OF BOSS KANEKO! IT IS YOUR FAULT IF MAMA IS HURT!
YOU'RE RIGHT.

I PROMISE YOU, MOMO, WE'LL SAVE HER.
SOB! SOB!
IT WILL BE DIFFICULT. THEY'LL BE EXPECTING US.
13

I TOLD YOU--
I DO NOT KNOW WHERE THEY ARE.

EVEN IF YOU DID, YOU NEED NOT TELL ME.
ONLY SOMEONE NOBLE OF HEART WOULD HAVE RESCUED MOMO.

I HAVE NO DOUBT SAKURA WILL TRY TO RESCUE *YOU* AS WELL.

THE TROUBLE IS THAT SHE MAY BRING HER *SAMURAI* FRIENDS WITH HER.

BUT EVEN IF THEY GET IN HERE, THEY WILL NEVER LEAVE.
THE *RONIN* WE HIRED ARE HERE, BOSS KANEKO.
14.

HEY-- MAKE SURE YOU STAY ALERT!
DON'T WORRY--WE'RE THE BEST THAT THE BOSS'S MONEY CAN BUY.
ANYONE WOULD BE A FOOL TO ATTACK US.
I'LL TAKE A LOOK AROUND THE CORNER.
HA HA! IT DOESN'T MATTER IF THEY SHOW UP OR NOT. WE'LL STILL GET PAID! GLUG! GLUG!
HEY-- PASS THAT JUG. I WANT SOME SAKE, TOO!
URK!
AHH-- THAT'S GOOD!
HEY--WHAT DO THOSE GUYS LOOK LIKE, ANYWAY?
GLUG! GLUG!
YOU'RE PATROLLING, AND YOU DON'T EVEN KNOW WHAT THEY LOOK LIKE?
THERE ARE TWO OF THEM. ONE IS A BIG GUY, AND THE OTHER IS A--
--A LONG-EARED SAMURAI WITH A...A...
GULP!
DO THEY LOOK SOMETHING LIKE US?
15

HELP! HELP!

NGGH--!

.....

WE DON'T WANT A FIGHT. WE JUST WANT THE WOMAN! EVERYONE ELSE CAN LEAVE.

KILL THEM!
16

YAHH!
URK!
HYAHH!

KRAK!
AUGH!

URK!
SNAP!
17

GET HIM! GET HIM!
UGH!
SURROUND HIM!
HE'S ONLY ONE GUY!

WHERE IS THE WOMAN?!
GAK!

GAH!

FLOOK!
WE GAVE YOU A CHANCE TO LIVE--

EGAK!
--YOU SHOULD HAVE TAKEN IT!
CHOP!
18.

WHERE IS SHE?

YOU! YOU LOOK LIKE YOU WOULD KNOW WHERE THE WOMAN IS BEING HELD!

I'LL KILL YOU!
THERE'S A LITTLE GIRL WHO WANTS HER MOTHER!

TELL ME WHERE SHE IS!
AHH--K!

NOW YOU'RE STARTING TO MAKE ME ANGRY.
19

GYAHH!
EYAHH!

HIYAHH!

FWAPHHS!
SHHH--!

CRAK!
YAHH--! MY FACE!

WHERE ARE YOU, BOSS KANEKO?
20

GASP!
BOSS KANEKO!

THE STOREHOUSE IS MY ONLY CHANCE.

YOU CAN'T HIDE FROM ME, BOSS KANEKO.

STAY BACK, SAKURA, OR I'LL KILL HER!
WHIMPER!

VERMIN LIKE YOU SHOULD LIVE ONLY IN THE DARK.

I CAN'T SEE A THING! OPEN THE DOOR! OPEN IT, OR I'LL SLIT HER THROAT!

I CAN HEAR YOU MOVING ABOUT! YOU CAN'T GET CLOSE TO ME WITHOUT ME KNOWING IT!

DON'T MESS WITH ME, WOMAN! I MAY NOT BE ABLE TO SEE YOU, BUT YOU CAN'T SEE ME EITHER!
21

SHOW YOURSELF, OR SHE'S A DEAD WOMAN!
NO! NO!

YOU'RE CORRECT--I CAN'T SEE IN THE DARK--
WHAT?!

--BUT YOUR INCESSANT TALKING LED ME RIGHT TO YOU!

!

NO! NO!

TWANGG!
SNAP!
URK!

WHO ARE YOU?

I AM YOUR DAUGHTER'S FRIEND.
22.

HEY-- YOU OKAY?
YEAH. THE REST OF THEM RAN OFF.
BUT WHERE'S SAKURA?

HERE.

BOSS KANEKO?
DEAD.
WHERE'S MY DAUGHTER?

MAMA!

I WAS HIDING OUTSIDE, AND I SAW ALL THOSE GAMBLERS RUNNING AWAY!

MOMO!
23.

WHAT NOW?
WITH BOSS KANEKO DEAD, THOSE TWO WON'T HAVE TO LEAVE THIS TOWN...
...BUT WE SHOULD LEAVE BEFORE THE AUTHORITIES ARRIVE.

WHAT ABOUT YOU, SAKURA?
I'VE GOT TO RESUME THE SEARCH FOR MY BROTHER.

SO LONG.
POOR GIRL. I HOPE SHE FINDS HER BROTHER SOON.

SHE NEVER WILL.
OH? WHY NOT?

SHE NEVER HAD A BROTHER.

完

SNITCH

HOW MUCH DO WE HAVE LEFT, USAGI?

WE'VE GONE THROUGH ALMOST ALL MY MONEY.

BY "**WE**" I ASSUME YOU MEAN **ME**.

THEN WE HAD BETTER FIND A JOB...

...OR SOMETHING.

"MURAKUNI--
WANTED FOR
PETTY
ROBBERY."
A TWENTY
RYO REWARD--
IT'S NOT MUCH,
GEN.
YEAH, BUT
WHEN YOU'VE GOT
NOTHING--
--TWENTY
RYO IS A
LOT. I KNOW
WHAT YOU
MEAN.
BUT I'VE
NEVER BEEN
KEEN ON BOUNTY
HUNTING.
THEN IT'S
LUCKY YOU'RE WITH
A PROFESSIONAL
HUNTER.
THE
PROBLEM IS
THAT WE ARE
NEW AROUND
HERE.
SO WE
HAVE NO
IDEA WHERE
MURAKUNI
MIGHT BE
HIDING.
RIGHT.
WHAT WE NEED
IS SOMEONE WHO IS
FAMILIAR WITH THIS
AREA.
PSST--!
EH?
?
2

I COULDN'T HELP OVERHEARING. I'LL GLADLY ASSIST YOU WITH SOME INSIDE INFORMATION...
...FOR A SMALL FEE, OF COURSE.

HMM... DON'T I KNOW YOU FROM SOMEWHERE?

OH...UH... YOU MUST BE THINKING OF MY TWIN COUSIN WHO LOOKS JUST LIKE ME.
YOUR COUSIN, HUH?
WELL, OKAY. YOU'RE HIRED.

I'LL NEED AN ADVANCE.
GIVE HIM A COIN, USAGI.
WELL... OKAY.

CHOMP!
AH! GOOD, GOOD.

I'LL GET ON IT RIGHT AWAY! I'LL MEET YOU BACK AT THIS INN! OKAY?
DON'T KEEP US WAITING TOO LONG!
3

AHEH, HEH, HEH, HEH.
THERE'S SOMETHING ABOUT HIM I DON'T TRUST.
HE LOOKS OKAY TO ME. YOU'RE JUST NATURALLY GROUCHY AND SUSPICIOUS OF EVERYBODY.
COME ON. LET'S GET SOMETHING TO EAT.
AHEH, HEH, HEH, HEH.
HEY, BOSS! I'M BACK!
IT'S ABOUT TIME!
WELL? HAVE YOU FOUND OUT ANYTHING?
4.

MORE BOUNTY HUNTERS HAVE ARRIVED, AND ARE AFTER MURAKUNI AS YOU ARE.
COMPETITION, EH? AND FOR SUCH A PALTRY REWARD.
BUT IT WOULD DIMINISH MY REPUTATION FOR OTHERS TO CLAIM MURAKUNI'S BOUNTY.

YOU HAD BETTER KEEP AN EYE ON THEM.
SLURP!

NOW GET OUT OF HERE AND FIND OUT WHERE MURAKUNI IS HIDING!
YES, BOSS, SURE!

AHEH, HEH, HEH, HEH!

5

BOSS! HEY, BOSS!
THAT WAS FAST!
DID YOU FIND MURAKUNI?

NO, BUT YOU HAVE COMPETITION. I FOUND THERE IS ANOTHER BOUNTY HUNTER IN TOWN, AND HE'S ALSO AFTER MURAKUNI!
WHAT?

ANOTHER HUNTER, HUH? I DON'T LIKE IT. I LOST THE BOUNTY FOR INAZUMA, AND I'M NOT GOING TO LOSE THE REWARD FOR MURAKUNI... NO MATTER WHAT IT COSTS!

HEY! I JUST HAD A GREAT IDEA! SUPPOSE I OFFER MY SERVICES TO THAT OTHER BOUNTY HUNTER?
HOW WILL THAT HELP US?

WHAT IF I SUPPLY HIM WITH FALSE INFORMATION?
HA! HE'LL BE RUNNING AROUND IN CIRCLES, WHILE WE'RE FREE TO CATCH THE CRIMINAL!
GOOD IDEA!

OF COURSE, I EXPECT TO BE COMPENSATED FOR MY IDEA!

YEAH. I GUESS THAT SEEMS FAIR.
PAY HIM, USAGI!
WHAT?

DON'T WORRY. YOU'LL BE REPAID AFTER WE COLLECT THE REWARD.
WELL...

OKAY, BUT WE'D BETTER GET SOME RESULTS--AND FAST!
YOU BET, BOSS!

AHEH, HEH, HEH!

7.

HEY, BOSS! I'VE GOT A **GREAT IDEA**!
OH?

AND SO...
AHEH, HEH, HEH!

AND AGAIN...

AND AGAIN, AGAIN...

YOU'VE BEEN HERE **THREE TIMES**, AND YOU STILL HAVE NOT GIVEN US ANY REAL INFORMATION!

I'M HOT ON MURAKUNI'S TRAIL! I...UH... JUST NEED A FEW MORE COINS TO BRIBE SOME INFORMANTS.
OKAY, BUT THIS IS THE LAST TIME! YOU WON'T GET ANYTHING MORE UNTIL WE GET MURAKUNI!

AHEH, HEH, HEH. IDIOTS.

I DON'T TRUST HIM. FOR ALL WE KNOW, HE COULD BE LOSING ALL OUR MONEY IN A GAMBLING HALL! I'M GOING TO FOLLOW HIM!
I'LL GO WITH YOU.

KEEP UP WITH HIM!
I'M TRYING, BUT HE RUNS LIKE THE WIND.
AHEH, HEH, HEH!

I HOPE WE GET THERE SOON, OR WE'LL LOSE HIM FOR SURE!
AHEH, HEH, HEH, HEH.

HUFF! HUFF! AT LAST! WE ALMOST LOST HIM FOR A WHILE!
SHOULD WE PEEK IN THROUGH THE WINDOW?
HE JUST GOT HERE. LET'S WAIT A MINUTE.
9.

WHAT?
!

AND DON'T COME BACK WITHOUT SOMETHING USEFUL!
YES, BOSS, YES!
?

SHOULD WE FOLLOW HIM?
I'M MORE INTERESTED IN WHO HE CAME HERE TO SEE.

COME ON.

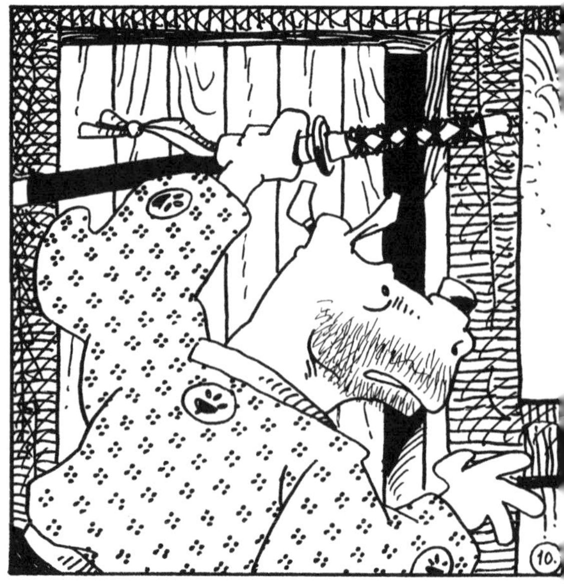
10.

ALL RIGHT! WHAT'S GOING ON?

GEN?!

STRAY DOG?
WHAT?

USAGI?

STRAY DOG!

WHY, YOU ROTTEN FILTH, I OUGHT TO--
YOU DIRTY LOW-LIFE SCUM, I'M GOING TO--
11.

WE'VE BEEN PAYING THAT SNITCH FOR INFORMATION ABOUT MURAKUNI!
I'VE BEEN BUYING INFORMATION FROM HIM AS WELL!
I'LL TEACH YOU TO INTRUDE ON MY BOUNTY!
IT'S MY BOUNTY! I WAS HERE BEFORE YOU TWO!
YOU'VE INTERFERED IN MY BUSINESS LONG ENOUGH!
THAT DOES IT! I'LL TAKE CARE OF YOU ONCE AND FOR ALL!
LET ME AT THAT SCUM!
STOP IT, YOU TWO! YOU'RE ACTING LIKE CHILDREN!
GET OUT OF MY WAY, USAGI!
12

WHY, YOU--!
IF YOU WANT TO BE MAD AT SOMEONE, BE MAD AT THE PERSON WHO DESERVES IT!
HUH?
Y-YOU'RE RIGHT!
WHERE'S THAT SNITCH? HE PLAYED US FOR FOOLS!
COME ON! LET'S FIND THAT GREEDY WEASEL!
WAIT! WE WON'T HAVE TO SEARCH ALL OVER TOWN TO FIND HIM!
WHAT?
I WANT TO GET MY HANDS ON THAT FILTHY SLIME!
WHY EXHAUST OURSELVES LOOKING FOR HIM? HE'LL COME BACK TO US... HE ALWAYS COMES BACK.
YEAH!
13

SO THOSE BOUNTY HUNTERS WON'T GIVE ME ANY MORE MONEY, HUH? WELL, THEY'RE NOT MY ONLY SOURCE OF CASH.

WH-WHO'S THERE?
DON'T WORRY. IT'S ME.
ARE YOU ALONE?

OF COURE I AM. I WOULD NEVER BETRAY YOU, SO PUT YOUR SWORD AWAY...

...MURAKUNI!

I KNOW YOU WOULDN'T TURN ME IN, BUT I'M GOING CRAZY HIDING OUT HERE WITH NO FOOD AND NO ONE TO TALK TO.

YOU'LL HAVE TO STAY PUT A WHILE LONGER. THE AREA IS CRAWLING WITH BOUNTY HUNTERS LOOKING FOR YOU--TEN OR TWELVE OF THEM, AT LEAST!
SO MANY, FOR SO SMALL A REWARD?

THESE ARE DESPERATE TIMES, BUT YOU'RE PAYING ME TO KEEP YOU INFORMED ABOUT BOUNTY HUNTERS IN THE AREA. I TORE DOWN ALL THE WANTED PLACARDS YESTERDAY, SO NO MORE OF THOSE GREEDY SCUM WILL KNOW OF YOU. I'LL TELL YOU WHEN IT'S SAFE TO LEAVE.
14.

DID YOU BRING ME SOMETHING TO EAT, AT LEAST? I'M **STARVING** OUT HERE! MY STOMACH HAS BEEN RUMBLING ALL DAY!
I BROUGHT YOU A RICE BALL JUST YESTERDAY. OKAY, GIVE ME MORE MONEY, AND I'LL BUY YOU SOME FOOD.

I SHOULD NOT HAVE STOLEN THAT MONEY IN THE FIRST PLACE. IT'S BROUGHT ME NOTHING BUT LONELINESS AND MISERY AND HUNGER.
I'M SO HUNGRY.

AND NOW I DON'T EVEN HAVE THE MONEY.
I GAVE YOU THE LAST OF WHAT I STOLE WHEN YOU WERE HERE YESTERDAY.
WHAT?

ARE YOU SURE YOU DON'T HAVE ANYTHING TO EAT?
NO, BUT I'LL BE BACK REAL SOON WITH FOOD! LOTS AND ***LOTS OF FOOD!***
REMEMBER-- ***STAY HERE!***

OOH...I HOPE HE COMES BACK FAST. I'M SO HUNGRY...
...BUT WHAT A GREAT GUY HE IS TO HELP ME LIKE THIS!

HA, HA! ***SUCKER!***
15.

NOW IT'S TIME TO SELL OUT MURAKUNI TO THOSE STUPID BOUNTY HUNTERS FOR THE BIG REWARD! WHAT A SMART GUY I AM!

I GOT ALL OF MURAKUNI'S MONEY!
I TOOK A LOT OF CASH FROM THOSE HUNTERS!
I BET I COULD EVEN TRICK THEM OUT OF THE ENTIRE BOUNTY IF I TRIED HARD ENOUGH!
HA! I LOVE MONEY! MONEY, MONEY, MONEY!

HEY, BOSS! IT'S ME, AND I'VE GOT GOOD NEWS!

YOW!
ZIP!

YOU DIRTY SLUG! YOU'VE BEEN PITTING US AGAINST EACH OTHER--
--AND CHARGING US FOR IT!
16

¡GULP!¡
I WOULD WRING YOUR SKINNY NECK, IF I DIDN'T ADMIRE YOU SO MUCH!

WAIT! WAIT! I KNOW WHERE HE IS! THAT'S WHAT I CAME TO TELL YOU! I KNOW WHERE MURAKUNI IS HIDING!

OKAY, LET HIM GO.
BUT NO MORE OF YOUR TRICKS!
THUD!
OW!

NO TRICKS. NO TRICKS. COME ON! FOLLOW ME, BOSS!

I SHOULDN'T BE DOING THIS! I ALWAYS GET PAID BEFORE I GIVE OUT INFORMATION!
YOU'LL GET PAID AFTER WE CAPTURE MURAKUNI!
AND IF THIS IS A TRICK, WE'LL DEMAND ALL OUR MONEY BACK!
17

HE'S IN THERE--IN THAT HUT!
IT LOOKS DESERTED.
HE'S PROBABLY ASLEEP! YOU CAN CATCH HIM UNAWARES!

WELL, I HELD UP MY END OF THE BARGAIN! I'LL MEET YOU BACK AT THE INN, AND YOU CAN GIVE ME MY SHARE OF THE REWARD!
NO! YOU DON'T!

CUT THAT OUT!
I DON'T TRUST YOU! YOU'RE STAYING WITH US!
COME ON. LET'S GO.

MMMPH!
QUIET, YOU! WE ALL PAID YOU FOR INFORMATION, AND WE WANT TO MAKE SURE YOU'VE TOLD US THE TRUTH THIS TIME!

18.

ALL RIGHT, MURAKUNI! DON'T MOVE!

WHERE IS HE?
THIS PLACE IS EMPTY!
THAT SNITCH LIED TO US-- AGAIN!

AUGHH! HE TRICKED US AGAIN!
I'LL KILL THAT GREEDY SCUM! WHERE IS HE?

I JUST LEFT HIM OUTSIDE-- NOW HE'S GONE!
JUST WAIT UNTIL I GET MY HANDS ON HIM--

YOUR HANDS ON HIM?!
YOU HAD HIM IN YOUR HANDS, AND YOU LET HIM GO!
I HAD TO RELEASE HIM TO DRAW MY SWORD!
19

WHY DON'T YOU WEAR YOUR SWORDS LIKE A NORMAL PERSON?!
I LIKE TO CARRY MY BLADE.
LIKE AN IDIOT!
YOU'RE THE IDIOT!
WELL, YOU'RE THE ONE WHO LET THAT SNITCH GET AWAY!
YOU CAN'T BLAME ME! YOU SHOULD HAVE BEEN WATCHING HIM, TOO!
IDIOT!
WHY, YOU-- I OUGHT TO--
JUST TRY IT, YOU INCOMPETENT BUFFOON!
STOP IT, YOU TWO! I'VE HAD ENOUGH OF YOUR ARGUING!
YOU'RE WORSE THAN CHILDREN!
20

USAGI IS RIGHT, BUT WHAT RANKLES ME IS THAT HE GOT THE BETTER OF US!
YEAH, BUT I'VE LOST BOUNTIES BEFORE, AND SO HAVE YOU, I IMAGINE.
TRUE, BUT NEVER LIKE THIS.
IT'S NO USE GOING AFTER HIM... GIVEN HOW FAST HE RUNS.
I HEARD THERE'S A MURDERER UP NORTH, WITH A TWO HUNDRED RYO REWARD FOR HIS HEAD!
I'VE HEARD OF HIM--TANIGUCHI THE KILLER, RIGHT? HE'S SUPPOSED TO BE REALLY TOUGH.
IT WILL PROBABLY TAKE AT LEAST TWO HUNTERS TO GET HIM.
YEAH. YOU'RE RIGHT.
PARTNERS?
SURE.
HOW ABOUT YOU, USAGI? DO YOU WANT TO JOIN US?
COUNT ME OUT! I'VE HAD ENOUGH OF YOU AND YOUR REWARDS THAT NEVER HAPPEN!
I'VE SPENT ALL MY MONEY, AND HAVE NOTHING TO SHOW FOR IT!
I'M LEAVING!
WHAT'S WRONG WITH HIM?
DON'T MIND USAGI. HE'S JUST NATURALLY GROUCHY AND SUSPICIOUS OF EVERYBODY.
IDIOTS.
21.

HUFF! HUFF! HUFF!
HUFF! HUFF! HUFF!
UH... I CAN'T RUN ANY MORE. HUH...HUH... HUH...

HA! THOSE IDIOT BOUNTY HUNTERS DID NOT EVEN NOTICE THAT I RAN OFF AS SOON AS I SAW THAT THE HUT WAS EMPTY!

BUT MURAKUNI LIED TO ME! HE PROMISED TO STAY IN THE HUT!

THAT PROVES THAT SOME PEOPLE JUST CAN'T BE TRUSTED!

JINGLE! JINGLE!
WELL, AT LEAST I MADE A NICE, TIDY PROFIT OFF THOSE GUYS!
HA, HA, HA!

SNAP!
JINGLE! JINGLE!

WH-WHO'S THERE?

GULP!
22.

MURAKUNI!
I-I'M...ER...GLAD TO SEE THAT ¿GULP!¿ YOU'RE SAFE!
I GOT TOO HUNGRY WAITING FOR YOU. I HAD TO FIND SOMETHING TO EAT.
I GOT OUT JUST BEFORE YOU ARRIVED WITH THOSE BOUNTY HUNTERS.
IF YOU HAD BOTHERED TO SPEND EVEN A FEW COINS ON FOOD, I WOULD HAVE BEEN CAUGHT!

TH-THOSE BOUNTY HUNTERS FORCED ME TO LEAD THEM TO YOU!
I DIDN'T WANT TO--IN FACT, I FOUGHT THEM TOOTH AND NAIL...BUT THEY WERE TOO STRONG FOR ME!

I SAW YOU LEAD THEM TO THE HUT, AND I HEARD HOW YOU DECEIVED ALL OF US!
NOW HAND OVER ALL THAT MONEY YOU TRICKED FROM US!

B-BUT YOU SAID YOU REGRETTED STEALING IN THE FIRST PLACE--THAT IT WAS THE CAUSE OF ALL YOUR PROBLEMS!
ROBBING HONEST PEOPLE IS ONE THING--BUT STEALING FROM A THIEF AND A LIAR IS ANOTHER!

NOW GIVE ME THE MONEY, OR I'LL GIVE YOU A DEADLY BEATING!
23.

......

HEY, I SAID, **YOUR MONEY OR YOUR LIFE!**

I'M THINKING! I'M THINKING!

I'VE HAD IT WITH YOU AND YOUR TRICKERY!

GULP!

POW!
BOP!
OW! EEE! AHH! OW! YAHHHHH! AHH! AHH! AHHH!
BAM!
BEAT!
POW!
PUNCH!

WHAT'S THAT SOUND IN THE DISTANCE?

IT SOUNDS LIKE THAT SNITCH--PROBABLY LAUGHING.
NO DOUBT HE'S CELEBRATING BECAUSE HE GOT THE BETTER OF US.
BUT, ONE DAY, HE'LL GET WHAT HE DESERVES!
I HOPE THAT DAY WILL BE SOON.
完

THE END

THERE IS STILL A LOT OF DAYLIGHT LEFT. IT'S NOT WORTH SPENDING THE NIGHT HERE.
HOPEFULLY, THE NEXT TOWN IS NOT TOO FAR AWAY.

THE BEGGAR
松林

...ANYTHING FOR A HOMELESS MENDICANT?

LEAVE MY INN, YOU FILTHY BEGGAR!
GET AWAY FROM HERE!

SALT! BRING ME SOME SALT!

FILTHY BEGGAR!
SKAAAA!

HARUMPH!
SHE PURIFIED HER DOORWAY! SHE MUST REALLY HATE BEGGARS!
4

ANOTHER TOWN AT LAST! IT FEELS LIKE I HAVEN'T EATEN IN DAYS!
5

THIS LOOKS LIKE A GOOD, **CHEAP** INN!

WHA--?!

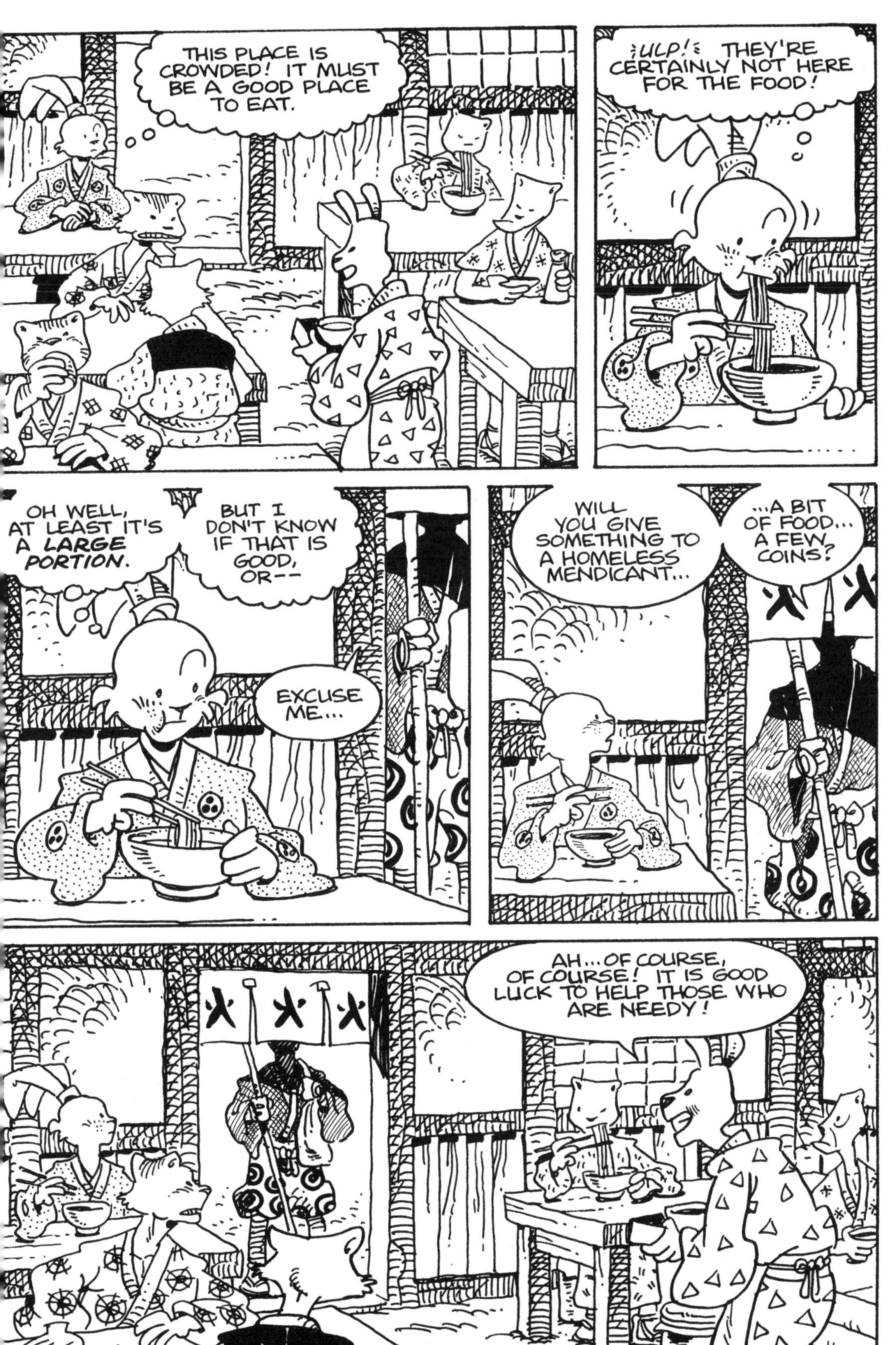
THIS PLACE IS CROWDED! IT MUST BE A GOOD PLACE TO EAT.
ULP! THEY'RE CERTAINLY NOT HERE FOR THE FOOD!
OH WELL, AT LEAST IT'S A **LARGE PORTION**.
BUT I DON'T KNOW IF THAT IS GOOD, OR--
EXCUSE ME...
WILL YOU GIVE SOMETHING TO A HOMELESS MENDICANT...
...A BIT OF FOOD... A FEW COINS?
AH... OF COURSE, OF COURSE! IT IS GOOD LUCK TO HELP THOSE WHO ARE NEEDY!
7.

YOU'RE IN LUCK! I HAVE SOME DELICIOUS SCRAPS YOU CAN HAVE.

YOU'LL HAVE TO EAT IN THE KITCHEN, THOUGH -- WOULDN'T WAN TO DISTURB MY PAYING CUSTOMERS!

COME ON INTO THE BACK. I'LL FIX A NICE BOWL FOR YOU.
THANK YOU.

THAT'S CERTAINLY A DIFFERENT RECEPTION THAN HE GOT IN THE LAST TOWN.
SLURP!

EVERYONE SEEMS INTERESTED IN THAT BEGGAR.
I GUESS KINDNESS TO THOSE LESS FORTUNATE IS RARE ENOUGH TO WARRANT SOME INTEREST.
8

HOURS LATER...
THIS WAS A NICE, QUIET TOWN.

IT'S TOO BAD I CAN'T AFFORD A NIGHT AT AN INN, OR I WOULD STAY A WHILE.

MORE HOURS LATER...
THAT OLD TEMPLE LOOKS LIKE A GOOD PLACE TO SPEND THE NIGHT.

OH--!

I'M SORRY TO DISTURB YOU. I JUST WANTED TO GET OUT OF THE COLD.

I'LL STAY ON THIS SIDE, SO AS NOT TO BOTHER YOU.
9.

ZZZZ...

I KNOW YOU ARE OUT THERE. IF YOU ARE A FRIEND, COME IN AND JOIN US.

IF YOU ARE NOT, LEAVE US ALONE!

10.

I DON'T SENSE THEIR PRESENCE ANYMORE.
I GUESS THEY'VE GONE.

BUT I WON'T BE SLEEPING MUCH TONIGHT.

EH--?

THE BEGGAR IS GONE!

HE MUST HAVE CLIMBED UP THE RAFTERS AND OUT THE ROOF!
WHY WOULD HE DO THAT?

WHOEVER HE IS, THERE IS MORE TO HIM THAN IT FIRST SEEMS.
11.

THE NEXT DAY, IN THE NEXT TOWN...
HERE YOU ARE, SIR!
EH?
!
HE WAS SURPRISED TO SEE ME HERE, SO HE IS DEFINITELY **NOT** FOLLOWING ME.
BUT WHO IS HE?
12.

AND SO...
AHH... THAT WAS DELICIOUS.

AND IT WASN'T VERY EXPENSIVE AT ALL!

WELL, I'VE GOT A LONG ROAD AHEAD OF ME.

13

LATER...
THERE HE IS. IT MIGHT JUST BE COINCIDENCE THAT WE ARE GOING THE SAME WAY, BUT I DON'T WANT HIM BEHIND ME.
I WANT TO KEEP MY EYES ON HIM.
14.

I'LL LET HIM GET FAR ENOUGH AHEAD OF ME BEFORE I CONTINUE ON.

HYAHHH!
KIIYAHH!
15

KILL HIM! KILL HIM!
I KNOW WHAT YOU'RE AFTER...
...AND YOU WON'T GET IT!
UH--!
GHAA!
COME OUT! I KNOW THERE ARE MORE OF YOU AROUND!
16.

NEKO NINJA!

IF THERE IS ONE THING I KNOW, IT IS THAT THE NEKO NINJA ARE UP TO NO GOOD.

GAK!

17.

URT!

.....

WOK!
OW!

KILL HIM! KILL HIM AND GET THE BOOK!

UGH!
!
HIYAAHHHH!
WHAT?!
ARGH!
18.

IT'S THAT LONG-EARED RONIN! HE HAS INTERFERED WITH OUR AFFAIRS IN THE PAST!
BUT NEVER AGAIN!
ULK!

URK!

......

HE'S UNCONSCIOUS, BUT OTHERWISE UNHURT.
EH? WHAT'S THAT?

THIS MUST BE THE BOOK THEY WERE AFTER.
19.

THESE ARE NOTES ON PEOPLE IN THIS AREA.

AND **I'M** IN IT!

HE WROTE ABOUT GEN AND MY ENCOUNTER WITH SAKURA...AND WITH STRAY DOG AND THAT SNITCH.

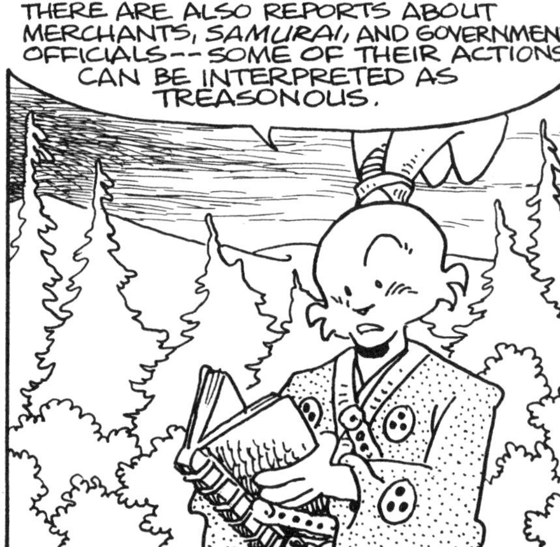
THERE ARE ALSO REPORTS ABOUT MERCHANTS, *SAMURAI*, AND GOVERNMENT OFFICIALS--SOME OF THEIR ACTIONS CAN BE INTERPRETED AS TREASONOUS.

HE WAS NOT FOLLOWING ME...
...BUT I KNOW **WHAT** HE IS NOW.
20

HUH!

WHAT HAPPENED?!
I CAME UPON YOU UNCONSCIOUS ON THE ROAD, WITH THE BODIES OF DEAD NEKO NINJA.
YES. I REMEMBER.
THEY ARE DEADLY. YOU'RE LUCKY TO STILL BE ALIVE.

I HAD SOMETHING...

THEY MUST HAVE TAKEN WHATEVER YOU WERE CARRYING...BUT WHY WOULD *NINJA* STEAL FROM A BEGGAR, UNLESS...

...YOU'RE NOT A BEGGAR AT ALL! YOU'RE A **METSUKE***!
21.

*SHOGUNATE SPY

YOU ARE RIGHT. IT IS NO USE DENYING IT.
I GATHER INFORMATION FROM OUR AGENTS IN VARIOUS TOWNS, AND REPORT IT TO OUR CENTRAL OFFICE.

INNS ARE THE BEST SOURCES OF INFORMATION. SO, MANY OF OUR AGENTS ARE STATIONED THERE.

IF THEY HAVE INFORMATION TO PASS TO YOU, THEY INVITE YOU IN?

EXACTLY. BUT IF THEY HAVE NOTHING TO REPORT, THEY SEND ME AWAY.

THE *SHOGUN* MUST BE PARANOID ABOUT KEEPING HIMSELF IN POWER.

WOULDN'T YOU BE? WHO KNOWS WHAT LORD MIGHT BE PLOTTING A REVOLT OR AMASSING A SECRET ARMY?

SO ALL SUSPICIOUS ACTIVITIES ARE REPORTED.
I WAS EVEN LEERY OF ***YOU!***

WHO? ME?

I FIRST NOTICED YOU IN THE DISTURBANCE WITH THAT WOMAN GAMBLER, SAKURA.
YOU WERE IN THAT TOWN? I NEVER NOTICED YOU!

IN OUR SOCIETY PEOPLE GO THROUGH GREAT PAINS **NOT** TO NOTICE BEGGARS.

IT IS THE PERFECT DISGUISE FOR SOMEONE WHO NEEDS TO TRAVEL INCONSPICUOUSLY.
BUT WHY WERE THE NEKO NINJA AFTER YOU?

THE NEKO NINJA CLAN CRAVES POWER, AND INFORMATION IS THE KEY TO POWER. WHAT I DO NOT UNDERSTAND IS... HOW COULD THEY HAVE DISCOVERED ME?
I THINK I HAVE THE ANSWER. I FELT I WAS BEING WATCHED IN ONE OF THE TOWNS.

THE NEKO NINJA MUST HAVE DISCOVERED ONE OF YOUR INFORMANTS, THEN STAKED OUT HIS INN UNTIL YOU ARRIVED.

THAT MAKES SENSE. WE WILL HAVE TO CLOSE DOWN ALL OUR INNS. I AM IN YOUR DEBT. I AM CALLED MATSUTANI.
AND MY NAME IS--
I KNOW YOUR NAME, USAGI-SAN.
23.

I REGRET MY BELONGINGS WERE TAKEN.
YES. THAT IS TOO BAD.
FAREWELL.
FAREWELL.

BRR... IT'S GETTING CHILLY.

AH... IT FEELS MUCH WARMER ALREADY.

THE END

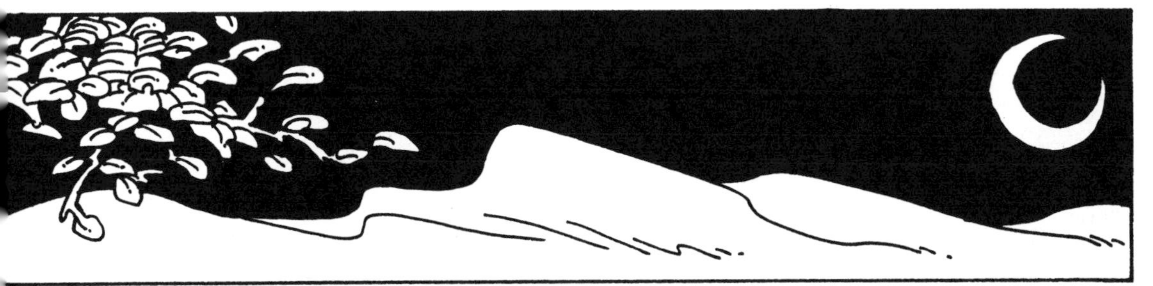

THE FORTRESS

SPASH!

SPASH

SPLASH!

SPLASH!

SPASH!

SPASH!

1.

UH!
SPLASH!

GHAK!

KASHIRA* CHIZU! IT'S ME!
WHO ARE YOU?

I AM ONE OF MANY WHO WOULD SUPPORT YOU TO REGAIN LEADERSHIP OF THE NEKO NINJA CLAN.

KIMI!
IT IS GOOD TO SEE YOU AGAIN, KASHIRA.
2.

*CHIEF

SO... THE CLAN STILL WANTS ME DEAD. HOW DID YOU KNOW I WAS IN THIS AREA?
WE DIDN'T. WE WERE ONE OF TWO GROUPS SENT HERE ON A MISSION!
OH?
WE WERE NOT HUNTING YOU AT ALL.

WE THREE WERE TO OVERSEE A GROUP ORDERED TO RECOVER A BOOK FROM A METSUKE*. IT CONTAINED DETAILS OF ONE OF OUR FUTURE PROJECTS.
*SHOGUNATE SPY

WE FAILED TO RECOVER IT, THANKS TO YOUR LONG-EARED FRIEND.
USAGI? IS HE AROUND HERE?

YEAH. THE STRANGE THING IS THAT HE BURNED THE BOOK, SO OUR MISSION WAS NOT A TOTAL FAILURE AFTER ALL.

I MUST REPORT TO JONIN* KAGEMARU, BUT DON'T WORRY, I WILL KEEP OUR ENCOUNTER A SECRET.
THANK YOU, KIMI, BUT ONE MORE THING BEFORE YOU GO...
EH?

WHAT IS THE MISSION OF THE OTHER GROUP?
3.

*LEADER

AH... SUCH A BEAUTIFUL VIEW!
EH--?
A PROCESSION. I WONDER WHO THEY ARE.
DEAD MEN.
WHAT?
IT IS GOOD TO SEE YOU AGAIN, USAGI.
CHIZU!
4.

THAT IS LORD AWASE AND HIS *SAMURAI*.

WHY CALL THEM ***DEAD MEN***?

THEY ARE WALKING INTO A ***TRAP***!

WHAT?

LORD WAKAME OF THE NEIGHBORING PROVINCE DIED WITHOUT AN HEIR, SO IT FELL UPON THE *SHOGUN** TO DIVIDE HIS HOLDINGS. MOST OF THE LAND WAS GIVEN TO A RELATIVE...

* MILITARY DICTATOR

...BUT THE ***RED CLOUD CASTLE***, ONE OF THE OUTLYING FORTRESSES, AND THE LANDS SURROUNDING IT WERE GIVEN TO LORD AWASE WITH THE PROVISO THAT HE TAKE PHYSICAL POSSESSION OF IT. IF HE DOES NOT, IT WILL BE GIVEN TO ANOTHER.

WHY GIVE IT TO LORD AWASE AT ALL?

THERE IS A HISTORY OF ANIMOSITY BETWEEN THE TWO CLANS, BUT THE *SHOGUN* OWED LORD AWASE A REWARD FOR SUPPORTING HIM IN THE RECENT WARS.

WHY WOULD THAT CAUSE THE DEATH OF THOSE *SAMURAI*?
5

AWASE OPPOSES HIKIJI, THE **SHADOW LORD,** WHO DOES NOT WANT HIM TO GAIN MORE LANDS... MORE POWER.

HIKIJI?!

YEAH. LORD HIKIJI HAS SENT HIS NEKO NINJA TO ASSASSINATE AWASE BEFORE HE TAKES POSSESSION OF THE RED CLOUD CASTLE.

WE CAN'T STAND BY AS THOSE SAMURAI MARCH TO THEIR DEATH! WE'VE GOT TO WARN THEM!

WHY? WHAT HAVE THEY TO DO WITH ME? I AM AN OUTCAST OF THE NEKO NINJA, AND HUNTED BY MY FORMER CLAN. STILL, I WILL NOT INTERFERE IN THEIR AFFAIRS. I CANNOT UNDERSTAND YOUR DESIRE TO GET INVOLVED.

!

I CAN'T JUST STAND BY AND DO NOTHING.
OF COURSE YOU CAN...
...BUT YOU NEVER DO.
6.

STOP! COME NO CLOSER!

I WISH YOU NO HARM! I COME TO WARN YOU!
7.

WHO ARE YOU? WHY DID YOU STOP OUR PROCESSION?

I AM MIYAMOTO USAGI, A *RONIN*. WHOM AM I ADDRESSING?

I AM MORIKAWA, A VASSAL OF LORD AWASE. NOW... ANSWER MY QUESTION!

THERE ARE NEKO NINJA AHEAD! YOU ARE WALKING INTO AN **AMBUSH**!
YOU MUST TURN BACK!
AND HOW DO YOU KNOW THIS?

I WAS INFORMED BY A...UH... RELIABLE SOURCE.

FEH! TURN BACK? ON THE WORD OF A ***RONIN?!***
8.

WELL... I TRIED TO WARN YOU!
STOP! SURROUND HIM!
CHH
NO MATTER HOW SKILLED YOU ARE, YOU CANNOT FIGHT ALL OF US!
I DON'T KNOW WHAT YOU'RE UP TO, RONIN, BUT I WANT YOU WHERE I CAN KEEP AN EYE ON YOU.
SHEATHE YOUR WEAPON, USAGI. YOU'LL JOIN OUR PROCESSION UNTIL WE ARRIVE AT THE RED CLOUD CASTLE.
AGREED.
YOU'LL WALK NEXT TO ME, RONIN. MAKE EVEN ONE SUSPICIOUS MOVE, AND I'LL KILL YOU.
9.

YOU DON'T BELIEVE ME.

NO, I DON'T.

WHY WOULD I **LIE** TO YOU?

WHY WOULD YOU **HELP** US?

I TOLD YOU-- YOU'RE HEADING INTO A TRAP. WHY NOT TURN BACK JUST TO BE SAFE?

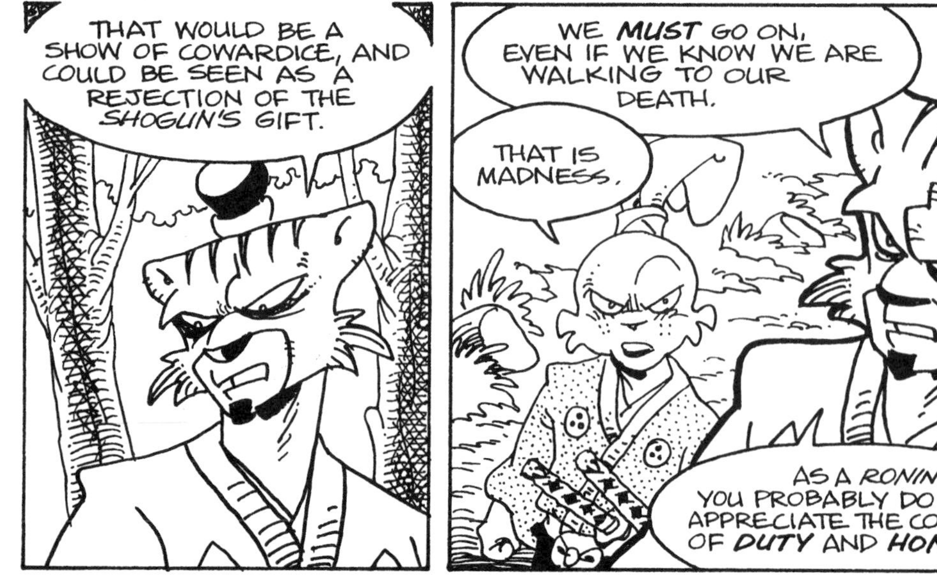

THAT WOULD BE A SHOW OF COWARDICE, AND COULD BE SEEN AS A REJECTION OF THE *SHOGUN'S* GIFT.
WE **MUST** GO ON, EVEN IF WE KNOW WE ARE WALKING TO OUR DEATH.
THAT IS MADNESS.
AS A *RONIN*, YOU PROBABLY DO NOT APPRECIATE THE CONCEPTS OF **DUTY** AND **HONOR**.
10.

WE'RE BEING WATCHED.

11.

ALERT! ALERT!

TWZZZ!
TWIZZZ!
TWIZZZ!

GET THE LORD TO SAFETY! GET LORD AWASE TO SAFETY!
THUK
THUK
WHINNY!

UH--!
LOOK OUT!
YAHH!

GYAHH!
BACK! GET BACK! GO THE OTHER WAY!
CRASH!
12.

YAH!
GYAHH!
AHH!
UH--!
GHAH!
LORD AWASE!

UH--!
EEG!
YARK!
THUD!

UHH....
TONO*!
*LORD

I- I AM ALL RIGHT, MORIKAWA... JUST A BIT BRUISED.
WE'VE GOT TO GET YOU AWAY FROM HERE!
HELP ME OUT!

TAKE COVER BEHIND THE PALANQUIN, LORD AWASE!
13

PROTECT THE LORD! PROTECT LORD AWASE!

FWTT!
FWTT!
FWTT!

UH--!
TANG!
THUK!
TANG!

HIYAHHHHHHHH!
14.

RALLY! RALLY AROUND LORD AWASE!

PROTECT THE LORD!
EYAH!

SKASH!
OOK!
GUH!

HYAHH!

KANG!

GAHH!
15.

LORD AWASE!
.....
GASP!

USAGI!
GAHH!
LOOK OUT!

16.

HYAHH!
GYUK!

KIAII!
GHAA!

UH-OH!

EYAHH!
CHIZU!

YOU SAID YOU DO NOT CARE ABOUT THE AFFAIRS OF OTHERS!
I DON'T-- BUT YOU'RE A FRIEND!
17.

HAHH!!
ULK!

GYAH!

GYAH!
TCHAK!

UH--!
TWIZZ!

POOF!

TONO!
ALL THE NEKO NINJA HAVE DISAPPEARED!
18.

.....
LORD AWASE!
THE NEKO MUST BELIEVE LORD AWASE TO BE DEAD.
THEY MAY SOON BE CORRECT.

GET OUT OF THE WAY!
WHO ARE YOU?

CHIZU IS SOMEONE WHO CAN HELP.
THIS TIME I WILL TAKE YOUR WORD FOR IT.
IT IS A BAD WOUND. FORTUNATELY, THE *SHURIKEN* WAS NOT POISONED.

UH...
THIS IS ALL THAT I CAN DO. HE NEEDS MORE HELP THAN I CAN GIVE.

A THIRD OF YOU--STAY BACK TO HELP THE WOUNDED. THE REST, ORGANIZE YOURSELVES. WE MUST GET LORD AWASE TO THE RED CLOUD CASTLE AS QUICKLY AS POSSIBLE.
19.

AND SO...
HURRY! IT'S NOT FAR NOW!

STOP! THERE MAY BE RESISTANCE FROM LORD WAKAME LOYALISTS. MANY WERE AGAINST GIVING THIS FORTRESS TO OUR LORD.
BUT WE NEED HELP FROM THOSE WITHIN THE CASTLE.
WAIT HERE WHILE I INVESTIGATE.

CHIZU AND I WILL ACCOMPANY YOU.
THEN COME ON!
20.

STRANGE. THERE ARE NO GUARDS.
IT COULD BE A TRAP.

THE GATE IS AJAR!

GODS!
21.

WHAT COULD HAVE HAPPENED?

ISN'T IT OBVIOUS?
EH?

HONOR DICTATED THAT THEY NOT TURN OVER THE FORTRESS TO THEIR ENEMY, BUT THEY HAD A DUTY TO OBEY THE *SHOGUN*.

THEY TOOK THE ONLY HONORABLE OPTION THEY HAD.
*SEPPUKU**--RATHER THAN THE DISGRACE OF SURRENDERING THE FORTRESS--AND AS A PROTEST AGAINST THE *SHOGUN'S* DECREE.
WHO ARE YOU?
*RITUALIZED SUICIDE

I AM MITSUHITO, AN EMISSARY OF HIS HONOR, THE *SHOGUN*. I WAS SENT AS AN OBSERVER OF THE TRANSFER OF THE RED CLOUD CASTLE.

WHY DIDN'T YOU STOP THEM?
AS AN OBSERVER, I HAVE NO RIGHT TO INTERFERE.
22.

MORIKAWA-SAN!
THE PROCESSION!
LORD AWASE MUST CLAIM OWNERSHIP OF THE FORTRESS, OR IT WILL BE GIVEN TO AN ALLY OF LORD HIKIJI!

WELCOME TO THE RED CLOUD CASTLE, LORD AWASE.

PLEASE TAKE POSSESSION OF THE FORTRESS, MY LORD. THE FUTURE OF OUR CLANS RESTS ON IT.

23

THE END

THE OUTLAW

WHAT I'M SAYING IS: WHY SHOULD A CRIMINAL LIKE TANIGUCHI RETURN TO THE PROVINCE OF HIS CRIME?

ANYBODY WITH HALF A BRAIN WOULD HAVE LEFT THIS AREA.

WHO CAN FATHOM THE MENTALITY OF A *KILLER*, GEN? ALL I KNOW IS THAT HIS TRAIL LEADS HERE.

LOOK, STRAY DOG, I JUST HOPE WE'RE NOT WASTING OUR TIME!

I'M GOING TO COLLECT THAT REWARD. YOU CAN LEAVE IF YOU WANT TO.

OH, NO, YOU'RE NOT GETTING RID OF ME THAT EASILY. HALF OF THAT REWARD IS **MINE!**
;GLUG! GLUG!;
YEAH, AND IT'S A **BIG** REWARD.

WHICH MEANS THERE WILL BE OTHER BOUNTY HUNTERS AFTER TANIGUCHI--A **LOT** OF OTHER BOUNTY HUNTERS.
I'M NOT WORRIED. WE'RE SMARTER THAN THEY ARE...AT LEAST, **I AM!**
1.

A CROSSROADS. WHICH WAY SHOULD WE GO?
WHO SAYS WE HAVE TO STAY TOGETHER?
YOU'RE SUGGESTING WE SPLIT UP?
WE'LL COVER MORE AREA THAT WAY.
YEAH... AND WITH OTHER HUNTERS AROUND, WE'LL HAVE TO FIND TANIGUCHI AS FAST AS POSSIBLE.
WE'LL MEET BACK IN TOWN TOMORROW, OKAY?
BUT I'M NOT GIVING YOU HALF THE REWARD IF I GET HIM!
THEN THE ONE WHO FINDS TANIGUCHI GETS THREE QUARTERS OF THE REWARD. AGREED?
AGREED.
SO LONG, PARTNER.
GOOD LUCK.
SAVE YOUR LUCK FOR YOURSELF, GEN.
I HAVE A FEELING YOU'LL NEED IT MORE THAN I WILL.
2.

GRR... I HATE THAT STRAY DOG'S ARROGANCE. I HAVE **GOT** TO FIND TANIGUCHI BEFORE HE DOES.

THOSE GUYS SMELL LIKE BOUNTY HUNTERS TO ME.
HEY-- I KNOW ONE OF THEM.

AKATSUKI...
GEN-- YOU BIG GRAY SLIME-- WHAT ARE YOU DOING HERE?
DON'T COME ANY CLOSER!

I'M HERE FOR THE SAME REASON YOU ARE, I BET.
I LOST OUT ON INAZUMA'S REWARD BECAUSE OF YOU! I'M NOT MISSING OUT ON **THIS** ONE.

YOU'RE NOT WELCOME HERE, GEN. WE FOLLOWED TANIGUCHI'S TRAIL TO THAT OLD HUT. INTERFERE WITH US, AND YOU'LL BE DEAD BEFORE HE IS!
INTERFERE? **ME?!** I MIND MY OWN BUSINESS.
I'LL JUST STAY BACK, AND OBSERVE YOUR EXPERT TECHNIQUE.
3.

COME ON-- LET'S GET HIM!
CAREFUL-- HE'S SUPPOSED TO BE A SKILLED SWORDSMAN!
HE CAN'T STAND UP AGAINST THE SIX OF US!
IT'S EMPTY!
ARE YOU SURE?
A HUT THIS SMALL-- DO YOU THINK I NEED TO LOOK TWICE TO BE SURE?
LET'S GET OUT OF HERE!
WHAT'S THE MATTER? WASN'T HE IN THERE?
GRR... NOBODY LIKES A WISE GUY, GEN.
4.

SMIRK! YOU'LL HAVE TO BE LOTS SMARTER IF YOU WANT TO CATCH TANIGUCHI!
ABANDON THE HUNT, GEN! STAY OUT OF OUR WAY!

HA! WHAT A BUNCH OF DOLTS!

LET'S SEE IF THERE ARE ANY CLUES THAT WILL POINT ME TO TANIGUCHI'S PRESENT LOCATION.

I DON'T EVEN KNOW IF HE WAS REALLY IN HERE OR NOT.

?

EMPTY. I GUESS THE OUTLAW GOT AWAY, AFTER ALL.

5

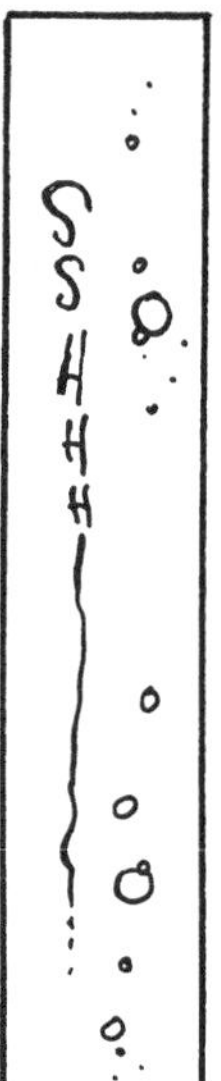
SSHHH——

HA! THEY'RE ALL GONE--THOSE IDIOTS...

...FALLING FOR A SIMPLE TRICK LIKE HIDING IN THE DARK RAFTERS.

HOLD IT, TANIGUCHI!
WHAT?

I'VE HEARD YOU'RE REAL GOOD WITH A BLADE, SO HAND OVER YOUR SWORD--SLOWLY.

NO SUDDEN MOVES. REMEMBER--THE REWARD IS THE SAME WHETHER YOU ARE ALIVE OR DEAD.
6.

YOU THINK HUNTERS ARE IDIOTS?! ANY THINKING CRIMINAL WOULD NEVER HAVE RETURNED TO THE SCENE OF HIS CRIME.
I HAVE MY REASONS.
YEAH. STUPIDITY.
MY WIFE HAD TO MOVE INTO A COUNTRY HOVEL...
...AND I RECEIVED WORD THAT MY SON WAS BORN LAST WEEK.
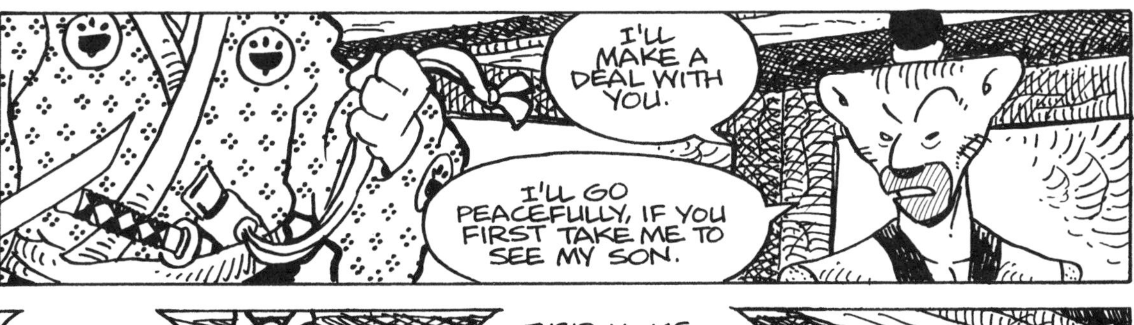
I'LL MAKE A DEAL WITH YOU.
I'LL GO PEACEFULLY, IF YOU FIRST TAKE ME TO SEE MY SON.

WHAT ARE YOU TALKING ABOUT?
THEIR HOME IS NOT FAR FROM TOWN--ALMOST ALONG THE WAY.

FEH! WHO DO YOU THINK YOU'RE TRYING TO FOOL? YOU DON'T HAVE A SON. YOUR GANG IS PROBABLY HOLED UP IN THAT HUT, AND YOU'LL LEAD ME INTO AN AMBUSH.
I DON'T HAVE A GANG.

OR SO YOU SAY.
NOW TURN AROUND, AND PLACE YOUR HANDS BEHIND YOU.
7.

ONE WRONG MOVE, AND YOU'RE DEAD.

LET ME SEE MY SON, AND I'LL COOPERATE.
SHUT UP.

I'M NOT FALLING FOR YOUR LIES! YOU HAVE NO SON.

SOON.
WHAT'S THAT UP AHEAD?
IT LOOKS LIKE THOSE WOODCUTTERS' CART HAS A BROKEN WHEEL.
PLEASE PAUSE A MOMENT TO HELP US, SAMURAI.
WE'VE GOT TO COME TO THEIR AID, GEN.

AND GIVE YOU A CHANCE TO ESCAPE? NO WAY!
YOU CAN'T BE AS HEARTLESS AS YOU SOUND, BOUNTY HUNTER.

YOU WOULD BE SURPRISED AT HOW HEARTLESS I CAN BE.
YOU LOOK LIKE A DECENT GUY--NOT AS RUTHLESS AS THOSE OTHER HUNTERS.
COME ON. LET'S HELP THEM.
8.

UGH!
REMEMBER-- DON'T TRY ANYTHING, OUTLAW!
NNNGH!

KEEP THAT SWORD ON HIM. CUT HIM DOWN AT THE FIRST WRONG MOVE.
GULP! Y-YES, BOUNTY HUNTER!

ARE YOU ALL RIGHT, HUSBAND?
I WILL --UGH!-- MANAGE, WIFE.
NNGH! HURRY WITH THAT WHEEL! THIS CART IS HEAVY!

OH!
IT'S TOO HEAVY FOR HIM!

DON'T LET GO, BOUNTY HUNTER. YOU MAY DROP IT ON YOURSELF!
HEY!
9.

I'LL TAKE CARE OF THIS, WOOD-CUTTER.
I'LL KILL YOU FOR THIS, TANIGUCHI! I KNOW YOU'RE TRYING TO ESCAPE!

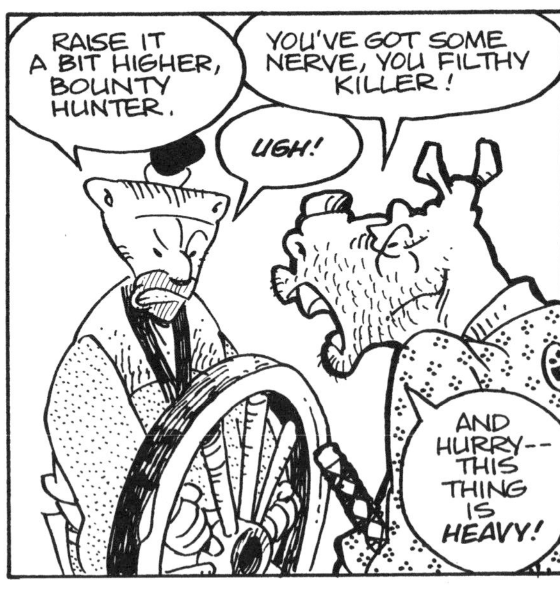
RAISE IT A BIT HIGHER, BOUNTY HUNTER.
YOU'VE GOT SOME NERVE, YOU FILTHY KILLER!
UGH!
AND HURRY-- THIS THING IS HEAVY!

THE PIN IS IN. YOU CAN LET IT DOWN NOW-- SLOWLY.
I OUGHT TO KILL YOU FOR WHAT YOU DID!

WHAT DID I DO, EXCEPT HELP A PEASANT COUPLE REPAIR THEIR CART?
SHUT UP AND TURN AROUND--HANDS BEHIND YOUR BACK.

PULL SOMETHING LIKE THAT AGAIN, AND YOU'LL BE SORRY.
HE NEEDED HELP, SO I HELPED HIM.
10.

FUNNY, YOU DON'T LOOK LIKE A MURDERER.
I AM A POOR, LOW-RANKING *SAMURAI*.

THE ARROGANT SON OF A *HATAMOTO** WAS BULLYING A POOR INNKEEPER. I DON'T LIKE BULLIES, SO I STEPPED IN TO HELP. THE BULLY WAS WITH FRIENDS, AND TRIED TO INTIMIDATE ME.
*HIGH-RANKING SAMURAI

WHEN HIS FRIENDS LAUGHED AT HIM BECAUSE I WOULD NOT BACK DOWN, HE CHALLENGED ME TO A ***DUEL***.

BUT HE WAS AN INEPT SWORDSMAN, AND I SLEW HIM. HIS FRIENDS ACCUSED ME OF MURDER, EVEN THOUGH IT WAS BECAUSE OF THEM THE DUEL TOOK PLACE. THE *HATAMOTO*, ANGERED AT THE DEATH OF HIS HEIR, PLACED A LARGE REWARD ON MY HEAD.

YEAH, AND I'M GOING TO COLLECT IT!
WE MAY AS WELL GIVE UP AND LEAVE THIS AREA.
YEAH.
11.

WE'VE LOST TANIGUCHI'S TRAIL COMPLETELY.
WHERE COULD HE HAVE DISAPPEARED TO?
¡GLUG!
EH--?
AKATSUKI-- LOOK!
HUH? WHAT IS IT?
GEN... AND HE'S WITH THE OUTLAW!
HE CHEATED ME OUT OF ONE REWARD. HE'S NOT GOING TO CHEAT ME OUT OF ANOTHER!
COME ON-- WE'LL CUT HIM OFF AT THE CROSSROADS!
THE HUNTERS!
GEN! YOU FILTHY SLIME!
AKATSUKI!
12

WE'LL NEVER BE ABLE TO OUTRUN THEM. THEY ARE *PROFESSIONAL KILLERS!* YOU'VE GOT TO HAND ME OVER TO THEM!

NO! I'M NOT GOING TO GIVE UP MY REWARD WITHOUT A FIGHT!
THEN YOU'VE GOT JUST *ONE OPTION!*

GIVE ME MY SWORD, AND I'LL STAND WITH YOU!
WHAT?! ARE YOU CRAZY?!

THEY'LL KILL YOU ANYWAY! WHAT HAVE YOU GOT TO LOSE?
.....

TURN AROUND AND HOLD STILL.
THERE. YOU'RE FREE.

HERE'S YOUR BLADE, THOUGH I DON'T KNOW WHY I'M RETURNING IT. YOU'LL PROBABLY SLAY ME WITH IT!
OF COURSE I WON'T!
13.

HIIYAHHHHH!
FLOOP!
ARGH!
GLIK!
HYAA!
UH--!
CHAK!
ULK!
14.

GYAHH!

I TOLD YOU TO STAY OUT OF THIS, GEN! I ONLY GIVE ONE WARNING!
LET'S JUST SAY I'M HARD OF HEARING!

I'LL KILL YOU!
DID YOU HEAR THAT?
ULP!

HIYAHH!

.....
15

YOU COULD HAVE LET HIM KILL ME, AND GOTTEN AWAY.

MAYBE I WANTED TO SLAY YOU MYSELF.

GULP!

BUT I GAVE YOU MY WORD OF HONOR. LET'S GO.
UH... SURE.

YOU REMIND ME OF A FRIEND. HE HAS AN OBSESSION WITH HONOR AS WELL, THAT LONG-EARED IDIOT.
NOW... GIVE ME BACK THAT SWORD.
16.

WHY DID YOU SIDE WITH ME BACK THERE? THE OUTCOME FOR YOU IS THE SAME, NO MATTER **WHO** BRINGS YOU IN.
SIX AGAINST ONE? AS I SAID, I DO NOT LIKE BULLIES.

HMMM...

DO YOU REALLY HAVE A SON, OR WAS THAT A RUSE TO LURE ME INTO A TRAP?
I DID NOT LIE.

WHAT'S HIS NAME?
HE DOES NOT YET HAVE A NAME, BUT I WANT TO CALL HIM **FUKUO**.

FUKUO--*"MAN OF GOOD FORTUNE"*--THAT IS A GOOD NAME.
YEAH.

I HOPE HE MAKES SOMETHING OF HIMSELF. ME, I WAS BORN UNDER AN UNLUCKY STAR, AND NEVER AMOUNTED TO MUCH.

I THINK YOU'VE AMOUNTED TO QUITE A LOT.
17

YOU SAID YOUR FAMILY IS NOT FAR FROM TOWN?
YEAH. THE LEFT FORK TAKES YOU TO TOWN, THE RIGHT TO MY WIFE AND SON.

HERE.
HERE'S YOUR SWORD. TAKE IT, AND GO TO THE *RIGHT.*
EH?

YOU UNDERSTOOD ME. TAKE YOUR FAMILY AND LEAVE THIS AREA. GET OUT OF HERE, BEFORE I CHANGE MY MIND.
THANK YOU, GEN-SAN.

I'M A FOOL. I KNOW I'LL REGRET THIS LATER, BUT THE WORLD WILL BE A BETTER PLACE WITH YOU ALIVE.

DON'T MAKE ME OUT TO BE A SAINT, BOUNTY HUNTER.

I HAVE SOMETHING FOR YOU AS WELL.
EH?

A *TANTO**?
I TOOK IT FROM ONE OF THE HUNTERS I KILLED.
18.

* DAGGER

I WOULD HAVE USED IT TO KILL YOU. I WOULD HAVE DONE ANYTHING TO GET BACK TO MY FAMILY.
SO LONG.
.....
BWA HA HA HA HA HA HA HA!
HEH, HEH. I LIKE HIM EVEN MORE NOW.
I GUESS I'LL HAVE TO TELL STRAY DOG THAT I HAD NO LUCK FINDING TANIGUCHI.
HYAHHH!
WHAT?
URK!
19.

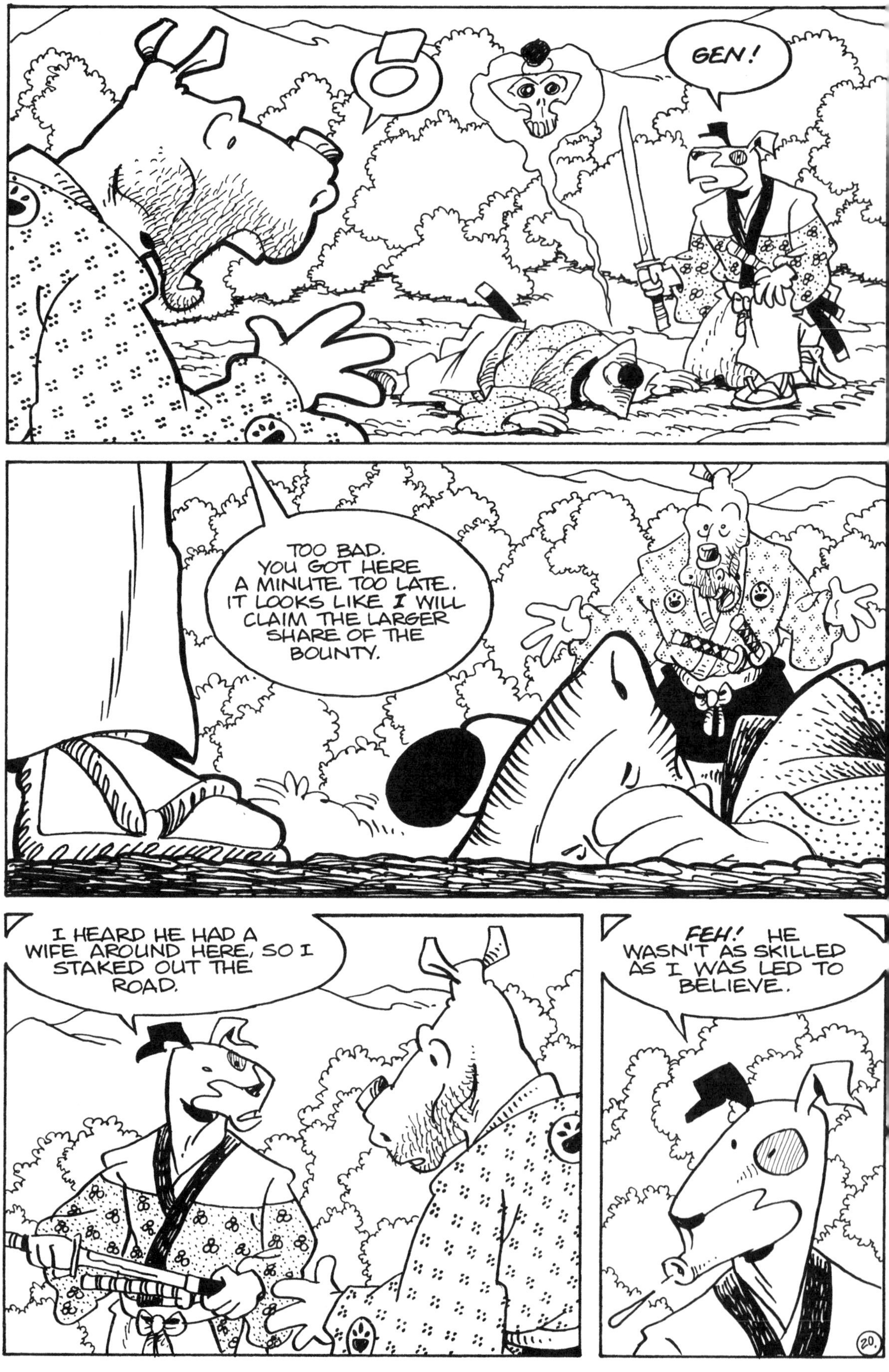

GEN!

TOO BAD. YOU GOT HERE A MINUTE TOO LATE. IT LOOKS LIKE *I* WILL CLAIM THE LARGER SHARE OF THE BOUNTY.

I HEARD HE HAD A WIFE AROUND HERE, SO I STAKED OUT THE ROAD.

FEH! HE WASN'T AS SKILLED AS I WAS LED TO BELIEVE.
20.

YOU TRAITOR!

I'LL KILL YOU FOR THAT!

21

SIGH...
A FIGHT WOULD BE FRUITLESS.

LOOK, I'M SORRY. I-I WAS UPSET THAT YOU BEAT ME TO TANIGUCHI.
UH... NO HARD FEELINGS?
GRR...!

THE EXTRA MONEY I'LL GET WILL SOOTHE MY SORE JAW.

BUT ONCE WE COLLECT THE REWARD, WE'RE SPLITTING UP! UNDERSTAND?
22

A DAY LATER...
EXCUSE ME. ARE YOU THE WIFE OF TANIGUCHI?
YES, I AM, SAMURAI-SAN. WHY DO YOU ASK?
I MET YOUR HUSBAND RECENTLY, AND HE ASKED ME TO GIVE THIS TO YOU.
WHAT? SO MUCH MONEY?
23

WHERE IS MY HUSBAND? IS HE ALL RIGHT?
I-I'M SORRY, BUT HE WAS KILLED SOON AFTER WE PARTED-- THOSE COWARDLY BOUNTY HUNTERS!
GASP! NO! NO!
BUT HE GAVE ME A MESSAGE FOR YOU. HE SAID TO NAME HIS SON FUKUO.
SOB!
"FUKUO"...
YES... THAT IS A FINE NAME.
FUKUO.
THE END

THE RAIN WILL RUST ITS EDGE,
AND THE SHEEN WILL FADE AWAY!
THE KEENEST BLADES ARE SHEATHED,
AND THAT'S WHERE THEY SHOULD STAY.
SO PLEASE, MR. SAMURAI,
DON'T DRAW YOUR SWORD TODAY!

SAYA 鞘

<SCABBARDS>

BY STAN SAKAI

COLORS BY TOM LUTH

CAW! CAW!

CAW!

PWEET!

HA! HA! HA!

DON! DAKO! DON!

1.

HA HA HA! YOU CAN'T CATCH ME! YOU'RE BOTH TOO SLOW!

HA! MOVE ASIDE, MISTER!
HEY!

TAK!

EH?

!
2.

HOW DARE YOU--A VAGABOND *RONIN**-- SULLY MY SWORD?! DON'T YOU KNOW IT IS AN INSULT TO ACCOST ANOTHER'S SCABBARD?
HA HA HA HA HA!
IT WAS AN ACCIDENT! THE CHILDREN--
*MASTERLESS SAMURAI

SILENCE! YOU CAN'T BRUSH OFF YOUR LACK OF COURTESY BY BLAMING OTHERS!

YOU ARE RIGHT. I APOLOGIZE FOR TOUCHING YOUR SCABBARD WITH MINE, AND FOR TAKING A SERIOUS BREACH OF CONDUCT AS LIGHTLY AS I DID.

FEH! YOU CALL THAT AN APOLOGY? GROVEL ON YOUR STOMACH LIKE A WORM, AND I ***MAY*** FORGIVE YOU.

IT IS CLEAR THAT NO APOLOGY I OFFER WILL SATISFY YOU. GOODBYE.
!
3.

YOU DARE TO TURN YOUR BACK ON ME? I'LL HAVE TO TEACH YOU A LESSON!
DRAW YOUR SWORD!

NOT HERE. WE SHOULD NOT RUIN THEIR SPRING RICE PLANTING.
THEN WHERE?

IN THE WOODS. THEY WILL NOT BE DISTURBED BY OUR COMBAT THERE.
VERY WELL.

THIS IS FAR ENOUGH.
DRAW YOUR SWORD.
4

I AM CALLED MIYAMOTO USAGI.
BAH! WHO CARES WHAT A DEAD RONIN IS NAMED?

YOU HAVE A FINE BLADE-- WELL HONED AND POLISHED.

WITH AN EDGE THAT WILL CUT YOU IN TWO. YOURS IS NO MORE THAN A RUSTY LENGTH OF STEEL.

SIGH YES. MY SWORD HAS BEEN DRAWN TOO OFTEN.

THEN THIS WILL BE THE LAST TIME!

HIYAHH--!
5

TANG!
TANG!
TANG!

YOU RONIN SCUM-- THINKING YOU'RE AS GOOD AS I AM!

STAY STILL, YOU!

AH--!

HA!
UH--!

HEH, HEH, HEH, HEH, HEH. GOT YOU!
6.

!
MY SWORD IS-- STUCK!

Y-YOU CAUGHT MY SWORD IN YOUR SCABBARD!
IMPOSSIBLE! NO ONE CAN DO THAT!

YAHH!
CHOP!
RYAHH!
WHAT KIND OF DEMON SWORDSMAN ARE YOU?

NO--STOP! PLEASE! I GIVE UP! DON'T HURT ME!

YOU ADMIRED MY SWORD-- KEEP IT! JUST LET ME GO!
7.

YOURS IS A FINE BLADE, BUT THE SWORD REFLECTS THE SOUL OF THE SAMURAI... IT IS THE SAMURAI'S SOUL...

YOU CHEAPEN YOUR SOUL.

ABAYO.*
*SO LONG

OH, PLEASE, MR. SAMURAI, DON'T DRAW YOUR SWORD TODAY. THE RAIN WILL RUST ITS EDGE, AND THE SHEEN WILL FADE AWAY! THE KEENEST BLADES ARE SHEATHED, AND THAT'S WHERE THEY SHOULD STAY.
SO PLEASE, MR. SAMURAI, DON'T DRAW YOUR SWORD TODAY!
DON DAN DOKO DOKO DAN
完

The Beggar

Me literally means "eye," and *tsuke* means "to apply." So the *metsuke* were literally the eyes of the shogun, charged with gathering information from the samurai and lower classes and investigating insurrection against the government. Five *ometsuke* dealt exclusively with the *daimyo*, or feudal lords, and the imperial court. Many *daimyo* were transferred to smaller fiefs or lost their lands altogether because of unfavorable reports. However, the *metsuke* were not immune to corruption themselves, and this became the basis for plays and TV shows.

Over time, the duties of the *ometsuke* changed to passing orders from the shogun to his *daimyo* and overseeing ceremonies and religious celebrations. The *metsuke* were abolished with the fall of the shogunate system and the Meiji Restoration in 1867.

The Fortress

The Bushido code lists seven traditional virtues for the samurai to live by:

Gi (justice): The ability to make the correct decision with fairness to everyone.

Yu (valor and courage): Confidence in one's ability to handle any situation. Never fear to act.

Jin (compassion): Consider others before oneself, and take every opportunity to help others.

Rei (courtesy and respect): Proper behavior toward everyone. Courtesy reveals one's true strength.

Makoto (honesty): Be honest with oneself, so one can be honest with everyone else. A samurai's decisions and actions reflect his true nature.

Meiyo (honor): An honorable heart leads to success and glory. Speaking and doing should be one and the same.

Chugi (loyalty): The foundation of all the virtues. A samurai's loyalty to his lord is unquestionable.

Other virtues include self-control, wisdom, and filial piety.

Saya

Touching a samurai's sword scabbard, even accidentally, was an offense in feudal Japan. The most famous incident of this type involved the swordsman Tsukahara Bokuden (1489–1571), founder of the Kashima style of fencing. He was on a ferry, crossing Lake Biwa, when a shift of the boat caused a peasant to touch a samurai's scabbard. The samurai was going to kill the terrified peasant when Bokuden intervened. When the samurai demanded to know the intruder's fencing style, Bokuden answered, "My style is fighting with no swords."

The samurai issued a challenge to a duel to settle the matter. Bokuden suggested they row to a nearby island rather than fight on the crowded ferry. As soon as they arrived, the samurai jumped onto the shore and drew his sword. Bokuden rowed back to the ferry, leaving the idiot stranded. If this story sounds familiar, you may have seen a variation of it in Bruce Lee's *Enter the Dragon*.

GALLERY

Stan Sakai's cover art for the issues collected in this volume. Colors by Tom Luth, except on Sakai's painted covers.

Usagi Yojimbo Volume Three #95

Usagi Yojimbo Volume Three #96

Usagi Yojimbo Volume Three #97

Usagi Yojimbo Volume Three #98

Usagi Yojimbo Volume Three #99

百

Usagi Yojimbo Volume Three #100

Usagi Yojimbo Volume Three #101

Usagi Yojimbo Volume Three #102

Usagi Yojimbo Volume Three #103

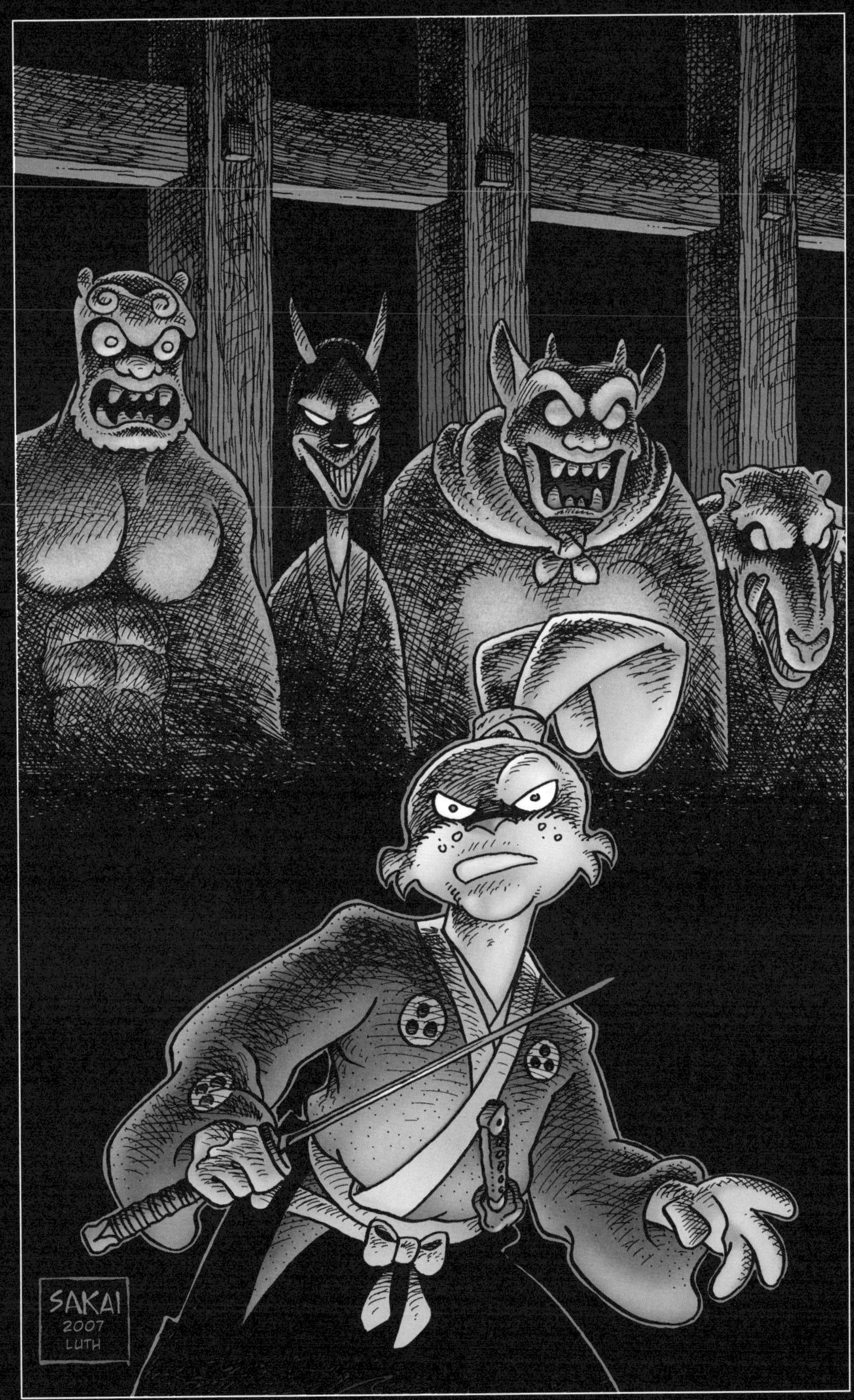

Usagi Yojimbo Volume Three #104

Usagi Yojimbo Volume Three #105

Usagi Yojimbo Volume Three #106

Usagi Yojimbo Volume Three #107

Usagi Yojimbo Volume Three #108

Usagi Yojimbo Volume Three #109

Usagi Yojimbo Volume Three #110

Usagi Yojimbo Volume Three #111

Usagi Yojimbo Volume Three #112

Usagi Yojimbo Volume Three #113

Usagi Yojimbo Volume Three #114

Usagi Yojimbo Volume Three #115

Usagi Yojimbo Volume Three #116

Usagi Yojimbo Book 23: *Bridge of Tears*

SAKAI

SAKAI

GROO VS. USAGI: WHO WOULD WIN?

This page was originally drawn for the 2007 Comic-Con International: San Diego souvenir book, in celebration of the twenty-fifth anniversary of Sergio Aragonés's *Groo.*

Story by Stéphane "Fanfan" Heude • Art by Laurent de Andrade

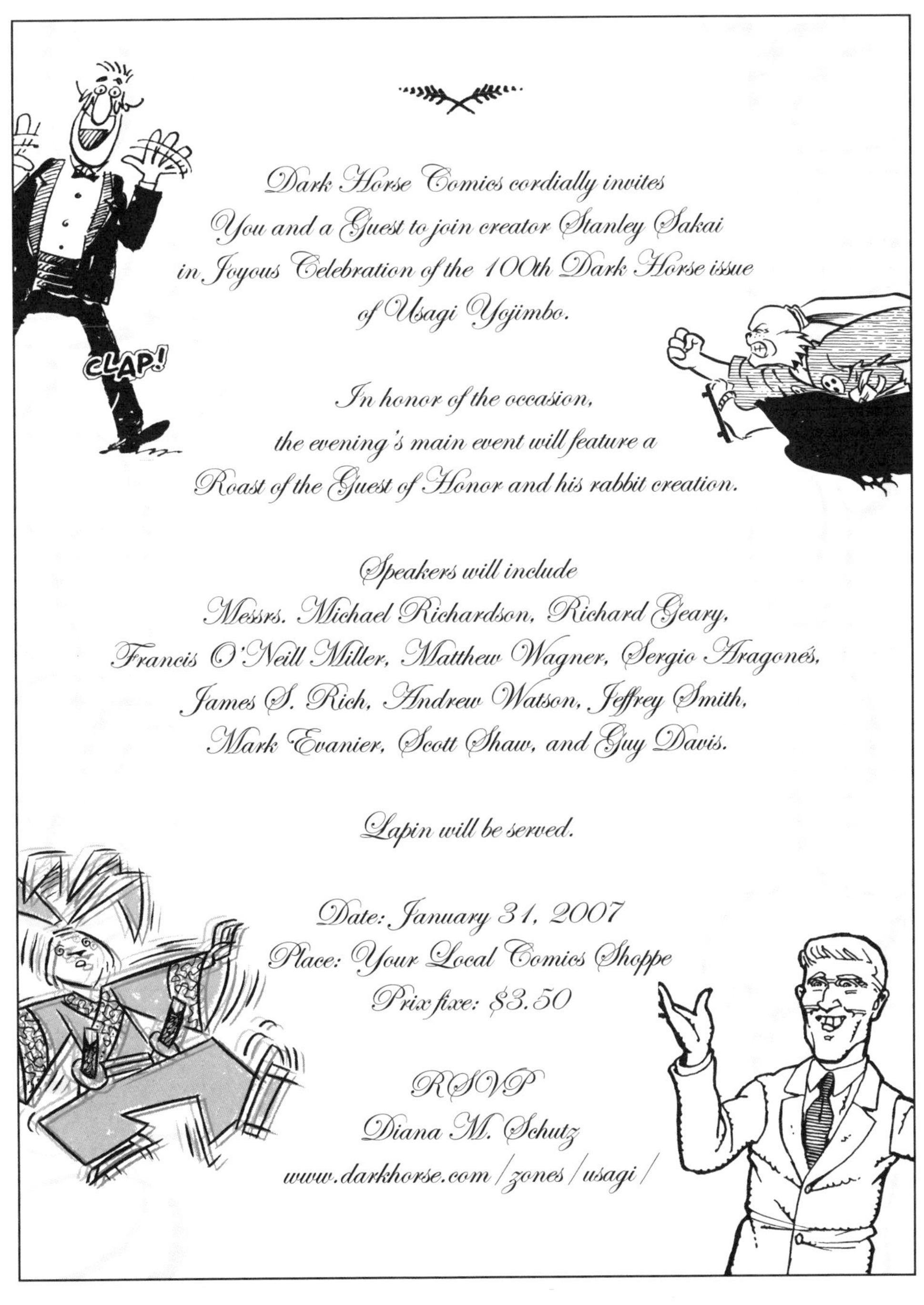

Dark Horse Comics cordially invites
You and a Guest to join creator Stanley Sakai
in Joyous Celebration of the 100th Dark Horse issue
of Usagi Yojimbo.

In honor of the occasion,
the evening's main event will feature a
Roast of the Guest of Honor and his rabbit creation.

Speakers will include
Messrs. Michael Richardson, Richard Geary,
Francis O'Neill Miller, Matthew Wagner, Sergio Aragonés,
James S. Rich, Andrew Watson, Jeffrey Smith,
Mark Evanier, Scott Shaw, and Guy Davis.

Lapin will be served.

Date: January 31, 2007
Place: Your Local Comics Shoppe
Prix fixe: $3.50

RSVP
Diana M. Schutz
www.darkhorse.com/zones/usagi/

Dark Horse's 100th issue of *Usagi Yojimbo* (January 2007) was cause for celebration, and editor Diana Schutz decided a guest "roast" was in order. This "invitation" ran in all Dark Horse comics that month.

HELLO, USAGI FANS! I'VE BEEN ASKED TO WELCOME ALL OF YOU TO THIS VERY SPECIAL COMIC BOOK!
Dark Horse Publisher Mike Richardson
USAGI YOJIMBO

AS I'M SURE YOU KNOW, WE'RE HERE TO CELEBRATE THE 100TH ISSUE OF STAN SAKAI'S USAGI YOJIMBO!

IN HONOR OF THE OCCASION, WE'VE ASKED SOME OF COMICS' BRIGHTEST STARS TO BE HERE.
MOST IMPORTANTLY, STAN HIMSELF IS HERE TO CELEBRATE WITH US! COME ON UP, STAN!

STAN, WE'RE SO GLAD TO HAVE YOU HERE... UH... STAN?
HI, MIKE!
USAGI YOJIMBO

COME ON, RICK! I'M SIX-FOOT-NINE! CAN'T YOU TRY AND DRAW THE PANEL SO THAT READERS CAN SEE BOTH OF US?!

HMMM... THIS ISN'T GOING TO WORK!
RICK, JUST PUT IT BACK THE WAY IT WAS!
SORRY, STAN!
SOMEBODY GET A BOX FOR STAN TO STAND ON!
RICK GEARY
THAT'S BETTER!

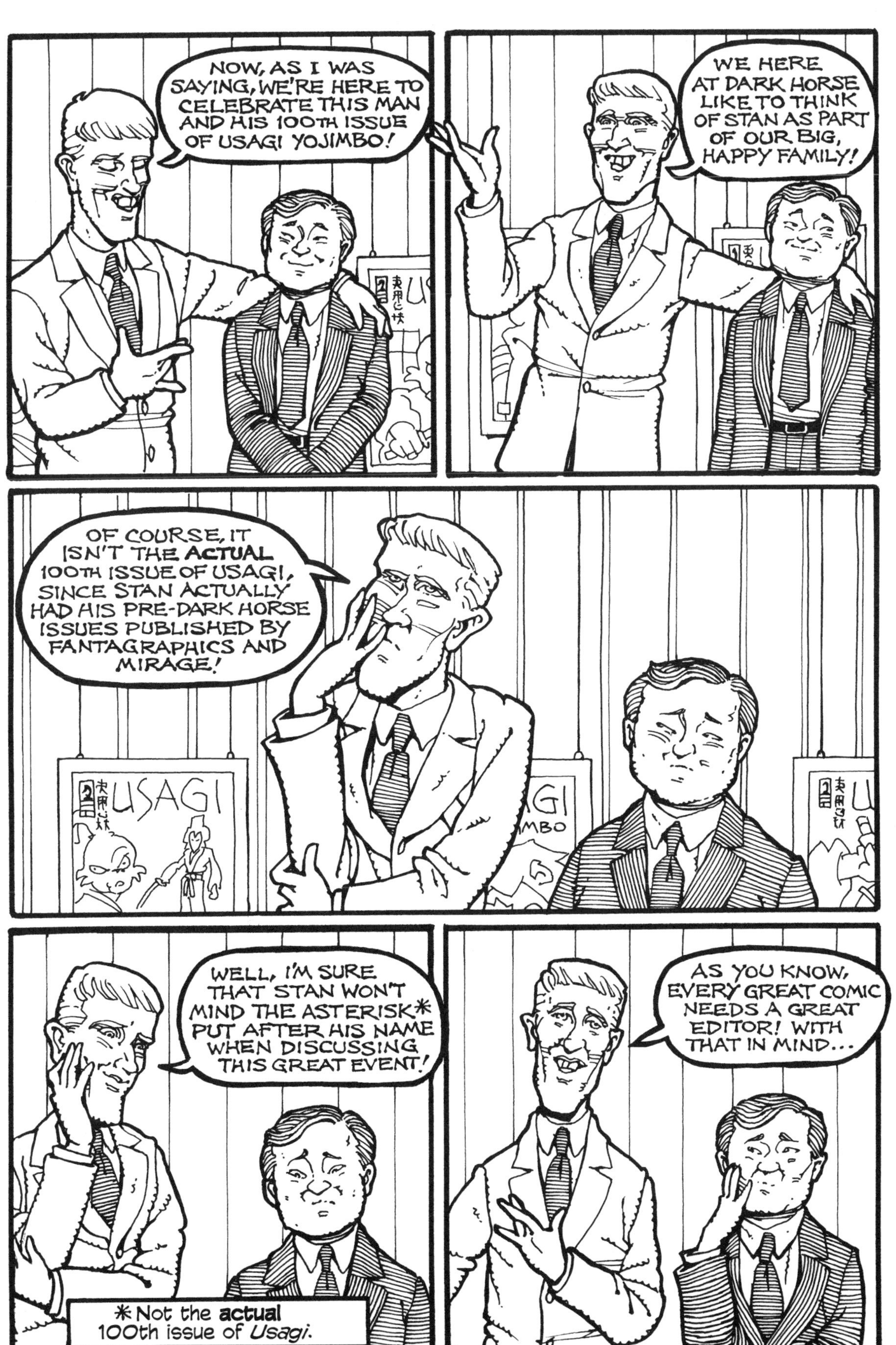
NOW, AS I WAS SAYING, WE'RE HERE TO CELEBRATE THIS MAN AND HIS 100TH ISSUE OF USAGI YOJIMBO!
WE HERE AT DARK HORSE LIKE TO THINK OF STAN AS PART OF OUR BIG, HAPPY FAMILY!
OF COURSE, IT ISN'T THE ACTUAL 100TH ISSUE OF USAGI, SINCE STAN ACTUALLY HAD HIS PRE-DARK HORSE ISSUES PUBLISHED BY FANTAGRAPHICS AND MIRAGE!
USAGI
WELL, I'M SURE THAT STAN WON'T MIND THE ASTERISK* PUT AFTER HIS NAME WHEN DISCUSSING THIS GREAT EVENT!
*Not the actual 100th issue of Usagi.
AS YOU KNOW, EVERY GREAT COMIC NEEDS A GREAT EDITOR! WITH THAT IN MIND...

MEET DIANA SCHUTZ!
USAGI
YOJIMBO

I CAN'T PRAISE DIANA'S EDITING ABILITIES ENOUGH! *
* And doesn't. -- Editor

ALTHOUGH... SINCE STAN SENDS IN EACH ISSUE COMPLETELY DONE, I'VE OFTEN WONDERED JUST WHAT IT IS DIANA DOES!
USAGI
YOJIMBO

WELL, SOMEONE HAS TO CARRY THE BOOK UPSTAIRS TO OUR PRODUCTION DEPARTMENT.

USAGI
CENSORED

THAT'S RIGHT, DIANA, WE **ARE** NUMBER ONE!

AS I MENTIONED EARLIER, WE'VE GATHERED SOME OF THE INDUSTRY'S GREATEST TALENTS TO HONOR STAN. *
WE'VE DECIDED THAT THE BEST WAY TO ACCOMPLISH THIS IS THROUGH A GOOD-NATURED ROAST!
* Not the actual 100th issue of Usagi.
AGI
IMBO
YOU KNOW, LIKE THE OLD DEAN MARTIN ROASTS, WHERE ALL OF THE GREAT CELEBRITIES CAME ON AND REALLY GAVE IT TO THE GUEST OF HONOR!
AND THROUGH THE MAGIC OF THE COMICS, WE WANT TO START OUT THE FESTIVITIES BY BRINGING ON OUR FIRST GUEST... THE STAR OF THIS COMIC... USAGI YOJIMBO!
?
USAGI?
OH... MY... GOD!

STAN*...?
*Not the **actual** 100th issue of *Usagi*.
USAGI YOJIMBO
PSST
NO, NO, NO! WHEN I SAID WE'RE ROASTING HIM, THAT'S NOT WHAT I MEANT!
PSST
UH... DUE TO CIRCUMSTANCES BEYOND OUR CONTROL, USAGI YOJIMBO WILL NOT BE JOINING US TONIGHT!
NOT TO WORRY, HOWEVER! THIS IS COMICS, AND THE WRITERS AND ARTISTS CONTRIBUTING TO THIS BOOK ARE CERTAIN TO... UH... BRING USAGI BACK!
USAGI YOJIMBO
I'D LIKE TO TAKE A MOMENT AND THANK STAN* FOR SHARING TONIGHT WITH US! WE LOVE HIM, AND WE LOVE HAVING HIS BOOK HERE AT DARK HORSE!
SO, WITHOUT FURTHER DELAY, LET'S GET ON WITH THE CELEBRATION!
*Not the **actual** 100th issue of *Usagi*.
HEY, SAVE SOME FOR ME! NEVER HAD RABBIT BEFORE!
STAN, I WANT TO TALK TO YOU ABOUT ISSUE #101... YOU'RE LATE!*
*Stan is **never** late. -- Editor

SUDDENLY--

FROM A PREVIOUSLY-UNNOTICED **SKYLIGHT**--

KRAAAT

GARR

GET OFF THAT **GRILL**, YOU STUPID **RABBIT!**

BOOT!

FM

THE RABBIT RONIN HAS WEATHERED MANY TRIALS IN HIS LIFETIME.
IN HIS WANDERINGS THROUGH FEUDAL JAPAN, USAGI HAS BRAVED COUNTLESS BATTLES AND SURVIVED TREMENDOUS BLOODSHED.
HE HAS FACED--AND OVERCOME--MERCILESS SWORDS AND THEIR WIELDERS, DEADLY NINJA BATS, AND FEARSOME DEMON WARRIORS, ALL WITH THE COURAGE AND DIGNITY BEFITTING A TRUE SAMURAI.
B
EDITORIAL
FLUMP!
AW!
SO CUDDLY...
SO CUUUTE!
POOR BUNNY.
BUT THIS... THIS "ROAST"...
...IS A FATE WORSE THAN DEATH!

BUT THE SHOW MUST GO ON...
I FIRST MET SERGIO ARAGONÉS ALMOST THIRTY YEARS AGO, WHEN I WAS JUST STARTING OUT IN MY FREELANCE ART CAREER. WE'VE BEEN GOOD FRIENDS EVER SINCE.

SERGIO IS ONE OF THE MOST RENOWNED AND MOST BELOVED CARTOONISTS IN THE WORLD...
100TH ISSUE

...SO I'M CONSTANTLY ASKED, "HOW DID YOU MEET HIM?"

WELL, TO MAKE A SHORT STORY EVEN SHORTER...

I FOUND HIS NAME IN THE PHONE BOOK!
TRUE!
100TH

DON'T TRY LOOKING HIM UP NOW, THOUGH. HE GOT HIS NUMBER UNLISTED SOON AFTER I CONTACTED HIM. I'VE OFTEN WONDERED IF THERE WAS A CONNECTION.

BUT BESIDES BEING A FRIEND, HE HAS BEEN A MENTOR TO ME.

IT IS BECAUSE OF HIM THAT I DO THE RESEARCH FOR MY STORIES, AND AM ABLE TO DRAW AS FAST AS I DO.

BUT HE DID NOT TEACH ME THROUGH EXAMPLE! OH, NO. HE TAUGHT ME THROUGH YEARS AND YEARS OF **CONSTANT RIDICULE!**

"YOU CALL THIS *SAMURAI ARMOR*? WHERE IS THE *WAKIBIKI*? THE *NODOWA* IS ALL WRONG!"
100TH

"YOU HAVE TO PENCIL EVERYTHING FIRST? HA! YOU DRAW TOO SLOW, LIKE A GIRLY-GIRL ARTIST!"

BUT WHO'S THE GIRLY-GIRL ARTIST NOW, HUH, SERGIO?!
100TH

I MADE IT TO ONE HUNDRED ISSUES!* DID YOU EVER HAVE ONE HUNDRED ISSUES?!
*LOTS MORE, ACTUALLY.

HUH? DID YOU? HUH? HUH?
100TH

SÍ! **GROO** FROM MARVEL.

OH.
OH, YEAH.
100TH

RATS!

THANK YOU, THANK YOU. GRACIAS. I'M VERY PROUD TO PARTICIPATE IN THIS HOMAGE TO...
CLAP!
CLAP!
CLAP!
CLAP!
CLAP!
CLAP!

...STAN SAKAI! WRITER, ARTIST, CALLIGRAPHER, AND CREATOR OF THIS GREAT COMIC BOOK THAT, WITH THIS TRIBUTE, CELEBRATES ITS ONE HUNDREDTH ISSUE*...
*NOT THE ACTUAL 100TH ISSUE.

...USAGI YOJIMBO!
CLAP!
CLAP!
CLAP!
CLAP!
CLAP!
CLAP!
CLAP!
CLAP!
CLAP!
CLAP!

AS IN ANY ROAST, MANY JOKES ARE GOING TO BE CRACKED ABOUT STAN AND USAGI, BUT I HAVE BEEN VERY FORTUNATE TO TRAVEL WITH STAN TO MANY COUNTRIES, AND IT HAS BEEN FUN.

"WE DO NOT TALK MUCH IN FLIGHT. WE FIND IT A VERY COMFORTABLE PLACE TO WORK, WITHOUT MANY INTERRUPTIONS.

"BUT WE TALK AT TAKEOFFS, LANDINGS, AND DURING MEALS.

THIS FOOD SUCKS!
I ALWAYS WANT TO BRING MY OWN FOOD, BUT I KEEP FORGETTING!

"BUT MEALS AT THE PLACES WE HAVE VISITED ARE SOMETHING ELSE. WHEN WE WERE IN HAWAII FOR A STORE SIGNING...

IS THIS HUMUHUMUNUKU-NUKUAPUA'A?
NO. JUST PLAIN DELICIOUS MAHI-MAHI.

OR IN MEXICO CITY, WHERE THE ORGANIZERS OF A WONDERFUL CONVENTION GAVE US AN UNFORGETTABLE BANQUET.
THESE TACOS ARE GREAT! WHAT ARE THEY?
A DELICACY-- "HUITLACOCHE"--THE FUNGUS OF CORN. JAMES BEARD CALLED IT THE MEXICAN TRUFFLE!

"AT A CONVENTION IN BERGEN, NORWAY, WE WERE SERVED A LOCAL DELICACY IN THE HOME OF OUR HOST.

SHEEP'S HEAD!

"NO POTATOES, SALAD, OR CONDIMENTS-- JUST THE BOILED HEADS.*

I WILL PLAY WITH IT LIKE WHEN I WAS A KID AND FAKE IT.
THANKS FOR THE ABUNDANT AKEVITT!
*TO READ MORE ABOUT THE HEADS, LOOK FOR STAN'S STORY IN DARK HORSE MAVERICK 2000.

"BUT STAN ATE IT. HE IS VERY ADVENTUROUS. HE WILL TRY ANYTHING ONCE.

NOT BAD. DIFFERENT, BUT NOT BAD.

OUR LATEST TRIP TOOK US TO GRANADA, SPAIN, FOR ANOTHER CONVENTION, OF COURSE.
AHH... SMELL THAT AROMA!
JUST LIKE MY MOTHER'S KITCHEN.
RESTAURANT La RANA
BAR PAELLA TAPAS
MAD

"BESIDES THE REGULAR MEALS, WE WERE TREATED TO A "PULPADA," A MEAL PREPARED BY A FAMILY OF FISHERMEN THAT HAS BEEN IN THE OCTOPUS BUSINESS FOR GENERATIONS.
THEY DROVE HUNDREDS OF KILOMETERS TO PREPARE THIS FEAST!
BEST OCTOPUS EVER!
Bitter KAS
VINO TINTO

EDICIONES GLENAT
USAGI
XI SALON INTERNACIONAL DEL COMIC DE GRANADA
WHAT DO WE EAT TONIGHT?
TAPAS!

"TAPAS! THOSE MAGNIFICENT LITTLE DISHES OF SPAIN! A CENTURIES-OLD TRADITION FROM THE ANDALUCIA REGION."
THIS LOOKS LIKE A GREAT PLACE.
TAPAS
RESTAURANT
MAD

CHORIZOS VARIOS.
ASSORTED SALAMIS.
CARACOLES.
SNAILS.
ACEITUNAS.
OLIVES.
QUESO MANCHEGO.
CHEESE.
TOROS GRANADA
VINO TINTO
BITTER KAS

AND THE RABBIT WITH ONIONS, MUSHROOMS, AND PORT...

...WAS DELICIOUS WITH THAT TOUCH OF GARLIC...

...AND...
UH-OH...

PLEASE WELCOME OUR NEXT PRESENTER!
YOU @X!#!
SERGIO MADE ME EAT IT!
END

Usagi Yojimbo

JAMIE S. RICH ANDI WATSON

UP NEXT, WE HAVE STAN'S FIRST DARK HORSE EDITOR...
...JAMIE S. RICH.
CLAP
CLAP
CLAP
I WAS A FRESH-FACED TWENTY-TWO WHEN STAN SAKAI BROUGHT HIS RABBIT TO DARK HORSE. I HAD NOT YET EDITED A COMICS SERIES ON MY OWN.
I WASN'T SURE WHAT EXACTLY TO EXPECT...

"...BUT PRETTY SOON DISCOVERED IT WAS THE SORT OF ASSIGNMENT EDITORS DREAM OF.
ABERNATHY! ADD A COMMA TO PAGE 18, PANEL 3, THEN GET IT UP TO PRODUCTION.

WE'RE ONLY A MONTH EARLY. WE'RE FALLING BEHIND!
YES, SIR!
BEN ABERNATHY FUTURE WILD-STORM EDITOR
DRING
DRING
MA

"THAT IS, UNTIL THE DAY IT ALL WENT HORRIBLY WRONG.
STAN! HOW THE HECK ARE YA, OLD BOY?
NOT GOOD.

STAN, BUDDY, WHAT'S WRONG?
I'M NOT GOING TO MAKE MY DEADLINE.
B-B-BUT WHY?
WELL, Y'SEE...

...I HAVE DOUBLE VISION.
IT MAKES IT HARD TO DRAW.
I'M GOING TO NEED ANOTHER WEEK. MAYBE TWO.
IF YOU'RE SURE, I GUESS WE'LL MANAGE.
"THE THING WAS, THE DEADLINE WAS ONE STAN HAD SET HIMSELF...
DOOM
"...AND IT WAS A MONTH EARLIER THAN WE NEEDED IT ANYWAY.
MOST PUNCTUAL
1st
STAN SAKAI
"SO, IMAGINE MY SURPRISE...
WHAT'S THAT?
THE NEW ISSUE OF USAGI.
FedAir
"...WHEN IT CAME A WEEK EARLIER THAN STAN'S ORIGINAL DEADLINE!"
FROM THAT DAY FORWARD, STAN SAKAI BECAME MY EDITORIAL BOOGEYMAN...
WHAT DO YOU MEAN, YOUR ROOT CANAL MADE YOU LATE?!
STAN SAKAI HAD DOUBLE VISION, AND HE WAS EARLY!
S. S.
ANDI WATSON FOLKS!
DON'T HURT ME.
...A DARK FIGURE USED TO SCARE SLACK-JAWED CARTOONISTS INTO SHAPE.

AGI
IMBO
THANK YOU, JAMIE AND ANDI!
I'M VERY HONORED THAT THE NEXT SPEAKER IS HERE.
100TH ISSUE

HE ENTERED THE COMICS FIELD SHORTLY AFTER I DID, AND HAS QUICKLY RISEN TO THE TOP WITH HIS BRILLIANT SERIES.

HE IS ONE OF THE MOST HONORED CREATORS WORKING TODAY...
100TH ISSUE

...AND I AM PROUD TO CALL HIM MY FRIEND.

HERE HE IS--TRULY A MAN WHO NEEDS NO INTRODUCTION!

100TH ISSUE

100TH ISSUE

UH... JEFF SMITH.
OH, ME!
CLAP! CLAP!
CLAP! CLAP! CLAP!
CLAP! CLAP!

"STAN IS ONE OF THOSE ARTISTS WHOSE SKILLS ARE LEGENDARY. HE IS ONE OF THE FASTEST CARTOONISTS WHO EVER LIVED. THIS IS A TRUE STORY FROM BACK WHEN STAN AND I WERE TRAVELING TOGETHER ON THE TRILOGY TOUR. ONE DAY WE WERE ALL ON A PANEL TOGETHER IN SAN DIEGO WHEN I LEARNED THE SECRET OF...

THE ASTONISHING STAN SAKAI!!

"STAN WAS POLITELY ANSWERING A QUESTION ABOUT WHETHER OR NOT USAGI HAD A TAIL UNDER HIS PANTS (APPARENTLY HE DOESN'T)...

"WHEN I HEARD A STRANGE SCRIBBLING SOUND COMING FROM UNDER THE TABLE.

SKRITCH SKRATCHY!
SKRITCH!
SKRIT!

!

"I PULLED UP THE CURTAIN IN FRONT OF THE TABLE AND SAW STAN **INKING A PAGE OF USAGI** WITH ONE FOOT, AND **LETTERING A PAGE OF GROO** WITH THE OTHER.

"IT REALLY HAPPENED!! ASK ANYONE!"

J.

...AND NOW, OUR NEXT SPEAKERS, WHO ARE SUCH GOOD FRIENDS OF STAN'S THAT THEY'LL DO PAGES IN THE BOOK FOR SHORT MONEY...
...HERE ARE MARK EVANIER AND SCOTT SHAW!

LET ME GO FIRST! I HAVE LOTS OF JAPANESE JOKES! REMEMBER, I WORKED ON THE PINK LADY T.V. SHOW!
UH, STAN GREW UP IN HAWAII! MAYBE IF YOU'D WORKED WITH JACK LORD...

AHEM! I DON'T KNOW WHY WE'RE GIVING THIS MAN A DINNER WHEN SOME OF THE GREATEST FIGURES IN COMICS NEVER GOT A DINNER!
ISN'T THIS RED BUTTONS' OLD ROUTINE?

THE INCREDIBLE HULK, WHO ONCE SAID, "HOW COME I CAN'T GET A TAN?" NEVER GOT A DINNER!
THE FLASH, WHO ONCE TOLD HIS GIRLFRIEND, "I'M SORRY I'M SO FAST!" NEVER GOT A DINNER!
RED BUTTONS JUST DIED AND YOU'RE DOING HIS BIT?

FORGET THOSE JOKES YOU GOT AT THE 99-CENT STORE AND SAY SOMETHING ABOUT STAN, A GREAT ARTIST, WRITER, AND LETTERER!
JUST SMILE AND PRETEND THEY'RE FUNNY, DEAR!

LETTERER?! YOU JUST REMINDED ME OF SOMETHING!
OH, NO! YOU'RE NOT GOING TO...
SMEK!

I'LL BE BACK IN A SECOND!
MARK, THIS IS A DINNER IN HONOR OF... YOU CAN'T...!

HI, STAN! WE NEED THESE GROO PAGES LETTERED RIGHT AWAY!
THE BOOK'S DUE IN ABOUT AN HOUR, AND SERGIO NEEDS AT LEAST HALF THAT TIME TO DRAW IT!

I'LL BRING YOU THE REST OF THE PAGES AFTER WE FINISH THIS STUPID SPEECH!
YOU CAN STOP PRETENDING THEY'RE FUNNY NOW, HANNAH!

OKAY, NOW, WHERE WERE WE?
WE WERE GOING TO INTRODUCE THOSE RABBITS WE BROUGHT!
RIGHT! SCOTT AND I JUST WOULDN'T FEEL RIGHT, ROASTING OUR OLD FRIEND STAN...
SO, BEING SCHOLARS OF FUNNY ANIMAL COMICS AND CREATORS IN THAT GENRE...
...WE DECIDED TO BRING ALONG SOME NEW RABBIT CHARACTERS WE'VE CREATED THAT WE'RE TRYING TO TRADEMARK!
AND HERE'S THE FIRST ONE-- RICKY RABBIT!
WHAT WAS WRONG WITH MY RED BUTTONS ROUTINE?
RED IS DEAD AND HE'S STILL FUNNIER THAN YOU ARE!
HELLO! I'M RICKY RABBIT (TM) AND I'M A LOT MORE ADORABLE THAN USAGI YOJIMBO! SO...
WHERE'S MY TOY DEAL?!? I WANT AN ACTION FIGURE! I WANT A LUNCH BOX WITH MY FACE ON IT!
AND I WANT A RESIN BUST AND A CARTOON SHOW AND T-SHIRTS! JUST LIKE STAN'S RABBIT!
OKAY, I'M OUTTA HERE! IF ANYONE NEEDS ME, I'LL BE AT THE LICENSING SHOW!
IT'S ALL YOURS, HARRY!
DUH... I'M HARRY HARE (TM) AN' PEOPLE TELL ME I'M KINDA SLOW...
SKRITCH! SKRITCH!
...BUT IF HARRY DON'T GET SAME DEAL AS USAGI...
--HARE STOMP!!!

HERE'S A REAL GEEZER OF A RABBIT THAT THEM GUYS CALL "THE OLD GREY HARE"!
...ENHHH... HUFF, PUFF! ...NGHH,... WHEEZE!

YOU CALL THIS A COMIC BOOK? WHY, IN MY DAY, THEY HAD COLOR! AND THEY WERE A DIME! AND THEY WERE ALL DRAWN BY JACK KIRBY!
NOT ONLY THAT, BUT--

ERRGGGHHH!!!
OH, MY HEART
NOW I REALLY WISH I HADN'T SIGNED UP FOR MEDICARE PART D!
PING!

LOOKS LIKE IT'S UP TO ME TO GET THIS ROAST BACK ON TRACK!
HIYA, FOLKS! I'M SATURDAY MORNING'S NEXT BIG STAR, RAPID-FIRE RABBIT!

WE'RE ALL HERE TO ROAST USAGI YOJIMBO... BUT PERSONALLY, I DON'T CARE FOR ROAST RABBIT!
HE WOULD MAKE A GOOD SHISH KEBAB, THOUGH! HE EVEN COMES WITH HIS OWN SKEWERS!
HA HA! HA HA! HA HA!
CANNED LAUGHTER

ARE YOU ENJOYING THIS, DAD?
LET'S PUT IT THIS WAY: I'M HAVING MORE FUN LETTERING THE MINSTREL'S DIALOGUE!
INK

MARK AND SCOTT HAVE NEW RABBITS FOR EVERY TASTE! CREATED ESPECIALLY FOR FANS OF UNDERGROUND COMIX, I'M BONGWATER BUNNY...
AT LEAST, I THINK I AM...

FLOPPY-EARS FANBUNNY HERE! I JUST HAD THE FIRST 99 ISSUES OF USAGI YOJIMBO "SLABBED" IN CLEAR LUCITE...
SNUK!
MAYBE I SHOULDA READ THEM FIRST...
USAGI YOJIMBO
NIGHT OF THE LEPUS

...AND I'M A FAMOUS SUPER-HERO RABBIT WHO CAN ONLY BE DEPICTED IN SILHOUETTE! I FEAR NOTHING... EXCEPT, OF COURSE, THE TIME WARNER LAWYERS!
THOSE GUYS ARE MEAN!

SORRY, **STAN**--WE **KID** BECAUSE WE **LOVE!** —**MARK EVANIER** AND **SCOTT SHAW!**

I'VE BEEN A FAN OF GUY DAVIS--
--FROM THE MOMENT I PICKED UP THE FIRST ISSUE OF **BAKER STREET**.
100TH ISSUE

WOW! LOOK AT THAT DRAFTSMANSHIP! HIS ARCHITECTURE IS AMAZING! HE'S INCREDIBLE!
BAKER STREET

"I WAS INVITED TO BE A GUEST AT A MOTOR CITY COMIC CON, AND--
WHAT? GUY DAVIS WILL BE A GUEST, TOO? YOU BET I'LL BE THERE!
SAMURAI
ISTORY of JAPAN
MYTHOLOGY

"THE ONLY THING I KNEW ABOUT GUY WAS THROUGH HIS ART, BUT I PICTURED US MEETING, TALKING SHOP, AND GETTING ALONG FAMOUSLY.
ORIGINAL ART

"BUT WHEN I SAW HIM...
ORANGE MOHAWK... LEATHER... CHAINS...
COMICS
DEN AGE

"IN MY MIND I IMAGINED GOING UP TO HIM...
ER... MR. DAVIS, SIR...
TAP! TAP!

WHADDAYA WANT, YA LITTLE PUKE?
WHO SAID YOU COULD TOUCH ME?
EEP!

"I ADMIT MY PREJUDICES GOT THE BETTER OF ME. A BIT INTIMIDATED BY MY IMAGINATION, I KEPT MY DISTANCE.
GULP!

"BUT I CONTINUED TO ENJOY GUY'S WORK.
JEEZ-- HE KEEPS GETTING BETTER AND BETTER!
SANDMAN MYSTERY THEATRE

"YEARS LATER, AT ANOTHER MOTOR CITY CON, I HAD A TABLE NEXT TO HIM.

"HE TURNED OUT TO BE ONE OF THE NICEST PERSONS I'VE EVER MET.

"EVEN MORE SURPRISING, HE TURNED OUT TO BE AS BIG A FAN OF MINE AS I WAS OF HIS!"

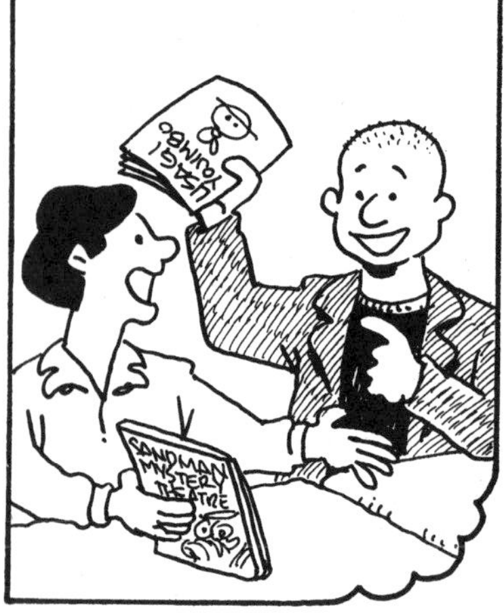
USAGI YOJIMBO
SANDMAN MYSTERY THEATRE

SO, WITHOUT FURTHER ADO, I WOULD LIKE TO INTRODUCE MY FRIEND, GUY DAVIS!
100TH ISSUE

YAWN! MAN, AM I BEAT!
100TH ISSUE

Z Z Z
?
!

PHOOEY! YOU CALL THIS A TRIBUTE?! THIS IS ALL I GET AFTER A HUNDRED ISSUES*?
*MORE, REALLY.

NO MENTION OF THE ACCOLADES I'VE RECEIVED? THE AWARDS I'VE WON?

THE BEST YOU ALL CAN SAY IS THAT I'M PUNCTUAL IN TURNING IN MY WORK?

EVEN COMIC-CON INTERNATIONAL: SAN DIEGO CALLED ME "ONE OF THE NICEST GUYS IN COMICS." SEE--IT'S WRITTEN RIGHT HERE IN THEIR UPDATE!
CCI: SAN DIEGO
2004

WELL, AFTER TWENTY-TWO YEARS, AND ALL THE STORIES AND CHARACTERS I'VE CREATED--

THERE'S ONLY ONE THING I CAN SAY--
TUG!
SWISH!
SWASH!

GO GET 'EM, GUYS!
¡AY CARAMBA!

RYAAAHH!?!
YOW!
GRR...
SIGH!
JUST ONCE I'D LIKE TO GO TO A PARTY WITHOUT IT ENDING IN A RIOT!

THANK YOU FOR SUPPORTING US THROUGH ONE HUNDRED ISSUES*!
S.
*AW, FORGET IT!

USAGI YOJIMBO #99 ALTERNATE ENDING

Alternate ending for *Usagi Yojimbo* #99 (see page 133). In the published story, Usagi does return to the bridge where he left Mayumi, but she had already left with the assassin Shizukiri.

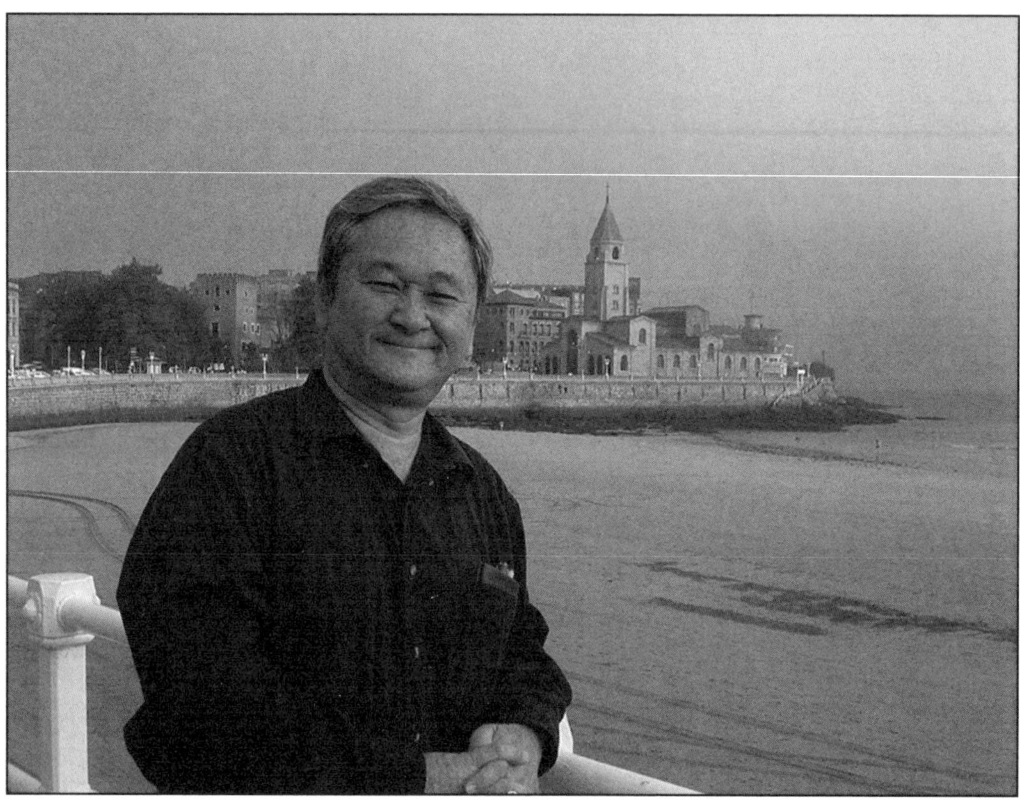

Stan Sakai in Gijón, Spain. Photo by Sharon Sakai.

STAN SAKAI was born in Kyoto, Japan, grew up in Hawaii, and now lives in California. He has two children, Hannah and Matthew. Stan received a fine arts degree from the University of Hawaii and furthered his studies at the Art Center College of Design in Pasadena, California.

Stan's creation *Usagi Yojimbo* first appeared in comics in 1984. Since then, Usagi has been on television as a guest of the Teenage Mutant Ninja Turtles and has been made into toys, seen on clothing, and featured in a series of graphic novel collections.

In 1991, Stan created *Space Usagi*, a series dealing with samurai in a futuristic setting, featuring the adventures of a descendant of the original Usagi.

Stan is also an award-winning letterer for his work on Sergio Aragonés's *Groo*, the *Spider-Man* Sunday newspaper strips, and *Usagi Yojimbo*.

Stan is the recipient of a Parents' Choice Award, an Inkpot Award, an American Library Association Award, a Harvey Award, five Spanish Haxtur Awards, several Eisner Awards, and an Inkwell Award. In 2003 he won the prestigious National Cartoonists Society Award in the Comic Book Division, and in 2011 Stan received the Cultural Ambassador Award from the Japanese American National Museum.

USAGI YOJIMBO™

Created, Written, and Illustrated by Stan Sakai

Available from Dark Horse Comics

The Usagi Yojimbo Saga Book 1
Collects *Usagi Yojimbo* Books 8–10
$24.99 | ISBN 978-1-61655-609-9

The Usagi Yojimbo Saga Book 2
Collects *Usagi Yojimbo* Books 11–13
$24.99 | ISBN 978-1-61655-610-5

The Usagi Yojimbo Saga Book 3
Collects *Usagi Yojimbo* Books 14–16
$24.99 | ISBN 978-1-61655-611-2

The Usagi Yojimbo Saga Book 4
Collects *Usagi Yojimbo* Books 17–19
$24.99 | ISBN 978-1-61655-612-9

The Usagi Yojimbo Saga Book 5
Collects *Usagi Yojimbo* Books 20–22
$24.99 | ISBN 978-1-61655-613-6

The Usagi Yojimbo Saga Book 6
Collects *Usagi Yojimbo* Books 23–25
$24.99 | ISBN 978-1-61655-614-3

The Usagi Yojimbo Saga Book 7
Collects *Usagi Yojimbo* Books 26–28
$24.99 | ISBN 978-1-61655-615-0
COMING SEPTEMBER 2016

Book 29: Two Hundred Jizo
$17.99 | ISBN 978-1-61655-840-6

Book 30: Thieves and Spies
$17.99 | ISBN 978-1-50670-048-9
COMING JULY 2016

Usagi Yojimbo: Yokai
$14.99 | ISBN 978-1-59582-362-5

Usagi Yojimbo: Senso
$19.99 | ISBN 978-1-61655-709-6

Space Usagi
$17.99 | ISBN 978-1-56971-290-0

The Art of Usagi Yojimbo
$29.95 | ISBN 978-1-59307-493-7

The Sakai Project: Artists Celebrate Thirty Years of Usagi Yojimbo
$29.99 | ISBN 978-1-61655-556-6

Gallery Edition Volume 1: Samurai and Other Stories
$125.00 | ISBN 978-1-61655-923-6

Gallery Edition Volume 2
$125.00 | ISBN 978-1-61655-924-3
COMING OCTOBER 2016

47 Ronin
Written by Mike Richardson
$19.99 | ISBN 978-1-59582-954-2

The Adventures of Nilson Groundthumper and Hermy
$14.99 | ISBN 978-1-61655-341-8

Available from Fantagraphics Books
fantagraphics.com

Book 1: The Ronin
Book 2: Samurai
Book 3: The Wanderer's Road
Book 4: The Dragon Bellow Conspiracy
Book 5: Lone Goat and Kid
Book 6: Circles
Book 7: Gen's Story

AVAILABLE AT YOUR LOCAL COMICS SHOP OR BOOKSTORE
- To find a comics shop near your area, call 1-888-266-4226. For more information or to order direct:
- On the web: DarkHorse.com • E-mail: mailorder@darkhorse.com
- Phone: 1-800-862-0052 Mon.-Fri. 9 A.M. to 5 P.M. Pacific Time. *Prices and availability subject to change without notice.

SAGI